SUPERNATURAL
DELIVERANCE

GUILLERMO
MALDONADO

WHITAKER
HOUSE

Cover Design: Juan Salgado

SUPERNATURAL DELIVERANCE:
Freedom for Your Soul, Mind, and Emotions

Guillermo Maldonado
13651 S.W. 143rd Ct., #101
Miami, FL 33186
http://kingjesusministry.org/
www.ERJPub.org

ISBN: 978-1-62911-598-6
eBook ISBN: 978-1-62911-599-3
Printed in the United States of America
© 2016 by Guillermo Maldonado

Whitaker House
1030 Hunt Valley Circle
New Kensington, PA 15068
www.whitakerhouse.com

Library of Congress Cataloging-in-Publication Data
Names: Maldonado, Guillermo, author.
Title: Supernatural deliverance : freedom for your soul, mind, and emotions /
  Guillermo Maldonado.
Description: New Kensington, PA : Whitaker House, 2016.
Identifiers: LCCN 2015046838 | ISBN 9781629115986 (trade pbk. : alk. paper)
Subjects: LCSH: Spiritual warfare. | Exorcism.
Classification: LCC BV4509.5 .M25625 2016 | DDC 235/.4—dc23 LC record available at
http://lccn.loc.gov/2015046838

2 3 4 5 6 7 8 9 10 11 12 ⨆⨆ 24 23 22 21 20 19 18 17

CONTENTS

I

THE REVELATION OF DELIVERANCE MINISTRY IN THE NOW

What is the most difficult problem you face? What issues in your life have you been struggling with for months—or even years? You may think you understand what you've been dealing with, but perhaps there is more to it than you have realized. Let me share with you my own journey of revelation into the ministry of deliverance that is available for every one of God's children, enabling them to live a life of freedom and fruitfulness.

The Scriptures promise abundant life and peace, but I struggled with feelings of fear and rejection. I loved God, prayed, and fasted, but even though I read in the Bible that I was a new creation in Christ and that all things had been made new in me, I wasn't free in those areas. I could not overcome them. I was still dealing with negative influences from my past.

I was just starting my ministry in the church, yet I faced the reality that my life was contrary to what the Scriptures teach it should be. In addition, I noticed the same pattern in the leaders who were under my care. A few of them used tranquilizers and sleeping pills, while some suffered from recurring depression. Others lived in cycles of sin that they could not break, participating in various forms of immorality, such as pornography, promiscuity, or homosexuality. Some had recurrent illnesses. Still others were afflicted by and in bondage to fears, just as I was. Something was wrong!

Why Don't Many Believers Experience Abundant Life?

During this time, I would ask myself questions for which I had no answers, such as the following: Why were born-again Christians who loved God and served Him unable to live in freedom or to exercise self-control in some areas of their lives? How could believers, who have been empowered by God's Spirit, be powerless to overcome addictions to food, smoking, prescription pills, or illegal drugs? If Christians were new creations in Jesus Christ, why did they still battle mental strongholds of fear, anxiety, and compulsive desires? Why were they still in bondage to the mind-set of the world and to sexual immorality, even to extreme behaviors? If Christ had already set them free, why were they still holding on to grudges and bitterness, unable to forgive others who had hurt them? Why was it so difficult for them to obey God and to be free of rebellion against Him and His ways? Why did they succumb to escapism and crippling feelings of guilt? Why did they experience nightmares and battle suicidal tendencies?

On the cross, Jesus Christ paid the penalty for our sins and our sicknesses, and His work is complete. His sacrifice was a legal transaction in the spiritual realm that delivered us from our bondage to sin. Yet, in experience, in practice, neither my staff nor I had fully entered into that freedom. Something was binding our wills and keeping us from pleasing God in certain areas of our lives.

I would spend hours, days, and weeks counseling the members of my staff, trying to deliver them from these conditions of bondage and defeat, but I saw no improvement. These leaders were unable to enjoy an abundant life of righteousness, peace, and joy, which are all characteristics of the kingdom of God. (See Romans 14:17.) In addition, I noticed another symptom that worried me. As I continuously tried to help people become free of their persistent, entrenched issues, the leadership of the church—as well as the members—was failing to experience growth in Christ. Something was holding them back. (See Ecclesiastes 7:7.)

As I sought to understand what was happening, and as I searched for solutions to our needs, the Lord began to reveal the answer—it was *the precious ministry of deliverance*. This is a ministry that Jesus brought to earth for all believers to avail themselves of and to use on behalf of others. Deliverance ministry is twofold: (1) It releases believers from oppression and demonization in the areas in which they experience persistent struggles. (2) It sets free those who are demon possessed or otherwise in bondage to the power of the enemy.

The Reality of the Existence of Demons and Evil Spirits

It wasn't as if I hadn't previously believed in deliverance through the power of Jesus Christ. I knew that Jesus and the apostles had practiced deliverance, freeing people from Satan's grasp. However, I had believed in it from an intellectual point of view alone, because I had never personally been delivered or ministered deliverance to others. I did not know how to access deliverance in the now—*today.* I hadn't yet received divine wisdom about the reality and origin of demonic bondage. As a result, I dealt with merely the "branches," or consequences, of people's problems, rather than with the root of them. Furthermore, I had tried to handle these matters directly with the people who were struggling— giving them advice and encouraging them to change their behavior. In reality, they were facing spiritual attack involving spiritual entities called "demons." Consequently, a spiritual response alone would be effective.

The Bible says, *"For we do not wrestle against flesh and blood, but against principalities, against powers, against the rulers of the darkness of this age, against spiritual hosts of wickedness in the heavenly places"* (Ephesians 6:12). Another Bible version translates this verse as follows: *"For we are not fighting against people made of flesh and blood, but against persons without bodies—the evil rulers of the unseen world…"* (TLB).

When I realized the true spiritual nature of the problem, the Lord instructed me to "clean" my leadership and the members of my church. I hope the following illustration will help to explain what we needed to do. After a fisherman takes a catch of fish, the first thing he does is to "clean" them. In other words, he removes their innards to prevent them from smelling bad. Likewise, the leaders and members of my church needed to be cleansed of the demonic influence and oppression that were afflicting them.

And so, the leadership (including myself) and the members of my church received deliverance. We were freed from our burdens, and, from that day forward, everyone began to grow spiritually. A revival was released in the church, thanks to the fact that everyone had been set free!

In my case, I had been a fearful man, but God completely changed me so that I became bold when evangelizing and preaching. I had the courage to take giant steps of faith. As the blindfold fell from the spiritual eyes of my ministers and other leaders, they recognized—and were delivered from—their own issues. Their leadership improved, and their minds were opened to receive wisdom and knowledge from God.

We often deal with merely the "branches,"
or consequences, of people's problems rather
than with the root of their issues.

Supernatural Deliverance

Perhaps you genuinely love God and are filled with the Holy Spirit, but you remain tied to the negative effects of your past, including emotional wounds and unforgiveness. Maybe you wrestle with mental strongholds, so that you continually deal with depression and/or feelings of rejection. Or, perhaps you struggle with sexual sin. Maybe you suffer from fears and phobias. It could be that you are experiencing hardness of heart, and you don't understand why. You can be delivered from any of these conditions!

Many born-again Christians have come to our ministry with a precious heart for God. They were faithful followers, and they sought to please Him, but because of their lack of knowledge about deliverance, they were in bondage in certain areas of their lives. Among them was an evangelist who shared the following testimony.

"My name is John McCormack. I am from Ireland, and I have been a follower of Jesus as a missionary in China for over fifteen years, teaching in schools and universities and for business associations. Although I knew God and had preached the gospel of Jesus for three years, I was really hard inside; my heart held a lot of pain and discouragement. I was unable to cry and could not feel the presence of God, so I grew distant in my relationship with Him. My understanding of Christianity was in a box, where I rationalized all that I saw and questioned everything, especially the purpose of giving tithes and offerings. I would reason and doubt, saying that maybe God would do something—and maybe He wouldn't. As an evangelist in China, I grew tired of talking to people and saying, 'Jesus loves you,' 'Jesus is real,' or 'Receive Jesus into your heart,' only to see no tangible manifestation or anything happen in the mission field or at church services. This physically exhausted me. It was painful.

"One morning, while watching teaching videos of Apostle Renny McLean on his Web site, I saw among the suggested videos a teaching from a man named Apostle Guillermo Maldonado. I watched one of his sermons, and my life was instantly changed. What I heard about deliverance, about the power of the supernatural, and about the true love of God has expanded my understanding of how big God really is. I was introduced to the supernatural power of God, which instantly broke the paradigms that religion, intellectualism, and the culture I was in had established as my environment. That moment, in my room, I encountered God in such a way that the walls around my heart were spiritually broken, and I was delivered from my bondages. For the first time in years, I cried in God's presence. The supernatural is much bigger than what I had believed it to be.

"Shortly after that encounter, I traveled to Miami, Florida, to receive ministry at Apostle Maldonado's Supernatural Fivefold Ministry School. I went looking for further healing and deliverance. During that weekend, I became a transformed man; even my question of giving tithes and offerings was resolved. God set my mind free, teaching me that it's not about me or about providing for myself or about other people providing for me—it's about looking to God. I learned that I had to be still and know that He is God! God removed the veil from my eyes—from my religious ways of knowing Him—and gave me the revelation of the supernatural, the revelation of God's power of deliverance and love. I am no longer the same man that I was before!"

Can a Christian Be Demon Possessed?

Many Christians recognize that deliverance ministry is needed (or they at least acknowledge that it was needed in New Testament times) to release from bondage those who are demon possessed. Yet there is much controversy over the question of whether a born-again Christian could ever be possessed by an evil spirit. How could a Christian be in a state of demonic bondage when the kingdom of God does not share territory with the kingdom of darkness?

If Jesus Christ completely paid the price of our salvation and deliverance when He died on the cross, if Christ dwells in our heart by faith, and if the Holy Spirit is our Counselor, shouldn't we be free of all demonic influence the instant we accept Jesus as Lord and receive God's Spirit?

Additionally, if Christ carried our sicknesses—as well as our sins—on the cross, why do we seem to inherit sicknesses and other types of bondage (such as arthritis or addictions) from our parents, grandparents, and other ancestors? Such sicknesses and bondages are often referred to as "generational curses."

Let us address these important questions, so that we will understand the nature of deliverance ministry. First, can a believer be *possessed* by a demon? The answer is no, because a born-again Christian belongs to the Lord Jesus Christ. The devil is no longer that person's lord and master. Jesus lives within the person's heart, or spirit, which is the throne of God on earth in those who have received His Son. In contrast, to be *possessed* by a demon means that your whole being is controlled by that evil spirit.

However, even though a Christian cannot be possessed by a demon, this does not mean that a believer might not have parts of his life that are being influenced by the power of a demonic spirit or that are inhabited by a demon. A demon can reside in any part of a believer except for his heart, or spirit. This is because there are certain areas of the believer's soul and body that he—knowingly or unknowingly—has yet to surrender to God. These vulnerable areas are not completely under Christ's lordship; they have not been fully redeemed. Consequently, the door has been left open for them to be "demonized." To be demonized means to be under the influence of a demon, or to be under attack by a demon.

For instance, if someone harbors unforgiveness, he opens the door for a demon to reside in his emotions, a situation that may also have an effect on his body. I recently ministered to a man who had been deeply hurt due to a betrayal. He had held unforgiveness in his heart, and he'd suffered from terrible arthritis pain. I led him in forgiveness, and then I rebuked the oppression in his emotions. He was instantly healed of the arthritis.

Two Greek nouns denoting a "demon," or a wicked or impure spirit, are *daimon* and *daimonion*. "Wicked spirits," "impure spirits," "evil spirits," and "demons" are interchangeable terms. In English versions of the New Testament, the Greek verb *daimonizomai* has been translated (among other variations) as *"demon-possessed," "possessed with a devil,"* or *"possessed by a demon."* (See, for example, Matthew 4:24 NIV, NKJV; Matthew 9:32 KJV; John 10:21 NIV.) However, I believe these are erroneous translations that cause many people to be confused about the activity of demons. Instead, I believe *daimonizomai* refers to demonization. A person does not need to be actually demon possessed to require deliverance from demonic attack.

In my experience, most Christians *do* need deliverance—and not just one time. Deliverance ministry is a feature of the kingdom of God that Christ came to release to us. In fact, I believe Jesus provided the marvelous ministry of deliverance as "daily bread" for His people. That means it is available to us all the time, whenever we need it.

A born-again believer cannot be possessed by a demon, but he can be influenced and/or attacked by one.

What Is Deliverance?

Deliverance is a term that is rarely used in the church today. It refers to the permanent removal of demonic spirits—unseen, evil entities without physical bodies—that deceive, influence, enslave, bind, torment, and sicken people. In the New Testament, we read, *"God anointed Jesus of Nazareth with the Holy Spirit and with power, who went about doing good and healing all who were oppressed by the devil, for God was with Him"* (Acts 10:38). When Jesus brought the kingdom of God to earth, He demonstrated that the ministry of deliverance always accompanies the presence of the kingdom. Deliverance is a manifestation that God's kingdom has arrived in people's lives and in the life of their communities, cultures, and nations. When we minister deliverance, we establish the kingdom of God in and among human beings. In chapter 2 of this book, we'll further explore the relationship between the kingdom and deliverance.

When most believers manifest a problem in their minds, wills, and/or emotions, their spiritual leaders merely counsel them, rather than discerning where there may be a demonic origin to the problem and setting people free by either casting out the demons or rebuking the influence of the demons in their lives.

> *Counseling, psychiatry, and psychology have replaced the ministry of deliverance in the church.*

Demonic spirits are the main cause of many emotional, spiritual, and physical problems with which people struggle. Until we discern this reality, we will continue to offer people solely counseling, psychology, and/or psychiatry in an attempt to patch up their wounds and ease their emotional pain. Yet we will fail to deal with the underlying cause of their problems. This approach is like removing a spider web from your home without killing the spider, or cutting off the branches of an invasive tree in your yard but never pulling up its trunk and roots. You will merely be beating the air without achieving any results.

Most believers love Christ but, for lack of knowledge, are still living in captivity. I have taken the time to investigate the need for deliverance among God's people, and I have concluded that approximately 80 percent of those in the church need deliverance, because they have one or more areas that are oppressed or enslaved by wicked spirits.

The enemy's greatest stronghold is man's ignorance of his deceitful ways.

The Importance and Necessity of Deliverance

Many people assume that after they have been born again and filled by the Holy Spirit, there is no possible way for them to be influenced by a demon. Such an idea is completely false. In fact, their belief in this lie is what keeps many of them in bondage. I have seen, heard, and experienced the need for deliverance in born-again Christians. I know that even after a person is saved, he must often also be set free. A good analogy is the experience of Lazarus (the brother of Mary and Martha), whom Jesus raised from the dead. When Lazarus was resurrected, he received new life; however, in order to live that life, he still needed to be released from the grave clothes that had been wrapped around him for his burial. (See John 11:43–44.)

To disguise his activities and attacks, Satan has made sure that most people today see deliverance as a superstitious practice—a medieval idea that only the ignorant hold to. The trap of this deception is that it makes many people believe that the devil doesn't exist. Some people believe that the devil is real but that *they* are exempt from his schemes—he couldn't possibly be exerting a negative effect on their lives. As a result, when the subject of deliverance is discussed, many people become offended by it, fearful of it, or defensive about it.

To better understand why deliverance is needed, we must recognize the nature of human beings and how they were created. The apostle Paul wrote, *"Now may the God of peace Himself sanctify you completely; and may your whole **spirit**, **soul**, and **body** be preserved blameless at the coming of our Lord Jesus Christ"* (1 Thessalonians 5:23). It takes spirit, soul, and body to make a whole person. Since each part of our makeup is unique, it needs to be individually treated, healed, and/or set free when it is demonized.

+ The *spirit* is the inner man, or the "spiritual man." It is where God comes to dwell when we are born again—it is the seat of His presence.

+ The *soul* is the seat of our will, with which we make decisions. The emotions and the mind (intellect) are aspects of the soul, also.

+ The *body* is the dwelling place of the spirit and the soul, and the means by which these two unseen parts of our being express themselves in the visible world as they manifest their uniqueness and their desires.

> *Man is a spirit with a soul who dwells in a physical body.*

When we were born again, it was our spirit—not our soul or our body—that was instantly regenerated. In order for God to *"sanctify [us] completely,"* our body often still needs to be healed, and our soul still needs to be renewed and set free from the effects of sin and Satan. In other words, the salvation and the transformation that took place in our spirit were immediate, forming a new creation (see 2 Corinthians

5:17)—but our soul is still corrupted by the sinful nature and needs to be progressively released and transformed.

Revelation for Deliverance Ministry

To understand the two-fold nature of deliverance ministry, we must receive revelation that enables us to do the following:

1. Discern the Difference Between Demonization and Demon Possession

Let us be clear about the distinction between demonization and demon possession. To be demonized means to be under the influence of, or under attack by, a demon. To be possessed by a demon means to be totally under the control of that demon in your spirit, soul, and body. For example, if you own, or "possess," a house, it belongs to you, and you have full authority and control over it.

We have noted that a believer cannot be possessed by a demon, because a born-again Christian belongs to the Lord Jesus Christ, and the devil is no longer that person's lord and master. Most of the time, if a believer is told that he is possessed by a demon, his reaction is anger, because he knows that Christ lives within him. However, there may be areas in a believer's life that are still under the influence of an evil spirit, because they have not been surrendered to the Lord's control. This, as we have discussed, is called "demonization."

For example, consider the following verse: *"And behold, a woman of Canaan came from that region and cried out to Him, saying, 'Have mercy on me, O Lord, Son of David! My daughter is severely demon-possessed'"* (Matthew 15:22). In this case, we should understand the term *"demon-possessed"* to mean being under the influence of a demon, rather than actual demon possession.

At one point, Jesus was presented with a man who was *"mute and demon-possessed"* (Matthew 9:32). The verb used in this verse indicates that the man was demonized, and the evidence of that demonization was that he was mute. The instant the demon was cast out, the man recovered his ability to speak. The man had not been possessed by a demon; rather, a specific area of his life had been under the influence of the wicked spirit.

Many of the people living in Palestine whom Christ set free from demonic oppression believed in the Lord Jehovah; they were waiting for the Messiah, the promised Redeemer. Unless they were Roman government officials or soldiers, most of them were farmers, fishermen, or businessmen—not criminals, lunatics, witches, or others whom you might ordinarily expect to be under the influence of Satan or subjected to his oppression. In fact, the Jews were forbidden to practice witchcraft or to engage in any aspect of the occult. In the Old Testament, such practices were punishable by death. (See Deuteronomy 18.) This means that, in Jesus' day, even some religious people who believed in the Lord were demonized.

Accordingly, when we encounter someone today who needs deliverance, we shouldn't assume that the person must be a criminal, a witch, a sorcerer, a prostitute, or an idol worshipper, like *"certain women who had been healed of evil spirits and infirmities—Mary called Magdalene, out of whom had come seven demons"* (Luke 8:2). Although there are people who are involved in such things and who allow Satan to influence and control them, there are also millions of "ordinary" people—such as educators, lawyers, doctors, artists, accountants, and secretaries—who need deliverance from the oppression of wicked spirits, just as the common people in the days of Christ needed to be set free from Satan's power. As I wrote earlier, I believe that the majority of the people in the church need deliverance from demonization; this is about the same percentage as need healing.

Again, demonization is not the same as demon possession, which refers to total dominion by an evil spirit. This takes place when someone is invaded and controlled by that evil spirit—when the individual's spirit, soul, and body are completely dominated by the demon (or demons). In the fifth chapter of Mark, there is an account of a man who was demon possessed. He did terrible things, against even his own body.

A man with an unclean spirit…had his dwelling among the tombs; and no one could bind him, not even with chains, because he had often been bound with shackles and chains. And the chains had been pulled apart by him, and the shackles broken in pieces; neither could anyone tame him. And always, night and day, he was in the mountains and in the tombs, crying out and cutting himself with stones.

(Mark 5:2–5)

This man was possessed, and not just by one demon but by a group of demons called *"Legion."* (See Mark 5:9.) When the demons that controlled the man's life saw Jesus and heard Him command them to come out of the man, they began to shout, *"What have I to do with You, Jesus, Son of the Most High God? I implore You by God that You do not torment me"* (Mark 5:7). Some people have told me that, before they visited my church, they hated me. Although they did not know me (I had never even spoken with them), and although I had never done anything to hurt them, they hated me. If they saw me up close, they wanted to hurt me. When people hate others for no reason, it is evidence of the presence of a demon. This may be why some people become angry at deliverance ministries and denounce them.

> *Anything that is anti-natural and compulsive is demonic. The greatest characteristic of demonic activity in a person is that the individual finds no rest for his soul.*

When Jesus set people free from Satan's power, the first thing they wanted to do was to tell their family members and friends about what had happened to them. Note what the man who had been possessed by the legion did after he received his deliverance: *"He departed and began to proclaim in Decapolis all that Jesus had done for him; and all marveled"* (Mark 5:20). This is how many people responded after Christ liberated them.

However, notice how the onlookers reacted when Christ delivered the man. They were so astounded that, instead of glorifying God that this man had recovered his self-control and no longer had to live in chains or be possessed by the demons that had tortured him, they preferred to react to the situation by "casting" Jesus out of the city! *"They were afraid....Then they began to plead with Him to depart from their region"* (Mark 5:15, 17).

These people refused to confront the reality of divine deliverance face-to-face. A similar situation occurs today. Some people feel no shame in consulting fortune-tellers, practicing outlandish occult rituals, or binding themselves with everything that Satan offers them; but when they have the opportunity to be set free from demonic oppression or possession, or to see others freed from evil spirits, they feel ashamed and/or become afraid. Christ instructed the man whom He had delivered to go and tell others everything he had received from God. He didn't tell him to keep it a secret. (See Mark 5:19.) Yet, today, after some people are set free, they feel too embarrassed about their former problems to share their testimonies with others. Consequently, many of them go back to the same condition—or to an even worse one—with which they were previously afflicted.

We must preach deliverance in the same way that Christ preached it. We must demonstrate the truth of the Scriptures and remove the stigma of deliverance, as well as the fear that prevents people from seeking it and receiving it. If the generation currently in leadership would do this, the next generation would follow its example, because young people today are tired of merely protecting their reputations and satisfying religious decorum. They want to know the true God, and they want to experience spiritual reality and freedom.

2. Discern Between the Effects of Demonic Attack and the Actions of the "Flesh"

When we minister to other people (as well as when we examine our own lives), it is essential for us to discern which negative behaviors and actions are prompted by demonic attacks, and which come from the *"flesh"* (see, for example, Galatians 5:16 NKJV, KJV), with regard to how they operate in our lives. The flesh does not refer to our physical bodies but to the corruption of sin working within us to pervert our thoughts, desires, and motivations.

Discerning between the work of demons and the fleshly nature is important because there have been two extremes in the Christian world regarding the existence and activities of demons. In the past, many people who ministered deliverance seemed to see a demon behind every bush. Other Christians completely dismissed the idea of demons, attributing every problem to the fleshly nature. Not all problems are demonic; neither are they all a result of the flesh. We need to recognize that either source can incite negative behavior, and then we must learn to identify the correct one in each situation.

Dealing with Demonic Attack

Demons work to destroy people's lives. As we read earlier in Ephesians 6:12 (TLB), demons are evil entities *"without bodies,"* so they desire to work through the bodies of human beings as a way to operate on the physical earth. Yet they are able to function outside human bodies, as well as inside them. Furthermore, demons have personalities, and they exhibit some characteristics similar to human beings. For example, they are self-aware, they have a will, they feel emotions, they have knowledge, and they even have the ability to think and to speak (using human instruments). In addition, as followers of Satan, their consciences are seared.

Throughout the Scriptures, we see evidence of the above characteristics of demons. A demon will tempt, deceive, enslave, torment, push, and corrupt a human being to do its will. The will of every demon responds to the will of its lord—Satan. Please understand that the will of Satan never includes the well-being of any man, woman, or child. He always wants to usurp people's authority in order to destroy humanity, as well as the earth. He wants to mock God and to annihilate everything that God loves, especially His most precious creation—human beings.

Demons try to keep people from recognizing and knowing the truth about Jesus Christ. They attempt to stop God's children from fulfilling their purpose and calling. They endeavor to prevent believers from serving Christ, placing obstacles to block them from becoming instruments of God who move in the power of the supernatural. Demons work to thwart believers from living an abundant life in Christ. The solution to such demonic attack and oppression is deliverance.

Dealing with the Flesh

The impulses of the flesh were set in motion in all human beings by the fall of humanity. This occurred when our first parents, Adam and Eve, listened to the lies of Satan and disobeyed God. (See Genesis 3.) Some synonyms for the flesh are the *"sinful nature"* (see, for example, Romans 7:18 NIV, TLB), the *"old man"* (see, for example, Romans 6:6), the "carnal self" (see, for example, Romans 7:14), the "Adamic nature" (see 1 Corinthians 15:22), and the "former you." In a later chapter, we will further explore the inner conflict between spirit and flesh, and we will learn how to have victory over the flesh.

When a sinful behavior is related to a carnal desire—rather than to demonic attack—the solution is to "die to self." We *can* "crucify" the flesh and cause it to be in submission to Christ. It will require daily death to self, but it is possible to exercise dominion over sinful desires.

The flesh is corrupt in itself, but it also attracts demons—just as the flesh of a carcass attracts vultures. Many people allow the sinful nature to become enthroned in their lives, so that they exclusively or primarily live to satisfy their fleshly desires. Such a lifestyle produces sin, complacency, and an eager pursuit of worldly delights, which are only temporary and ultimately lead to death. In contrast, when someone wholeheartedly pursues the life of the Spirit, he will experience peace and joy—not only on earth but also for all eternity.

> *The remedy for the flesh is to "crucify" it,*
> *but the cure for demons is to cast*
> *out the evil spirit(s).*

For those who are living according to the sinful nature, godly counsel about "crucifying" the flesh can be effective in helping them to live in line with the Spirit—if they heed that counsel. However, when demons are involved, something else is needed. Demons cannot be "counseled"; they must be cast out. The treatment used for the flesh will not bring the same results with demons. Many people are unknowingly trying to "cast out" the flesh and "crucify" demons! That will never work. The demon who was "counseled" will merely gloat, because it knows it is wasting your time. It will further establish its presence in the life of the person it is oppressing, while using that person to mock you.

For example, if you tell someone who is under the influence of a demon in the area of sexuality—perhaps manifesting in adultery—to deny the flesh, that individual will usually become frustrated, because his efforts will prove futile. Perhaps, for a little while, the person may be able to control the negative impulse. However, the instant that resolve disappears, he will fall into sin once more. People must first be set free from demonic control before they can learn to exercise self-discipline.

How can you discern whether you are fighting against your flesh or against a demon? Generally, if you are fighting a demon, you will not be able to exercise self-control, no matter how hard you try. You will be wrestling a compulsive desire that goes beyond your strength and your desire to please God and to show respect to your family. If you have prayed and fasted but continue to fall into the same sin, you are probably dealing with a demon that has somehow found an entrance to oppress the affected area of your life.

He who is slow to anger is better than the mighty, and he who rules his spirit than he who takes a city.   (Proverbs 16:32)

When the protective walls of our spirits are down, we are defenseless. Prayer, fasting, and self-denial will raise them back up again and strengthen us so we can rule over our flesh and keep the enemy away. Some people provide no protection for their spirits at all; therefore, they lose the ability to govern them, and they end up giving way and allowing wicked spirits to come into their lives.

> *Demons enter a person's life when the protective walls of his spirit are down.*

3. Recognize That Deliverance Is Part of the Finished Work of the Cross and the Resurrection

Deliverance is part of the finished work of the cross and the resurrection, in which Jesus won the war against sin, sickness, and death. The war is already over! All we need in order to enter into that victory is to appropriate (apply) Christ's perfect work in our lives by faith. Suppose a millionaire wrote you a check for a large sum as a gift. The only thing left for you to do in order to obtain that money would be to cash the check. If you never cashed it, you would not be able to do anything with the money that was given to you. On the other hand, if you were to cash it, the money would be yours to use. In a similar way, when Christ defeated the enemy through His death on the cross and His resurrection, He provided for every human need, including material provision, financial resources, good health, and deliverance from Satan. The next step for you is to apply the benefits of that victory by receiving it and "depositing" it—making it effective in your own life.

4. Understand That Deliverance Is "the Children's Bread"—the Provision of Our Heavenly Father

Jesus Christ once described deliverance as *"the children's bread"* (Matthew 15:26); this term refers to a family's daily meals. Jesus never said that deliverance was available for only a few special children. He said it was for *the* children. If you are a child of God—having believed in Christ and received Him as the Lord and Savior of your life—and if you need deliverance, then all you have to do is to take the bread that Christ offers you.

If you are struggling with fear, anxiety, rage, resentment, hate, or jealousy, you can be set free. If you are battling doubt, unbelief, procrastination, or depression, you can be released from your burden. If you are in bondage to your tongue, so that you habitually speak lies, slander, gossip, or blasphemy, you can repent and receive freedom. If you continually succumb to sexual immorality, involving yourself in pornography, adultery, homosexuality, fornication, or masturbation, you can be delivered. If you are enslaved by uncontrolled appetites, wrestling with an addiction to pills, alcohol, or nicotine, you can take the children's bread and be set free. You can be delivered—even right now!

Several years ago, Pastor Samson Paul from Bangalore, India, attended a convention held in Orlando, Florida. After the event, he asked where he could find a good church, and a friend took him to our congregation in Miami, King Jesus International Ministry. "It was a four-hour drive, but it was worth it," Pastor Samson says. That Sunday, he attended two of our services, and he grew interested in one of my messages about the resurrection and the supernatural power of God.

Ever since that day, he has remained connected to our ministry and has implemented in his church in India everything he has learned about supernatural power. He has boldly established baptisms and deliverances, and great miracles have taken place. After only a year and a half, his church grew from 4,500 members to 6,000 members, and he has opened seven daughter churches. Even some nonbelievers seek out Pastor Samson because they desire to receive a miracle. All this is taking place in one of the most pagan of nations. The following are two testimonies from Pastor Samson.

There was a "haunted house" in Pastor Samson's town. Any family who bought the house always ended up with problems. Family members experienced bankruptcy, discord, divorce, and/or despair, having no peace. At one point, a husband and wife purchased the home, completely oblivious to its history. While the wife was cleaning the house, she was possessed by what seemed to be the spirit of an eighty-eight-year-old man who had died there and who did not want anyone else to live in his house. This couple went to Pastor Samson's church looking for help, and, while the pastor was preaching, the woman began to manifest the evil spirit in a horrible way. People say that her eyes popped out and that her face became enlarged. When Pastor Samson mentioned the name of Jesus, the woman said that she knew Jesus. Her deliverance was very strong. She rolled around on the floor while making strange noises and foaming at the mouth, but the power of God set her free. The family moved to another house, and everything returned to normal.

Another testimony involves a woman who had terminal cancer and was in a coma in the hospital. To make matters worse, she was blind and deaf; she was essentially existing in a vegetative state. The doctors said there was nothing they could do for her, and they declared that she would die at any time. One day, while Pastor Samson and his wife were visiting the hospital, the pastor felt that they should pray for this woman. He did not dare pray in the hospital, but God had placed great compassion in his heart for the patients at that facility who were sick and without hope. He felt the love and compassion of God for them, and he began to pray. He declared the love of God for the comatose woman and cast out the spirit of death from her body. Suddenly, she began to react. Tears flowed from her eyes, and everyone realized that she could hear what people around her were saying. The pastor continued to pray, and, two weeks later, the woman miraculously began to see. Eventually, she was released from the hospital. Now, she is totally healed, to the glory of God.

Prayer of Deliverance

I would now like to lead you in a prayer of deliverance. Before you pray, it is important for you to understand that, without true repentance, there can be no deliverance. Repentance is not an emotion; rather, it is a change of mind-set. It is a voluntary decision to stop sinning and disobeying God. It means turning your back on sin, evil, the desires of the flesh, worldly attitudes, and anything else that displeases God, with the conviction that all these things are wrong and are harmful to your relationship with your heavenly Father. That includes any negative covenants, or "secret vows," which you have made with yourself, such as declaring, "I will *never* trust men again," or "I will *always* hate her for what she did to me." Repentance involves making a decision to submit to God, without reservation, with the belief that it is the right thing to do. If you repent of your sinful thoughts and sinful practices, please repeat this prayer:

> Heavenly Father, I come before Your presence with a humble heart. I recognize that I have sinned against You, and I repent of my wrongdoing. I confess my transgressions right now. I also forgive all those who have offended me, and I break any ties I have had with the occult and with secret vows. I ask You to forgive me and to cleanse me. Remove all sin from me—all iniquity and transgression—by the power of the blood of Jesus, which He shed on the cross on my behalf. Now, I receive Your forgiveness, and I apply the complete work of the cross and the resurrection to my life. I order every demon that has tormented me and influenced my life to leave, right now, and I declare myself free, in the name of Jesus. Amen!

2

THE KINGDOM OF GOD BRINGS DELIVERANCE

Before the first man and woman were created by God, a spiritual war took place in heaven. A being named Lucifer, whom God had created and appointed to be an archangel, became prideful and arrogant. Lucifer had been given beauty and wisdom and had been put in charge of the worship of God in heaven, but he began to desire equality with his Creator. More than that, he wanted to replace God so that he himself could rule over everyone and everything. His heart was filled with iniquity, and he fought against his Maker.

And war broke out in heaven: Michael [another archangel who was loyal to God] *and his angels fought with the dragon* [Lucifer]; *and the dragon and his angels fought, but they did not prevail, nor was a place found for them in heaven any longer. So the great dragon was cast out, that serpent of old, called the Devil and Satan, who deceives the whole world; he was cast to the earth, and his angels were cast out with him.* (Revelation 12:7–9)

Lucifer promoted a rebellion, and he seduced a third of God's angels to follow him, renouncing their loyalty to their Creator. Expelled from heaven, Lucifer and the other rebellious angels were thrown down to the earth. In the Scriptures, we read the following: *"How you are fallen from heaven, O Lucifer, son of the morning! How you are cut down to the ground, you who weakened the nations!"* (Isaiah 14:12), and *"[The dragon's] tail drew a third of the stars of heaven and threw them to the earth"* (Revelation 12:4).

The above verses show how Lucifer, who was once known as the *"son of the morning,"* became the *"adversary"* (1 Peter 5:8) who is often called the devil, or Satan. Once Lucifer and the other angels rejected God, they became a rival kingdom, one that continually opposes the kingdom of God. These fallen angels are now what we call "demons." I believe that their rebellion and banishment to the earth caused a divine judgment to take place upon the planet. Note the wording in the first chapter of Genesis: *"In the beginning God created the heavens and the earth.* ***The earth was without form, and void; and darkness was on the face of the deep.*** *And the Spirit of God was hovering over the face of the waters"* (Genesis 1:1–2). The emptiness and darkness was due to the presence of Satan and his angels.

Spiritual Warfare on Earth

Sometime after these events, God created life on the earth, including all vegetation, fish, birds, and animals. Last, He created human beings, saying, *"Let Us make man in Our image, according to Our likeness;*

let them have dominion over the fish of the sea, over the birds of the air, and over the cattle, over all the earth and over every creeping thing that creeps on the earth" (Genesis 1:26). The Creator placed the first man and woman, Adam and Eve, in the garden of Eden. They were created in the image of God, and they were given the role of stewards and guardians over the earth.

We should understand that when mankind was created, Satan had already been cast down to the earth. Thus, when God gave human beings dominion, He was giving them authority under His kingdom, the government of heaven, to rule in the world—including the ability to subjugate Satan and his kingdom of darkness.

The devil knew that he had not been authorized by God to rule on the earth; he was here only as a result of his punishment. To "legally" operate in the world, he would need to usurp the authority that human beings had been given by God. So, he tempted Adam, through Eve, to willingly disobey his Creator. Instead of exercising dominion over Satan, and thus subduing him—which he could have done—Adam chose to sin against God. He failed to use the authority that God had given him to rule over the enemy. (See Genesis 3.)

Mankind's spiritual war involves an enemy who usurped authority over the earth.

In contrast to what we read in the New Testament, we do not see any accounts in the Old Testament of the ministry of casting out demons. This is because Satan had won the legal authority to operate on earth. As a result of Adam's disobedience, human beings lost their right to govern over the world. No person had the authority to cast out demons or to subdue the devil, because Satan had established his wicked rule on the planet. Additionally, human beings had a sinful nature and were no longer in direct fellowship with their Creator. Consequently, they became subject to an enemy who exercised power over them. And, by surrendering their authority to Satan, they surrendered it, by extension, to his demons.

Jesus Christ Brought God's Kingdom and the Ministry of Deliverance

When God's Son, Jesus Christ, came to earth and confronted evil spirits, some of the demons yelled, *"What have we to do with You, Jesus, You Son of God? Have You come here to torment us before the time?"* (Matthew 8:29). These demons knew that, according to God's plans, they would ultimately be cast into the fires of eternal punishment. Christ did not argue their claim that it was *"before the time,"* because He was obedient to the will of the Father. He didn't torment the demons, but He did exercise authority over them. Meanwhile, Satan and his demons plotted to kill the Son of God in an attempt to thwart God's plan of redemption for human beings and to maintain their power over the earth.

Christ's spiritual battle was more difficult than that of Adam, because He was dealing with a legal enemy.

Jesus Christ, the Son of God, was able to cast out demons even before He went to the cross and defeated Satan, because the kingdom of God had arrived *with* Him, and because He was in perfect fellowship with His Father in heaven. When Jesus was resurrected from the dead after dying on the cross for our sins, He stripped the devil's authority from him, so that Satan returned to functioning under an illegal status.

After disarming, defeating, and dethroning the devil, Christ gave the church power and authority to deal with him. (See, for example, Luke 10:19; Matthew 28:18–20.)

Satan still has power, but now he has no *authority*; the use of his power on earth is unlawful. He can exercise power over us only when we give him a legal opening to do so through our disobedience to God.

When Christ brought the kingdom of God to earth with the manifestation of the casting out of demons, many people were left speechless. They had never seen anything like it. Some people asked, "'*What a word this is! For with authority and power He commands the unclean spirits, and they come out.' And the report about* [Jesus] *went out into every place in the surrounding region*" (Luke 4:36–37). Not even the great patriarchs of Israel—such as Noah, Abraham, and Moses—had ever delivered people from demons. I have read that many people who lived during Jesus' time considered a demon to be an "inferior deity." Therefore, the people reacted to Jesus' power to cast out of demons with either admiration (if they believed in Him) or mistrust (if they did not accept Him). Those who were under the influence of demons had a strong negative reaction to this overthrow of the kingdom of darkness.

> *The casting out of demons is a manifestation of the dominion of God's kingdom.*

Deliverance Came by the Preaching of the Gospel of the Kingdom

Jesus' preaching of the gospel of the kingdom produced five major types of miracles: the curing of deafness, blindness, lameness, and muteness, and the deliverance of the demon possessed. (See, for example, Isaiah 35:5–6; Matthew 4:23–24.) There is no record of any of these five categories of miracles being performed in the Old Testament. Yes, we read about certain miraculous events that occurred under the old covenant—the resurrection of the dead, supernatural provision, and miracles and signs over the elements and other aspects of nature. However, we do not read about the above-mentioned five miracles because, as stated previously, they came with Christ and His preaching of God's kingdom.

Jesus used the casting out of demons as a primary sign to confirm that the kingdom had arrived in a particular place or in a particular person to whom He was ministering. He said, *"If I cast out demons by the Spirit of God, surely the kingdom of God has come upon you"* (Matthew 12:28). When demons leave a place or a person, it is a sign of both overthrow and defeat—overthrow for the kingdom of God and defeat for the kingdom of darkness.

The casting out of demons is the greatest of the five miracles of the kingdom because it implies the removal of the evil governing kingdom.

To preach the kingdom of God without ministering deliverance would be a violation of the laws of God's realm and government, which demand the removal of Satan's kingdom. An announcement about the heavenly kingdom that is not accompanied by the casting out of demons is simply a motivational message. Yet, when we preach God's kingdom and demonstrate the conquest of Satan's kingdom, we will see the dominion of heaven arrive in people's hearts and lives, setting them free from every oppression and bondage. The power of the kingdom of God is able to confront Satan and his demons, subduing them and removing them from the various areas in which they are attacking people, whether it be their family life, finances, health, ministry, or anything else.

> The kingdom of God does not come
> without the overthrow of Satan,
> and vice versa.

Only when we receive the fullness of the kingdom we will be able to subdue Satan, because then we will be operating according to God's government, with our original authority restored to us. Jesus said, "*From the days of John the Baptist until now the kingdom of heaven suffers violence, and the violent take it by force*" (Matthew 11:12).

Thus, deliverance and the kingdom go hand in hand. When someone is healed and set free of any oppression, bondage, or affliction, it is a result of the arrival of God's kingdom. So, when the kingdom comes upon a person, it means that the enemy has been conquered; he has lost his power over that person's life. At that point, Satan's only option is to remain subdued and to obey the new kingdom. This is what it means to overthrow the enemy.

> The condition for subduing Satan
> and his demons is to remain in
> supernatural power and authority.

When we cast out demons, we take authority over evil spiritual entities in the invisible realm—"*persons without bodies*" (Ephesians 6:12 TLB) that torment the bodies, minds, and emotions of human beings.

As a citizen of the kingdom, you can exercise your rights and cast out the enemy from your life and from the lives of others. Again, if you are preaching the message of the heavenly kingdom but not demonstrating it by casting out demons, then the message you are proclaiming is incomplete. It is a misrepresentation of God's kingdom, which provokes a confrontation—a collision—between the government of light and the powers of darkness. Such confrontation ultimately results in the defeat of the enemy and the deliverance of those whom he has oppressed.

In the natural world, two kings, with their corresponding kingdoms, cannot reign over the same territory. Can a new kingdom take up residence in the territory of another kingdom without first defeating and removing the established kingdom? The answer is no. Jesus said, *"When a strong man, fully armed, guards his own palace, his goods are in peace. But when a stronger than he comes upon him and overcomes him, he takes from him all his armor in which he trusted, and divides his spoils"* (Luke 11:21–22).

Each of us must choose which king and which kingdom we will submit to—God's kingdom or Satan's kingdom.

> It is not biblical to preach the gospel
> of the kingdom without also demonstrating it
> by the casting out of demons.

The Presence of the King and His Kingdom

An important part of Jesus' commission on earth was to *"proclaim liberty to the captives…, to set at liberty those who are oppressed"* (Luke 4:18), and we see a fulfillment of that commission in the following passage:

And Jesus went about all Galilee, teaching in their synagogues, preaching the gospel of the kingdom, and healing all kinds of sickness and all kinds of disease among the people. Then His fame went throughout all Syria; and they brought to Him all sick people who were afflicted with various diseases and torments, and those who were demon-possessed, epileptics, and paralytics; and He healed them.   (Matthew 4:23–24)

Demonic spirits cannot withstand the presence of Jesus Christ, the King of Kings. An example of this truth is found in the gospel of Mark.

Now there was a man in their synagogue with an unclean spirit. And he cried out, saying, "Let us alone! What have we to do with You, Jesus of Nazareth? Did You come to destroy us? I know who You are—the Holy One of God!" But Jesus rebuked him, saying, "Be quiet, and come out of him!" And when the unclean spirit had convulsed him and cried out with a loud voice, he came out of him.   (Mark 1:23–26)

The man in the synagogue had at least two demons afflicting him—possibly more—since the *"unclean spirit"* spoke of itself as *"us"* and *"we."* Those demons recognized in Jesus the government of God, which had the power to expel and punish them. They knew who Jesus was, calling Him *"the Holy One of God."*

Today, in most churches, if a similar instance of the manifestation of a demon were to occur in a member of the congregation, the person would be removed from the sanctuary to prevent him from interrupting the service. But in the above situation, Christ immediately expelled the demons from the individual, allowing the delivered man to remain in the synagogue. He commanded, *"Be quiet, and come out of him!"* Interestingly, when Jesus stilled the storm on the Sea of Galilee, His words were much the same: *"Quiet! Be still!"* (Mark 4:39 NIV).

When the demons heard Jesus' command, they provoked a violent reaction in the man. They deliberately tried to defy God's order because they did not want to be removed from the person they were afflicting.

Such fierce manifestations are tangible evidence that a collision has occurred between the two invisible kingdoms and that they are engaged in battle. I often see this type of manifestation when I minster to those who are demonized or demon possessed.

When Christ brought the kingdom of God to earth, He exposed the existence of the kingdom of darkness while clearly demonstrating the superiority of the heavenly kingdom. Accordingly, after the demons initially resisted Jesus' command to come out of the man in the synagogue, they were forced to leave. In this account, we see the victory of the kingdom of light and the defeat of the kingdom of darkness. Whenever you observe demons leaving people, know that the kingdom of heaven has arrived.

Christ said, *"Behold, I cast out demons and perform cures today and tomorrow, and the third day I shall be perfected"* (Luke 13:32). In essence, He was declaring, "I will continue doing what God sent Me to do—preaching, teaching, healing, and casting out demons—until My ministry on earth ends." In fact, Jesus began and ended His ministry doing these very things. Likewise, evil spirits have to submit to the authority that Jesus delegated to believers.

> *When Christ brought the kingdom of God to earth, He exposed the existence of the kingdom of darkness while clearly demonstrating the superiority of the heavenly kingdom.*

Authority over the Enemy

As children of God and citizens of His kingdom, Christians have been given the same authority that Christ has, including power over demons. Today, some Christians preach, some teach, and, in certain cases, some heal; but not many Christians cast out demons. The deliverance that Christ introduced and demonstrated is no longer being practiced by the majority of believers. Yet there are so many people in need of deliverance—even more so than in the days when Jesus Christ walked on the earth.

Jesus never sent out any of His disciples to preach the gospel of the kingdom without first giving them the authority and the power to cast out demons.

When [Jesus] had called His twelve disciples to Him, He gave them power over unclean spirits, to cast them out, and to heal all kinds of sickness and all kinds of disease. (Matthew 10:1)

Then the seventy [disciples] returned with joy, saying, "Lord, even the demons are subject to us in Your name." (Luke 10:17)

As a believer, you are under God's government. Therefore, when you stand in the authority of Christ and say to a demon, "Leave, in the name of Jesus!" it has no other alternative—it has to obey. There is no place for it to hide. Jesus is the Son of God and the King of the kingdom. Recall that when the demons saw Him, they screamed, "[We] *know who You are—the Holy One of God!*" (Mark 1:24; Luke 4:34), because they recognized His heavenly rule. It will work the same way for us, but first we must appropriate our God-given authority. The demons will not leave until they recognize that we are truly governing according to Jesus' reign and power.

Jesus never sent anyone to preach the gospel of the kingdom without first giving them the authority and the power to cast out demons.

The Public Ministry of Deliverance

Most of the wonders that took place during the days of Jesus' ministry and the time of the New Testament church do not take place in the modern church. As we have seen, when Christ cast out a demon, violent manifestations would erupt: people would scream and fall down violently; they would tremble and shake. But those things never stopped Jesus from ministering. He did not prevent those manifestations from happening; He didn't worry about maintaining religious order and decorum. His sole concern was to help people. His disciples followed His example, both while they were with Him and after His ascension to heaven. In the book of Acts, we read the following about the disciple Philip:

> *And the multitudes with one accord heeded the things spoken by Philip, hearing and seeing the miracles which he did. For unclean spirits, crying with a loud voice, came out of many who were possessed; and many who were paralyzed and lame were healed.*
>
> (Acts 8:6–7)

Let us remember that one of Jesus' first encounters with demons was not in the streets but in the synagogue—among people who followed God. His ministry included casting out evil spirits from those who were demonized or demon possessed, not counseling them or giving them a psychiatric evaluation. And, Christ ministered deliverance in public. He did not need a private place or many hours of ministry in order to resolve a situation of demonic oppression or possession.

There are some leaders in the church today who are ashamed of ministering deliverance in public because they think that other people will be frightened away by it. But deliverance is an important part of the gospel of the kingdom, so we have nothing to be ashamed of when practicing it. I have concluded that since Christ delivered people in public, I will deliver people in public, also. We must participate in the ministry of deliverance as openly as we participate in the ministry of salvation or healing or any other aspect of the kingdom. If I have to choose between offending God and offending men, I choose to offend men. I must be on God's side. We are not better than Jesus!

Other church leaders are caught up in a "religious spirit" that does not really want to see deliverance. It prefers the old order of things and human works over a fresh anointing from God and supernatural works. Yet, just as Christ sent out His disciples and the believers of the early church to minister the kingdom, He is sending us, as today's citizens of the kingdom of God on earth, to cast out demons, to heal the sick, and to raise the dead. The only thing that remains is for you to decide to do it!

The first step you must take is to cast out every demonic influence from your family, your business, your finances, and every other area of your life. Then, you will be able to minister deliverance to other people. In Christ, you have the power and the authority, right now, to rebuke every demonic spirit and to establish the kingdom of God in your life! The following account is evidence of God's desire to deliver those who are oppressed by Satan.

"My name is Sally, and my life is a testimony of the fact that Jesus Christ has the power to set free a person's soul and to completely change that person's life. His presence transformed me to the point of enabling me to attain the happiness I had never experienced.

"From my earliest memories, I could not recall ever having been truly happy. I grew up in a dysfunctional home with abusive parents who were alcoholics. In addition to the abuse I suffered from my parents, I also experienced physical, mental, psychological, and sexual abuse from other people. At school, my schoolmates mocked me and sexually harassed me, and several men touched me in inappropriate ways. As a result, when I became a teenager, I decided that I didn't want to live anymore.

"I always looked for love in all the wrong places—in boyfriends and in material things. In reality, my soul needed peace and freedom. I didn't see any way out. When I was fourteen, I was diagnosed with depression and anxiety, and the doctors prescribed medication, which led to my becoming addicted. For years, I felt that I had lost my mind. I tried to commit suicide several times and would hurt myself by cutting my arms and other parts of my body. Three times, my parents utilized a law called the Baker Act, which allowed them to call the police and have them commit me to a psychiatric hospital, where I was kept drugged for seventy-two hours, until a doctor decided either to send me to jail, leave me in the hospital, or allow me to go home.

"During that period, for one reason or another, I spent my time going from one funeral to the next. There were sixteen deaths in my family in a span of five years. In addition, my boyfriend left me, and I fell into another deep depression. I was practically submerged in sin and darkness—everything was sadness, pain, and abandonment! That is why I didn't want to live anymore.

"When I was in tenth grade, I met a teacher named Jose who talked to me about King Jesus Church (Ministerio Internacional El Rey Jesús), but I didn't pay much attention to what he had to say. However, the seed had been planted, and, in time—as a last resort—I opted to get closer to God and to commit to obey His commandments. Since then, I have received deliverance and inner healing. God has restored me, piece by piece. He has set me free from the darkness and sin that had kept me unhappy and depressed. From the time I started to walk in His ways, my life was transformed. Now, my life makes sense; it has direction and purpose—and I am happy! God placed compassion and love in my heart for others, and I want to serve Him by helping people who are in the same type of situation I was in. God is everything to me, and I want to declare to the world that Jesus is my Lord and my Savior! Depression had taken control of me, a sense of loneliness and compulsive thoughts of death had surrounded me incessantly, but God arrived on time and rescued me. Today, I am a new person."

That is a tremendous testimony of what the ministry of deliverance can do in someone's life. It is a kingdom ministry that every Christian has the right to receive and to apply to his life. The body of Christ in America, in Europe, in Asia, and all over the world needs this precious ministry. When I traveled to Ukraine to speak at a conference on the supernatural, the country saw a powerful demonstration of the revelation of the supernatural! Healings, miracles, deliverances, and impartations of the "fire" of God were all evident.

One pastor named Vlad Grebenyuk shared the following testimony about how his ministry changed after he received the revelation of the ministry of deliverance. Although this pastor had been in ministry for twenty years, this was the first time he had encountered the supernatural power of deliverance with the manifestation of casting out demons, and he was confronted with the reality of the supernatural realm. He was shocked after witnessing at least two people manifest a demonic influence, and he went to the church to pray.

Later that evening, God told him that he was to participate in deliverance ministry. He knew that he would continue to see demonic manifestations, just as Jesus had, but that he would walk in the same authority as Jesus did to cast them out. One evening, after a group meeting, Pastor Vlad was speaking about repentance to a young boy in his congregation who was a new believer, and the boy asked if he could start repenting for some specific sins. As he began to do so, the young boy started convulsing and screaming at the top of his lungs. The demons that had kept him in bondage for years were starting to manifest. With the revelation that he had received concerning the power of the name of Jesus, Pastor Vlad rebuked the demons and cast them out.

That was the first time God used him to deliver someone from demonization. This incident created a hunger among the members of his church to see more supernatural manifestations of deliverance. So, they conducted a "Daniel Fast" for a whole week and also held a nonstop, twenty-four-hour time of prayer. One evening, as Pastor Vlad drove around his town, he declared that the town was going to belong to Jesus.

Pastor Vlad listened to recordings of my sermons, and he heard a testimony about breaking the power of influence. Instantly, the Holy Spirit told him that there were two strong spirits influencing and controlling his city: witchcraft and homosexuality. He started praying against the *"strong man"* (see Luke 11:21–22) of these powers, expecting to see a change. Within the next few weeks, a young man who had been invited to the youth House of Peace (home fellowship ministry) held at Pastor Vlad's home started to behave in a very strange way. They took the young man to another room and began to minister deliverance, leading him to renounce every evil spirit. Immediately, Pastor Vlad received instructions by the Holy Spirit to cast out the spirits one by one. That young man had a long line of generational curses, with voodoo practices, and he was set free for the first time in his life. Praise God! Pastor Vlad shared, "I believe it was a lesson from God to teach me about the reality of what is going on in the spiritual world." During the next two days, Pastor Vlad spent time in the presence of God, desiring to know more. In that small amount of time, God revealed to him more about deliverance than he had learned in his previous twenty years of going to church and practicing religion.

Recently, late on a Saturday night, Pastor Vlad received a phone call from one of the members of his church who asked if he would pray for a demon-possessed man. The afflicted man, who was in his early twenties, was so deep in sin that the devil had physically taken control of his body. The man held the palms of his hands so tightly against his ears to avoid listening to Pastor Vlad that his ears turned dark red. Also, at first, he spoke in an unusual dialect that was impossible to understand. The young man was out of himself and out of his mind.

As the night proceeded, this man was delivered and set free, and, the next morning, he woke up with a completely different attitude and was finally at peace in his body, his spirit, and his soul. He was astonished and did not know what had happened to him!

"This is just an example of how powerful the God whom we serve is, and how much power belongs to us as children of God. My desire is that my Slavic people in Ukraine will grasp the revelation Apostle Maldonado teaches on deliverance, imparting it all over the world into people's hungry hearts."

In Christ, you have the power and the authority, right now, to rebuke every demonic spirit and to establish the kingdom of God in your life!

Prayer of Deliverance

To conclude this chapter, say the following prayer out loud:

Lord Jesus, I believe that You are the Son of God and the King of the kingdom. I confess that You are my Savior and Lord. When You died on the cross for my sins and were raised from the dead, You completely defeated Satan and his demons. I acknowledge that the kingdom of light is completely superior to the kingdom of darkness. As a child of God and a citizen of His kingdom, I have been given authority over all the power of the enemy. In the name and authority of Jesus, I cast out every demonic influence from my family, my work, my finances, my ministry, my health, and every other area of my life. I rebuke every demonic spirit and command it to leave me, right now. The kingdom of God is fully established in my life! I have been delivered and set free, in the name of Jesus. Amen!

3

THE INTERNAL CONFLICT
BETWEEN THE FLESH
AND THE SPIRIT

In our ministry, I regularly hear about genuine transformation taking place in people's lives. A short time ago, a man named Josué came up to the altar during a service to testify about the power of God in his life. His testimony especially impacted me because of the restoration that Jesus had accomplished in him and the radical transformation that had occurred in his heart.

Josué explained that even though he had been raised as the son of a pastor, he had had no desire to follow the "rules" of religion. So, he had rebelled and fallen into the lifestyle of the world, including drug abuse. He began to live the college party life but, as a result, ended up in jail. His father visited him and gave him a Bible, insisting that he needed to change.

Josué spent more than a week in jail, but his mind was still set on continuing his fast lifestyle; he was ready to go back to the world. On his last day in jail, a Christian man was assigned to the cell across from him, and this man started speaking to him about Jesus. All at once, Josué was filled with the Holy Spirit; he encountered the Lord and started weeping. "I suddenly became happy and knew that once I was released, I needed to return to God," he said.

Ever since this encounter with God, Josué hasn't touched illegal drugs or fallen back into his old ways. "God has used me to speak to my old friends, presenting to them the truth of the gospel!" he exclaimed. He further testified that God has progressively restored his family. His mother, who had been schizophrenic for twenty-one years, was completely healed and delivered. His sister, who used to struggle with suicidal thoughts, was also delivered. Through Jesus Christ, Josué was reconciled to God. He now feels that sin has no power over him. He is a new man, thanks to the restoration Christ accomplished in him.

God's Original Intention

Please understand that whenever I talk about *restoration* in this book, I am referring to our returning to God's original intention for us, the original state in which we were created. Everything in God begins with His purpose, which never changes. The first human being, Adam, represents God's plan for humanity. However, even though Adam was the first person to be created, he was also the first person to forfeit the Creator's purpose for his existence. In contrast, Jesus, the "second Adam" (see 1 Corinthians 15:45), represents the restoration of God's original intent for human beings, which the first Adam failed to fulfill.

What was God's purpose for the human race? It was to reflect His *"image"* and *"likeness."* (See Genesis 1:26.) Throughout the Scriptures, we can see that God's intent was, in essence, to replicate Himself in a created being who had His own "spiritual DNA." This created being (1) would have intimate communion with God, (2) would govern and rule over everything God had created, and (3) would be fruitful, multiply, and fill the earth. (See Genesis 1:28.) Once we grasp this truth, we will realize that we cannot really talk about our being restored unless it is in the context of the original purpose of our Creator.

The English word *"image"* in Genesis 1:26 is translated from the Hebrew term *tselem*, among whose meanings is "resemblance"; it denotes "representative figure." The word also signifies "essential nature." Human beings were created with the essential nature, or qualities, of God.

Based on various dictionary definitions of *image*, as well as on revelation I have received about this concept, I believe the following meanings also shed light on the significance of our being made in God's image: (1) a *shadow*, in the sense of being "an imitation of something," or a "copy"; (2) "the representation of a substance," "a duplicate, likeness, or replica." These words represent an external appearance; in this case, that of God's. It is fitting to say that when Jesus came to earth, He specifically came in the form of a man, rather than in any other form or as any other created being, because it is human beings who represent the nature of God.

The word *"likeness"* in the creation account comes from the Hebrew term *demuwth*, which can mean "resemblance," "similitude," or "shape; figure; form; pattern." Perhaps *The Living Bible* best captures the sense of this word when it says, *"So God made man like his Maker. Like God did God make man"* (Genesis 1:27). God created man like Himself. Human beings are meant to be on earth as God is in heaven. This explains why He gave us power and authority to govern and rule over everything He has created.

Made in God's *"likeness,"* we are "patterned" after Him. One example of this concerns the Creator's triune nature: He is God the Father,

God the Son, and God the Holy Spirit. As we have previously noted, man is also made up of three parts: he is a *spirit* with a *soul* who dwells in a physical *body*: *"Now may the God of peace Himself sanctify you completely; and may your whole **spirit**, **soul**, and **body** be preserved blameless at the coming of our Lord Jesus Christ"* (1 Thessalonians 5:23).

The Origin of the "Flesh," or the Sinful Nature

We know that, tragically, human beings walked away from God's original intention for them. When Satan tempted Adam and Eve to disobey God, they succumbed to that temptation and fell, and the consequences were evident. Their spirits died, their souls were corrupted by the sinful nature, and their bodies became subject to aging, sickness, and death. They were banished from the garden of Eden—the garden of God's glory. Sometime later, Adam and Eve had children, to whom they transferred their sin nature by means of "the law of generational inheritance"—and their children subsequently passed along the same sin nature to their offspring; this has been the case from generation to generation to this day. So, the law of generational inheritance applies not only to physical genetics but also to our spiritual state. Every human being is born with a sinful nature because he was "conceived in sin." (See Psalm 51:5.)

> *Adam's decision to disobey God caused his spirit to die and his soul and body to be corrupted.*

As descendants of Adam, all human beings are born with a nature that is inherently rebellious toward God. This leads us to act independently of Him and to live mainly for selfish purposes, just as Satan separated himself from God, pursuing his own self-centered desires. Most people's biggest problem today is that they live *"according to the prince of the power of the air, the spirit who now works in the sons of disobedience,...*[being] *by nature children of wrath"* (Ephesians 2:2–3).

> *The flesh, or sinful nature,*
>
> *originated in the fall of mankind.*

Christ Came to Restore Humanity

On the cross, the "second Adam" paid the full debt for mankind's rebellion and sin. He did this to restore human beings to God's original design. This means that, through the work of Christ, if we repent, we can be reconciled with God. Without repentance, there can be no reconciliation, because a rebel cannot be restored as long as he is still resisting God. Without repentance, we can exhibit only an outer appearance of Christianity that is not genuine transformation. True reconciliation restores us to an intimate relationship with our heavenly Father, which the first man and woman once enjoyed. Furthermore, it gives us the power and authority to rule on earth and to be fruitful for God.

True reconciliation with the Father, through Jesus, revives our spirit, transforms our heart, and restores our relationship with Him.

Our Ongoing Struggle Against Sin

The apostle Paul wrote the following to the first-century Christians in Rome:

> *For what I do is not the good I want to do; no, the evil I do not want to do—this I keep on doing. Now if I do what I do not want to do,*

it is no longer I who do it, but it is sin living in me that does it. So I find this law at work: When I want to do good, evil is right there with me. For in my inner being I delight in God's law; but I see another law at work in the members of my body, waging war against the law of my mind and making me a prisoner of the law of sin at work within my members. What a wretched man I am! Who will rescue me from this body of death? (Romans 7:19–24 NIV)

These verses describe the internal battle between the flesh and the spirit experienced by Paul, one of the great apostles in the history of Christianity. But why did Paul, a believer redeemed by Christ, experience this conflict? Jesus defeated sin, the flesh, the devil, and the world through His death on the cross and His resurrection; His work to restore us to God has been fully completed. So, what type of conflict was the apostle Paul speaking of in Romans 7?

The conflict Paul described was the battle between the flesh and the spirit. As I explained previously, when someone accepts Jesus Christ into his heart, it is the spirit that is reborn; the spirit is also the place where God's own Spirit comes to dwell in the believer. Yet the person's soul (mind, will, and emotions) still needs to be delivered, renewed, and transformed. As we will see, the soul is the arena that remains corrupted by the flesh, and from which the fleshly desires often take control in our lives. Paul wrote, *"For the flesh lusts against the Spirit, and the Spirit against the flesh; and these are contrary to one another, so that you do not do the things that you wish"* (Galatians 5:17).

Paul touched on the topic of grace more than any other New Testament writer, but he also wrote much about crucifying the flesh. He spoke of dying daily (see 1 Corinthians 15:31), of putting off the "old man" (see Ephesians 4:22; Colossians 3:9), of dying to earthly things (see Galatians 6:14; Colossians 3:5), and of denying the carnal self (see Titus 2:12). Such ideas are not often mentioned in the modern church! Yet, to grow spiritually, we must not only continuously receive God's grace but also persistently deny our flesh so that it doesn't rule over our lives. Rejecting the sinful nature is an ongoing, daily process.

The first spiritual confrontation that a new believer faces is usually the inner conflict between the flesh and the spirit. Before his spirit was renewed, the believer may not have been aware of this conflict, especially if his conscience was dulled by sin. The painful battle that arises within a new Christian can take him by surprise, producing guilt and confusion. That is why we must understand the true nature of this conflict.

Have you experienced this inner conflict between the flesh and the spirit? Has the struggle discouraged you, because you want to please God but always seem to do the opposite of what He asks? You may desire to pray more, to learn how to fast, to seek God earnestly, to commit to Him on a deeper level, and to worship Him with greater freedom, but your flesh finds these things disagreeable, and you can't seem to make any progress in these areas. Perhaps you have certain ungodly feelings that you cannot defeat, sinful longings that seem uncontrollable no matter how hard you try to stifle them. Maybe you are unable to suppress a negative emotion that rises within you, such as anger, and this has prevented you from succeeding in your job or in your relationships. Maybe you battle thoughts of revenge, sexual immorality, or unbelief. Or, it could be that you struggle with anxiety or low self-esteem. If so, I want you to know that there is a key to fighting this battle between your flesh and your spirit, so that you can emerge from the fight victorious. We will discover this key as we progress through this chapter.

The biblical definition of the "flesh" is anything that lacks the control and influence of the Holy Spirit.

Humanity's Threefold Nature

Paul wrote, *"Therefore, if anyone is in Christ, he is a new creation; old things have passed away; behold, all things have become new"* (2 Corinthians 5:17). It might seem at first that this verse contradicts the idea of a conflict between the flesh and the spirit, but it makes sense when we understand our triune nature as human beings, as well as what takes place in the new birth. Let's now explore these three aspects of our makeup—the spirit, the soul, and the body.

The Spirit

The word *"spirit"* is translated from the Greek word *pneuma*, which literally means "breath," "breeze," or "wind," and figuratively indicates "spirit." The spirit is the part of the believer that God fully redeemed in salvation; it had been dead in sin, but it was restored to life in Jesus. The spirit is the center of a person, the inner man. It is the true "self." It is the spiritual heart, where God's Spirit—and therefore His presence—dwell. It is where our relationship with our heavenly Father takes place, including our communion with Him. (See 1 Corinthians 6:17.) It is the seat of our spiritual intuition, or perception, where we "feel," "hear," and "grasp" spiritual things; thus, it is the place where supernatural revelation is received, where God reveals His mind and heart. It is also the place of the conscience, which is the voice of our spirit that convicts us of what is evil and affirms to us what is right and good.

The Soul

The Greek word for *"soul"* is *psyche*, a word that denotes "life." In this case, it refers to the life of the soul—the mind, the will, and the emotions—or "the seat of personality." As mentioned earlier, in contrast to the spirit, the soul was not instantly redeemed at salvation; it must undergo a continuous process of transformation into the likeness of Jesus Christ because it has been corrupted by the sinful nature. That is why we need to receive deliverance in our mind, will, and emotions. God's Word is essential in this process because it is able to penetrate our very being, distinguishing between our spirit and our soul and revealing our true motivations. The Word *"is living and powerful, and sharper than any two-edged sword, piercing even to the division of soul and spirit, and of joints and marrow, and is a discerner of the thoughts and intents of the heart"* (Hebrews 4:12). Deliverance enables us to walk in continuous and progressive spiritual transformation.

"The natural man does not receive the things of the Spirit of God, for they are foolishness to him; nor can he know them....But he who is spiritual judges all things" (1 Corinthians 2:14–15). An individual who has not been born again, or a believer who is still bound by his soul and has not yet begun to be transformed, is often referred to as *"natural,"* *"soulish,"* or *"fleshly."* The Greek word for *"natural"* in the above verse is sometimes translated as *"sensual,"* as in James 3:15. The decisions of a *"natural,"* fleshly person are directed by his corrupt soul; consequently, his entire life is controlled by that corrupt soul. In contrast, a believer who is controlled by his spirit is called *"spiritual."*

> The "soulish" person is independent, selfish, and rebellious against the spirit.

In the Scriptures, Abraham's sons Ishmael and Isaac symbolize the opposition between the flesh and the spirit. The Angel of the Lord told Ishmael's mother that her son would be like a *"wild donkey"*—an animal characterized by stubbornness. (See Genesis 16:11–12 NIV, NASB.) A fleshly person is willful, prideful, selfish, egocentric, independent (from both God and His people), and rebellious. These characteristics describe the soul that has not been transformed, delivered from bondage, or healed from hurts. In contrast, the Lord told Abraham that He would establish His *"everlasting covenant"* (Genesis 17:19) with Isaac, the son of promise. It is God's covenant with us through Jesus Christ that gives us access to the freedom of life in the Spirit.

The following three expressions are representative of the soul, whether it is carnal or transformed: "I think" (the mind), "I want" (the will), and "I feel" (the emotions). These are the soul's three primary motivations. All Christians must (1) renew the mind according to the thoughts of Christ, (2) submit the will to God, and (3) yield the emotions to the desires of the Lord. Doing so will enable us to reflect the image of our heavenly Father.

The Mind

The mind is the intellect; it includes the processes by which we reason, as well as the sum of our conscious and unconscious thoughts. Our intellect has been established and shaped by various influences throughout our lives, such as the following: information and impressions we have taken in; knowledge we have attained through education and other means; the opinions we have developed based on our experiences; the opinions of others that we have been exposed to; the characteristics of the family, society, and nation in which we grew up; and the culture in which we currently live.

Someone who is operating according to a "natural," or "soulish," disposition does not discern or understand that which is supernatural, or spiritual. He perceives only the natural world—what he can identify with one or more of his five senses (sight, hearing, touch, taste, and smell)—or what he can reason out intellectually. Although such a person may be highly educated, he has no way of understanding the supernatural, because he operates according to the limited extent of human knowledge. The supernatural is above and beyond reason and natural laws; it can be understood only by the spiritual senses, such as faith or supernatural discernment.

A soulish person does not recognize that his spiritual senses are dead (in the case of someone who has not been born anew in Christ), or asleep (in the case of a believer who has not yet learned to die to the corruption of his soul). For such a person, the supernatural is a foreign world or environment that his reason and intellect do not accept. When he encounters something that cannot be explained or defined by the natural world, he considers it illogical or foolish. His conclusion is that the situation or event is not real and is unworthy of his attention. He rejects it completely.

Thus, the unredeemed mind accepts false ideas and develops wrong patterns of thinking that lead to mental strongholds in which one's perspectives are entrenched in error. So, even when an individual's spirit is born anew in Christ, his thought patterns may repeatedly return to concepts and ideas that go against the mind of God, and he may experience a continual battle in his mind between truth and error.

As we will see, the solution for a mind that has been corrupted by the sinful nature is renewal through revelation by the Word of God. We must break old mental patterns, false paradigms, and negative thinking habits and replace them with God's thoughts, until the mind of Christ is fully formed within us. (See Romans 12:2; Galatians 4:19.)

The "soulish," or "natural," man does not believe what his intellect cannot explain.

The Will

The will is our ability to choose. It refers to the decisions we make that lead to our actions. Our personal strength is housed in our will, and what we decide to do determines the quality of our character. The soulish person is directed by a will that is tainted by sin rather than by a will that is aligned with the heavenly Father and His Word. Even when someone has good intentions to do God's will, he can't sustain the power to do what is right by the exercise of his will alone. Somewhere along the line, his resolve will weaken. Later in this chapter, we will see how to yield our will to God's so that we can reflect and pursue His purposes.

The Emotions

The emotions are the organ of the soul that keep us in touch with ourselves and with other people. In the Scriptures, we see that God is a Being who has emotions—such as love, sorrow, and anger—and who expresses them. Because we are made in His image and likeness, we have emotions, too. Accordingly, we should not be afraid to express our emotions, either in public or in private, as long as they are healthy emotions and not destructive ones like jealousy or unrestrained anger.

Earlier, we talked about how most people go through life with numerous and repeated emotional wounds. A wounded soul often projects itself to the world in a negative way, creating new wounds, both for that person and for others. The solution for hurt feelings is inner healing and deliverance. Our emotions must be healed of their wounds and delivered from demonic oppression, so that we can be free to express our emotions in a healthy way.

I have noticed that our society is motivated mainly by emotions and feelings rather than by principles, values, and righteous convictions. The flesh expresses itself though emotions that are still under spiritual bondage. We've all heard the following slogans (or similar ones): "If it feels good, do it"; "If it makes you happy, buy it or take it"; and "Don't deny yourself something you want—you deserve it." When the corrupt soul rules your life, and when your emotions have more influence over you than your convictions, you need deliverance. You must reach the point where you unite with God against your sinful self, so that you can be transformed into your true self as a person made in God's image. There has to come a time when you take your emotions to the cross so that the life of Jesus can grow within you.

While every believer must go through a process of inner healing and deliverance in the soul, because that is the place from which many of our problems originate, such deliverance is most urgent and needed for people who have experienced, or are experiencing, the following: an abortion or an intention to have one; abandonment by one's parents; being orphaned; a difficult childhood as an adopted son or daughter; abuse, whether as a child, a teenager, or an adult; a chronic and/or hereditary disease; uncontrollable or compulsive habits; persistent fears; being plagued by feelings of rejection, depression, loneliness, desperation, or thoughts of suicide; recurring thoughts of guilt and condemnation; a rebellious spirit; difficulty forgiving; ongoing feelings of hatred and bitterness; constant anger or intense jealousy; obsessive desires to bring harm to others; planning or committing assault or murder. Other cases include those who frequently have thoughts or desires of a homosexual or bisexual nature; those who have engaged in immorality; those who have a history of sexual perversion; those who have been exposed to pornography; those who have participated in practices of witchcraft or other forms of the occult; those who have used mantras or have participated in the practices of yoga, transcendental meditation, or Eastern religions, such as Buddhism; those who suffer from schizophrenia; those who are addicted to alcohol, drugs, sex, or money; and those who are compulsive liars or gossips. I also recommend that war veterans receive deliverance from distressing or traumatic memories of experiences on the battlefield or of other aspects of their service.

The will must be surrendered,
the mind renewed,
and the emotions healed.

The Body

Let us now turn to the third part of humanity's triune nature: the physical body. God placed us in a physical world that operates according to natural properties and parameters. The essence of human beings is spirit. However, without a body, we could not operate on this physical earth. God created the body as a way for our spirits and souls to express themselves and as a means for us to govern the creation over which He has placed us as stewards. Of course, even though we live according to physical properties, this does not prevent the supernatural realm from intersecting with the physical world. When Jesus came to earth, He was born with a physical body. He operated in this world according to its physical boundaries and lived as all other human beings do, except that He was without sin. But He also continually manifested the supernatural on earth and taught us that we are to live in the power of the Spirit.

The body that God originally gave Adam was glorious, incorruptible, and eternal; but sin marred humanity's physical complexion, subjecting it to sickness, decadence, and corruption. Today, our bodies, as well as our souls, need to be redeemed. A person's body will please the desires of whichever aspect of his higher self is truly in control—whether the corrupt soul or the renewed spirit. If it is the corrupt soul, the body will indulge the desires of the flesh; if it is the renewed spirit, the body will submit to cleansing and strengthening so that it can be a vessel of honor for its Creator and receive the very life of Christ.

In order for our body to receive cleansing, strengthening, and renewal, we must present it to God as a *"living sacrifice"* (Romans 12:1). We must also worship God, pray, and fast. We need to subject our body to what the spirit wants, rather than allow the body to indulge fleshly desires.

The complete redemption of our spirit, soul, and body will take place when Jesus comes back for His church. (See, for example, 1 Corinthians 15:51–53.) Therefore, let us anticipate His coming by moving forward with the transformation of our whole being, which will happen as we go *"from faith to faith"* (Romans 1:17) and *"from glory to glory"* (2 Corinthians 3:18).

The body was created to be the temple of the Holy Spirit.

Overcoming the Fleshly Nature

Galatians 5:19–21 lists various works of the flesh: *"adultery, fornication, uncleanness, lewdness, idolatry, sorcery, hatred, contentions, jealousies, outbursts of wrath, selfish ambitions, dissensions, heresies, envy, murders, drunkenness, revelries, and the like."* These manifestations of the works of the flesh are representative. Let us review some additional ones, which we have previously discussed: unforgiveness, resentment, bitterness, unrighteous anger, self-pity, fear, anxiety, pride, compulsive lying, attention-seeking, rebellion, greed, gluttony, uncontrolled sexual passion, and others. The flesh manifests itself through undisciplined emotions, impure desires, and perverted thoughts that we allow to have free rein in our lives.

In its utmost expression, the fleshly nature is the coming together of an individual's body and soul to act independently from God. That independence opens the door to sin, which ends up dominating the person, sinking him into slavery, guilt, and condemnation. The enemy will always attack your life if he discovers that the fleshly nature is active—if he sees that there is something in your life to which you have allowed him legal access through disobedience or rebellion. We need to reach a point where we can say of Satan, as Jesus did, *"He has nothing in Me"* (John 14:30).

> *The non-crucified flesh is always an open door to demons.*

Here is the key to overcoming the fleshly nature. The apostle Paul wrote, *"I have been crucified with Christ; it is no longer I who live, but Christ lives in me"* (Galatians 2:20). Let us analyze Paul's statement *"I have been crucified with Christ."* This is a declaration of death to the sinful nature. The condition of being crucified with Christ must be a reality in our lives. *"It is no longer I who live, but Christ lives in me."* It is a fact that when the carnal self dies, the new man, which has been resurrected with Christ, can be fully in control, ruling over the soul (the mind, the will, and the emotions) and over the body, which will progressively obey the spirit more each time.

Being crucified with Christ does not mean that our personality disappears. It means that we are dead to sin and to our old ways of doing things that are contrary to God's ways, and that we live according to our "new man," which has been raised with Christ. We submit our will to God rather than ruling ourselves. We no longer do what the sinful nature thinks, wants, or feels but rather what Jesus thinks, wants, and feels. That is why Paul said, *"And the life which I now live in the flesh I live by faith in the Son of God"* (Galatians 2:20).

Allow me to give you a pearl of wisdom about "living by faith in the Son of God." It is *available* in the now; but, for it to be a *reality* in the now, the carnal self must be crucified. For many believers, this verse is merely theory; it is not part of their actual experience. The flesh dominates them, so that little or no transformation occurs in their lives. Legally, in the spiritual realm, Jesus has redeemed them, but His work will rest solely as potential until they make a decision to reject the flesh, to live according to the life of Christ, and to daily receive transformation. Likewise, many people try to believe for healing, miracles, supernatural provision, and other blessings in the now but are unable to because they have not yet crucified the flesh.

Where the carnal self is not yet crucified, we see manifestations of the works of the flesh. Where the carnal self is crucified, and Christ lives within, we see manifestations of God's kingdom here and now.

Consequences of Living According to the Flesh

It is essential to understand that when we live according to the flesh, it is not a benign decision—it has serious consequences, such as the following five results.

1. We Expose Ourselves to Demonic Powers

If we continuously yield to our carnal nature, we invite evil forces into our life. Paul counseled, *"Do not...give place to the devil"* (Ephesians 4:26–27). There is a point at which an individual can cross the line between indulging in a work of the flesh and being oppressed by the operation of an unclean spirit in that area of his life, because he has left the door open to such an operation. That line can be crossed by a repetition of the sinful act. If a person regularly practices a particular work of the flesh, sooner or later, he will be demonized.

The only area in which the enemy can gain ground is that in which the flesh has not been crucified.

2. The Power of the Flesh Is Multiplied

The anointing of God increases and multiplies as we surrender to Christ and die to our carnal self. But the opposite effect also occurs. When we fail to crucify the flesh, its power increases, and it begins to live for itself. The more we allow it to do so, the more it will dominate us.

3. It Puts Us Under a Curse

"Cursed is the man who trusts in man and makes flesh his strength, whose heart departs from the LORD" (Jeremiah 17:5). This verse describes the person who trusts in his own carnal nature, relying solely on his own strength, skills, talents, wisdom, money, position, or goodness rather than on God. When his heart turns away from God, he falls into a curse.

The apostle Paul addressed a similar situation in the second and third chapters of Galatians. The Galatian believers had started out living according to the Spirit, and God had moved among them with miracles, signs, and wonders, so that the supernatural had become a lifestyle for them. But then some legalistic Christians came among them and persuaded them to rely on aspects of the Old Testament law for their righteousness, rather than on faith and grace. (See Galatians 2:11–16.) This led them to fall under the curse of self-reliance. (See Galatians 3:10–13.) When the members of the church in Galatia succumbed to living according to the law, this impeded the flow of the supernatural power of God in their lives. In Christ's love, Paul taught them how to return to living by grace. (See Galatians 3:11–29.)

Characteristics of Those Who Live in Legalism

Living according to the law affects people in the following significant ways.

They focus on outward acts instead of inward transformation. I believe that legalism is one of the greatest problems in the Western church, as well as the biggest stumbling block for new believers. This mind-set is an expression of carnality, because it leads people to trust in their own ability to follow God's laws. The legalistic mind-set focuses on outward acts rather than on inward transformation. That is why legalistic churches institute various "rules" for their members, such as "Don't wear make-up" or "Don't dance." These churches may also promote acts of obedience to God that are in line with Scripture; however, the motivations they encourage for carrying them out do not usually include love and thankfulness to God and a reliance on His grace but rather a sense of obligation, a fear of punishment, and a striving after human perfection.

When someone is legalistic, he tries to do what he believes will please God and to *not* do what he believes offends God. His outward behavior may deceive both himself and others because, while it might appear to be righteous, it is really empty effort. Every time a person tries to sanctify and justify himself before God solely by following rules, the only thing he pleases is his own ego. He is living in the flesh! Additionally, legalism produces bondage to perfectionism. If you want to be justified by living according to God's law, you will have to keep the law 100 percent *perfectly*. To fail to do this is to fall into a curse. (See, for example, Deuteronomy 27:26.)

If your focus is on complying with rules and laws, your faith will not be in operation, and you will be condemned, because you will either trust in your own ability or your own organization or your own denomination or your own plans, rules, talents, intellect, educational diplomas, and so forth. This way of living will not transform your heart; neither will it count toward righteousness on your behalf.

But there is another way of living, a way of peace and freedom. It is to live by faith and by grace. As Paul reminded the Galatians, *"The just shall live by faith"* (Galatians 3:11), and as he told the Ephesians, *"For by grace you have been saved through faith, and that not of yourselves; it is the gift of God"* (Ephesians 2:8).

They become carnal. Legalism and carnality go hand in hand. All the works someone does while in a carnal frame of mind, as good as they may be, are not accomplished for God but rather for the purpose of satisfying the demands of the "self." These are *"dead works"* (see Hebrews 6:1; 9:13–14); they have no value to the Lord. Furthermore, as we have seen, it is impossible to reach perfection by using human effort and strength. Even if such perfection could be reached, nothing in our carnal self can substitute for the work of Jesus on the cross to cleanse us completely and to give us His righteousness. When He died, He paid the price that our flesh never would—and never could—pay.

4. We Are Unable to Please God

The following is a very strong declaration, but it is true: Anyone—including a believer—who walks according to the fleshly nature cannot please God. (See Romans 8:8.) If you want to please Him, you must make a decision to "kill" the works of the flesh in your life and live by the Spirit. The carnal nature cannot produce anything that would bring pleasure to God. You may be very "religious," but you will never please the Lord while you are working in your own strength!

5. It Leads to Death

The final consequence of living according to the flesh is death. *"To be carnally minded is death"* (Romans 8:6). One way or another, living according to the flesh leads to physical, emotional, and/or spiritual demise. In a heartrending passage of Scripture that we read earlier, Paul called the rebellious nature *"this body of death"* (Romans 7:24). It is a lie to think one can live in the flesh without suffering mortal consequences. But there is always hope in Jesus Christ.

At our church's annual youth conference last year, we heard testimonies from many people who had been rebellious and stubborn—set in their own ways and living in the world—before coming to salvation. One of those who testified was a young man named Giancarlo.

When Giancarlo was a boy, his parents never really believed in God or in church. Yet, soon after moving to Florida, they were introduced to the gospel and started attending church, where their lives were transformed through Jesus Christ. When his parents became youth leaders, Giancarlo struggled to keep up a Christian image in front of his family and other people. He would go to church services during the day but then do his own thing at night; he was living a double life.

"I didn't care what the church, my parents, or God had to say about me," Giancarlo said. He got tattoos on his body and many piercings on his face. At the age of twelve, he began experimenting with homosexuality. When he was nineteen, he was diagnosed with human papillomavirus (HPV). This virus can develop into cancer, but Giancarlo's doctors found it early. He underwent surgery and was told to stay away from sexual intercourse with men for a period of time, so that the virus could clear from his stomach. But Giancarlo didn't follow the advice, and the virus resurfaced. His symptoms were stomach pain, cramps, difficulty eating, and anxiety.

Trying to cover up the fact that he had this virus became a difficult burden for Giancarlo as he lived his double life. It was at this time that he attended our youth conference. There, he experienced the presence of God, and the Holy Spirit spoke to him. When the youth pastor gave an altar call, Giancarlo knew it was his time for healing. He shared, "I felt a burning sensation traveling throughout my whole body. It shook me to my core. I knew that I was healed of the virus. Now, the pain is gone, I can eat normally, and I don't have anything to fear anymore!" While he was testifying at the conference, he decided to remove all his piercings as a sign that he was leaving his old ways behind and bringing God into his life. "I feel changed. I feel new. I was delivered from homosexuality. I don't look at guys in the same seductive way that I used to anymore. I see them as God's sons and my fellow brothers in Christ!"

> *The opposite of trusting in the flesh is trusting in the supernatural grace of God, which empowers us to do what we cannot do in our own strength.*

How to Walk in the Spirit

What is the process by which we leave the fleshly nature behind so that we can please God and live in freedom? Jesus told His disciples, *"If anyone desires to come after Me, let him deny himself, and take up his cross daily, and follow Me. For whoever desires to save his life will lose it, but whoever loses his life for My sake will save it*" (Luke 9:23–24). The following are four principles for walking in the Spirit.

1. Deny Yourself and Take Up Your Cross

In the above Scripture passage, *"whoever loses his life"* does not refer to physical death but rather to leaving behind the "life" of the sinful nature that operates in the corrupt soul. We must lose that old life in order to win the life of the Spirit and follow after Jesus.

Denying our flesh is a *daily* necessity. Jesus won complete victory over sin, and it is a reality in the eternal realm; but until He returns and completely transforms us, we have to appropriate His victory and execute it in the temporal realm on earth, progressively making it a reality in our lives. Every day, when you wake up, take authority in Jesus' name over your soul (your mind, will, and emotions) and order it to submit to the will of your "new man" in Jesus Christ. You are the only one who can do this. Once you take that authority, God will give you supernatural grace to empower you to deny the carnal self.

Taking up one's cross is a personal decision. Doing so is *your* decision—God will not impose it upon you. What does it mean to take up your cross? It means to submit to God anything in which your will crosses with His will; in which your thoughts rebel against His thoughts; in which your emotions are not aligned with the fruit of His Spirit. Taking up your cross is a voluntary sacrificial offering before God. It is a rejection of the operation of the fallen soul, which causes you to be separated from God, and it is a choice to receive the eternal life of the Spirit, which brings you into oneness with Him. Then you will be free to pursue the purposes of God.

Taking up one's cross is a personal decision. Doing so is your decision—God will not impose it upon you. Taking up your cross is a voluntary sacrificial offering before God.

So, *"make no provision for the flesh, to fulfill its lusts"* (Romans 13:14). Instead, voluntarily choose to crucify your flesh each day. In other words, do not feed it, so that it cannot be activated. Do not try to justify or defend any selfish, rebellious action. When you do, you are yielding ground to the sinful nature. Instead, take the flesh to the cross, because, *"those who are Christ's have crucified the flesh with its passions and desires"* (Galatians 5:24; see also Ephesians 4:22; Colossians 3:5).

> *Crucifying the flesh means applying the cross of Jesus to the carnal self as a decision of your will.*

2. Exercise Personal Discipline and Self-Control

The carnal nature has a perverted and insatiable appetite; it always wants everything in excess: food, drink, sex, sleep, and so forth. Therefore, we must dominate and subjugate our fleshly nature. Again, when you cannot govern your carnal self, you are living more in the flesh than in the Spirit; the "old man" has risen up to rule. You must crucify it. Place your flesh under submission to Jesus Christ and begin to take greater authority over your life. Paul wrote, *"God did not give us a spirit of timidity, but…of self-discipline"* (2 Timothy 1:7 NIV).

3. Yield Your Total Being to God

When you yield yourself to God, you surrender your rights to Him. This includes the "rights" that the carnal self demands. We must put aside the "natural," soulish life in order to live in the supernatural. Therefore, yield to God your unbelief, your fears, your doubts, your insecurities, your bitterness, your self-hatred, your weaknesses, and any other manifestations of the sinful nature. Yield everything to Him.

"*Christ suffered for us in the flesh,…that* [we] *no longer should live the rest of* [our] *time in the flesh…but for the will of God*" (1 Peter 4:1–2). To cease from a particular sin, we must continually deny the flesh until it dies; then we will have the freedom to do God's will in that area of our lives. In this process, our flesh will suffer because its desires and its control will be denied. This can be a painful experience to endure. However, we have only two options—the short and the long—in regard to denying the flesh.

The short method consists of crucifying the flesh the moment we know that there is something in our life that does not please God. The long method is to keep doing what's wrong, knowing that it is harmful to us and against God's will, with the idea of pleasing our flesh—only to eventually realize that in order to spiritually stay alive, we must die to ourselves. The second method causes us much distress and wastes valuable time in which we could have served God in freedom.

A good illustration of the second method may be seen in the following example. Suppose a young Christian woman who loves God and wants to please Him meets an attractive young man who does not believe in God and does not care about sinning against Him. If she wants to please God, she will not become involved with this young man, even though her carnal self may want to. She will choose to make her flesh suffer so that her soul can be renewed and strengthened. This is the short, less painful option. The long method would be for her to enter into a relationship with the young man but, sooner or later, have to acknowledge the great differences between them. If she chooses that method, she will allow that unhealthy relationship to separate her from God for a time, likely causing a long period of negative consequences, until finally, she will be forced to leave that relationship and deal with much greater pain than if she had immediately denied her flesh.

We have to surrender our mind, our will, and our emotions to God every day, just as Jesus Christ surrendered His life completely to the Father. (See, for example, Luke 22:42.) Then, we must ask God's Spirit to help us to choose to do what is right in each situation. When we choose God's way, He will empower us by His Spirit to live in freedom and integrity. Again, every decision implies an action, and every action has consequences. It could be that you will choose between heaven and hell today. If you place your trust in God and surrender your will to Him in faith, making the decision to love and serve Him, God will make that decision a reality in your life through His mighty power.

> *The surrendering of our life to God*
> *is continuous and progressive.*

A woman named Alana from Trinidad and Tobago was living independently from God and following the works of the flesh until she repented and gave her life to the Lord. The following is her testimony.

"I was raised in church, but I had never seen any change in my life. I would go to church and sit there, waiting for the service to end. Being twenty-two years old, I thought I could handle life on my own, so I moved out of my house. I met a guy who seemed very nice but made me experience the worst six years of my life. For him, I started drinking and doing obscene things that were against God, to the point where I contracted cervical cancer. I forgot my worth as a woman and how to love myself. I hated my appearance; I hated who I was becoming. So, I tried to commit suicide. Finally, I went home to my mother. She prayed for me and invited me to a service at King Jesus Ministry. I went but became offended, and I returned to the world to do whatever my flesh desired. My life spiraled away. I was struggling, depressed, and trying to make ends meet. I asked God to please help me, and I promised to do anything, even return to church.

"I did get a job but never fulfilled my promise to God; eventually, I lost everything. I also lost all my faith and hope and turned to partying to escape. Partying became my idol; it was more important to me than sleeping, eating, or working. I didn't care about life; I grew more aggressive and would get into fights with my mother and others.

"During a Halloween party in South Miami, I met a team of evangelists who were there sharing the gospel. At first, I didn't want to hear what they had to say, but then one of them began to prophesy to me, and I felt the presence of God. I was convicted of my sin and began to cry; I felt God's pain and the consequences of my sin. That night, I left the party and made the decision to leave that world. The same weekend, I returned 'home' to church with my mother. God healed my heart, delivered me, and set me free from living by the flesh. I became obedient to God's direction for my life, and He became my source of prosperity. He supernaturally healed me of the cervical cancer and cancelled a $2,000 debt of medical bills! Words cannot express how happy I am today. I am a new creature in Him. I cry with joy and thank God for saving me. He is good!"

To yield to the Spirit is to let God be God.

4. Choose to Walk in the Spirit and Not in the Flesh

We are either being led by the Holy Spirit or controlled by the flesh; if we are not living according to the Spirit's guidance and character, then we are allowing the flesh to dominate us. We can lead only one of two lives: the life of faith or the life of the flesh. Therefore, you will live the abundant life to the degree that you are willing to die to your carnal self. So, choose blessing and not a curse!

Walking in the Spirit will enable you to be set free from sin so that you may do the will of God. And, when you walk in the Spirit, you can live completely free from condemnation. (See Romans 8:1.) To walk in the Spirit, you must live in the Spirit. This means living according to a supernatural flow of the power and presence of God. Our heavenly

Father provides this ongoing supernatural flow as an expression of His relationship with us as His children. *"For as many as are led by the Spirit of God, these are sons of God"* (Romans 8:14).

> The supernatural transformation of
> the believer is based on an exchange of life.
> You decrease so that Jesus may increase in you.

The Final Challenge

We must accept the fact that we will experience a certain amount of suffering in regard to sin. We will either suffer temporary "deaths" by denying sin while we are here on earth, refusing to let it reign in our lives, or we will suffer eternal death because we chose to maintain a lifestyle of sin during our time here. To put an end to sin's control over us, we must endure the pain of rejecting the desires of the flesh. If you obey God, denying yourself and taking up your cross, you will receive the life of Christ; but if you disobey God and continually indulge your flesh, you will be on the path to everlasting death.

Are you willing to "lose your life"—the operation of the sinful nature within you—in order to gain the life of the Spirit and be restored to God's original design for you? Are you willing to "crucify" your flesh daily? Are you willing to deny yourself anything you know displeases God? Think about the areas of your life that the enemy often attacks. Do you indulge in pride, rebellion, or self-pity? Are you still operating according to soulish motivations? The only way to overcome the "old man" is to place it on the cross of Jesus so that your new man, resurrected in Christ, can govern your life.

The choice lies before you today. Say no to your flesh and yes to the life of the Spirit, following Jesus in both His death and His resurrection.

Prayer of Deliverance

Each day, after I have worshipped and communed with the heavenly Father, I always say the following prayer in order to break the flesh's dominion over my life. I encourage you to pray it daily, as well.

Lord, I voluntarily crucify my flesh and deny myself. I take up my cross and follow You. I declare that the "old man" does not control my life. I submit my flesh to the finished work of Jesus on the cross and receive His grace to live in righteousness before You. I willingly choose to yield to Your Spirit rather than to the carnal nature. I pray this in the name of Jesus Christ, amen.

4

DELIVERANCE FROM THE SPIRIT OF REBELLION, SEDITION, AND WITCHCRAFT

I want to start this chapter by identifying the days in which we live. Our generation is experiencing the greatest period of innovation and progress the earth has ever seen. Improvements that previously seemed impossible have become commonplace. Many processes that formerly had been complicated have been simplified; endeavors and procedures are being accomplished easier, faster, and better. The abundance of knowledge and the advancements of science and technology have made the peoples of the world seem much more closely connected, and almost any achievement appears to be within our reach. Yet, despite these innovations and accelerations, I believe that this generation is the most rebellious against God that the world has ever known.

An Environment of Lawlessness

This is a prophetic time when spiritual warfare between the kingdom of light and the kingdom of darkness has intensified. Among the primary marks of our generation are a lack of order, an absence of respect for the law, a rejection of boundaries, and a refusal to submit to authorities established by God. I believe that we have left ourselves exposed to powerful evil spirits from Satan's kingdom that have never before operated upon the face of the earth. These malignant spirits have now been released because we are in the end times. This situation fulfills the prediction of the Scriptures that there will be an increase in rebellion and iniquity in the last days. (See, for example, 2 Timothy 3:1–5.)

If we want to be potent vessels through which God saves, heals, and delivers others, we need to be delivered from the spirit of rebellion that has enthroned itself in our generation and has infiltrated the lives of even the people of God. We must identify this spirit of rebellion and take action to be free from its influence.

The Antichrist Spirit of Rebellion

The apostle John wrote, *"As you have heard that the Antichrist is coming, even now many antichrists have come, by which we know that it is the last hour"* (1 John 2:18). Many of the systems on which our world operates today have been infiltrated by *"the spirit of the Antichrist"* (1 John 4:3). The antichrist spirit is preparing the way for the eventual appearance of the person of the Antichrist, who will embody it. Satan knows that his time is limited, and as the *"ruler of this world"* (John 12:31; 14:30; 16:11), he has unleashed this destructive spirit. When we observe the operation of the antichrist spirit, we see that we are dealing with the essential character of Satan himself. It is his nature that is governing the evil powers and principalities subverting our society.

Before our own eyes, we are witnessing the effects of the spirit of antichrist. This spirit does not submit to God-given authority; it rejects authority. It is in direct contradiction to the spiritual principles and laws of the kingdom of heaven. When I refer to "laws" in this context, I am not referring to the religious legalism we discussed in the previous chapter but to the godly principles of the Bible and to the moral laws that nations have enacted to protect their citizens and to enable them to live honest, upright lives. The spirit of antichrist is lawless; therefore, it seeks to distort the good laws of our nations and to create corrupt ones in its own favor.

The most prominent characteristic of the antichrist spirit is that it rebels against God's laws.

Have you ever wondered, *Why is my life always filled with such conflict?* I know many people who have asked themselves this question. If they're not experiencing strife in one area, they're experiencing it in another. Many couples seem to constantly struggle in their marriage, in their relationship with their children, in their relationship with their parents, or in their relationship with their siblings, often over an inheritance or some other family issue. And, if they are not fighting another human being, they seem to be battling some problem related to money, health, or another area of life. Similarly, many businessmen seem to be continuously hindered by conflicts related to the management of their companies or the state of their finances. Besides all this, many countries are being thrust from one crisis to another, from natural or economic disasters to political upheavals to terrorist attacks and more.

Although conflict and strife have been in existence on earth since the fall of man, I believe the spirit of antichrist is increasing the intensity of these battles in our day. For the same reason, we are seeing an increase in rebellion in the home, in society at large, and even within the church. When people oppose the authorities that have been delegated by God, and when they refuse to submit to good laws and to proper order, they are under the influence of the spirit of antichrist.

God's Restoration Plan

When God created the world, He established it in beauty and order. Previously, we saw that the archangel Lucifer became full of pride and arrogance, desiring to be equal with God. He seduced a third of God's angels to renounce their loyalty to the Creator and then led a rebellion against Him. God overthrew Lucifer and his angels and cast them down to the earth. These rebellious angels became a rival—though inferior— kingdom that opposes God's kingdom to this day. Moreover, Lucifer's rebellion and banishment to earth resulted in a divine judgment upon the world, in which the earth became *"without form, and void"* (Genesis 1:2). Thus, the spirit of rebellion initiated by Satan wreaked devastation on the earth.

God allowed this to occur, but it was not His ultimate purpose for the world He had created; His plan was redemption and restoration. Beginning with the command *"Let there be light"* (Genesis 1:3), He reestablished beauty and order by which the earth would function, founding it on His own nature. He created human beings and gave them the position of rulers and stewards over the earth, with the ability to subjugate Satan and his angels and to maintain and establish a well-ordered world that reflected His character.

The first human beings were given great freedom, as well as healthy limitations by which to live. (See Genesis 2:15–17.) However, after being tempted by Satan, Adam and Eve fell into sin and became subject to corruption and death. Since that time, every member of the human race has been born with a fallen nature that is inherently rebellious against God. In addition, when human beings disobeyed God, they relinquished their authority over the earth, allowing Satan the right to rule on earth until Christ defeated him at the cross.

When God created the universe,

He established law, order,

and boundaries.

When Jesus won the victory over sin and death, He restored to human beings their dominion on earth, including the power to "bind and loose"—to constrain Satan's activities and to release people from his power, thus defeating the enemy. (See Matthew 16:19; 18:18.) Although Satan retains his power until Christ returns, he no longer has authority on the earth unless human beings grant him that right through their rebellion and disobedience against God. Instead, he now has to use the same tactics he employed in the garden of Eden, which are to trap, to trick, and to seduce people to rebel against their Creator. And he uses those schemes against us over and over. Once more, I believe that we are witnessing the highest expression of the spirit of rebellion the world has ever seen.

The reason why life is always so full of conflict is that we are in the midst of a spiritual war that is being fought over the territory in which we live—earth. The origin of this war was Satan's uprising in heaven against the kingdom of God. That war was initially waged between God and Satan, but it has become our war, as well. If we want to live in victory regarding each of the conflicts we face, and if we want to address the crises and conflicts affecting our family members, our society, and our world, we must understand the spirit of rebellion that Satan has unleashed and learn what it means to live under God-given authority.

The root of rebellion is spiritual immaturity,

which is made evident by pride and arrogance,

as was the case with Lucifer.

Human Authorities Are Appointed by God

The Scriptures teach that God sets in place human authorities to be His representatives of righteousness on earth, and that He takes such authority seriously.

> *Let every soul be subject to the governing authorities. For there is no authority except from God, and the authorities that exist are appointed by God. Therefore whoever resists the authority resists the ordinance of God, and those who resist will bring judgment ["condemnation" NASB] on themselves.* (Romans 13:1–2)

God is the One who has ordered and established every authority in heaven and on earth. For example, in the church universal, the highest authority is Jesus, and He appoints human leaders under His authority in order to build and to strengthen the church. (See Ephesians 4:11–12.) He established authorities in other realms of life, as well. In His plan for the family, He appointed the husband/father as the authority. In the workplace, the business owner or manager is the authority; in a country, the leader—the president, the prime minister, the king or queen, the governing body of legislators, and so forth—is the authority. Whoever resists these authorities opposes God and the order that He has established.

For Christians who live under patently wicked leaders or evil laws, there are serious issues to consider in regard to the proper response. But harboring a spirit of anger and rebellion is never the solution. The apostle Paul lived under persecution, but he instructed the first-century believers to pray for *all* human authorities, that the believers might live *"a quiet and peaceable life in all godliness and reverence"* (1 Timothy 2:2).

The Spirit of Rebellion

God will not bless anyone who lives in a state of rebellion. In my experience, the spirit of rebellion manifests in three ways: (1) by open rebellion, (2) by sedition, and (3) by "witchcraft," the meaning of which I will describe shortly. Each of these aspects is an expression of the spirit that rebels against God and against the authorities He has established on the earth.

We must be able to identify these three manifestations of the spirit of rebellion so that we can be delivered from them and prevent them from taking hold in our lives.

Open Rebellion

The dictionary defines *rebellion* as "opposition to one in authority or dominance," and "open, armed, and usually unsuccessful defiance of or resistance to an established government." From a spiritual standpoint, the definition of rebellion is very similar, but the government that the spirit of rebellion seeks to defy and to resist is the kingdom of God. Rebellion against God's kingdom can be traced to either a work of the flesh or to the activity of a demonic spirit.

The spirit of rebellion opposes every form of authority and doesn't answer to any law. It desires to do as it pleases without being told that it is wrong. Its purpose is to destroy, and it will ultimately ruin any human being whom it uses to defy authority, if the person doesn't recognize the error he is in, repent, and receive deliverance.

When someone is in a state of rebellion against God, His Word, and the authorities He has established on earth, his heart has been perverted. We must all be on alert against a spirit of rebellion within us, because the Bible says, *"The heart is deceitful above all things, and desperately wicked; who can know it?"* (Jeremiah 17:9). Tragically, it is possible for those who were previously walking in the Spirit to end up walking according to the flesh as a result a rebellious heart, thereby putting themselves on a direct path to their own demise.

> *"Spirituality" that rebels against authority is perverted spirituality.*

One biblical example of the spirit of rebellion is the group of people who built the tower of Babel. Rather than honor God, they desired to make a name for themselves, defying Him and the purpose He had given them to fill the earth. They wouldn't follow God's plan voluntarily, and they ended up being *"scattered"* over the earth. (See Genesis 11:1–9.)

Rebellion is an attitude that comes from spiritual immaturity and fleshly desires. Again, if it is not recognized and repented of, it will end up causing division and destruction, whether in the family, the church, the workplace, or any other entity. We must realize that rebellion does not usually manifest suddenly; rather, it is something that a person progressively develops, whether knowingly or unknowingly.

Let's look at an example of how a rebellious spirit can develop. Many times, rebellion takes hold in people who possess great gifts and who believe that their abilities place them "above the law," or on a level where they are not answerable to authority. Yet it is God who has given us all of our abilities and talents. We did nothing to earn, deserve, or obtain them, and they do not make us exempt from submitting to Him or to the authorities He has appointed.

A problem often arises when people confuse gifts with character. While gifts relate to what you can *do*, character relates to who you *are*. Your true nature is who you are on the inside, even if it is not evident to others. And whereas gifts are inherent, good character has to be cultivated over time. Where someone's character is immature, the spirit of rebellion often finds a vulnerable area to exploit, so that the person becomes ruled by his corrupt ego and dominated by his flesh. An immature character is an ideal environment for the spirit of rebellion.

Let me give you a word of caution: You might have many abilities; you might even do miracles, prophesy, and cast out demons; but if you are not submitted to God's authority, you are catering to the corruption of your soul, the condition we discussed in the previous chapter. Anyone who becomes his own authority, who ceases to be accountable to anyone, who lives independently from God and trusts exclusively in his own knowledge, wisdom, and abilities, will fall into deception and error—and, ultimately, destruction.

> *Perverted spirituality is often born of a rebellious heart that lacks the maturity of character to subject itself to an authority appointed by God.*

When we observe other people, it is often easier to recognize their gifts than their true character. Usually, a person's character becomes evident when he is under pressure. Problems, anxieties, injustices, and crises force it to the surface. When testing comes, the true self is illuminated. If an individual's character is weak, and he allows himself to be governed by it, it can tear down everything he has built with his gift.

Immature character is not something to take lightly. In our society, a gifted individual is often put into a position of influence over others solely on the strength of his abilities; however, without mature character, that person's use of his gifts can cause disaster. I have had that experience with some of the leaders in my ministry. At the beginning of our association, I identified their gifts and potential, adopted them into my spiritual family, and worked to train them and guide them to maturity. Yet I made the mistake of putting them into positions of leadership mainly on the basis of their gifts, only to find out later that they lacked strength of character. At first, I did not realize how grave their character deficiencies were, because their immaturity was hidden behind their gifts. But these deficiencies led to a rebellious spirit.

The sad result was that they hurt many people and ended up tainting the ministry work while causing division in the church. The spirit of rebellion within a congregation leads to much disunity and can cause a congregation to splinter as the rebellious leader breaks off to start a new ministry. Today, a large number of churches and ministries seem to have been born out of a spirit of rebellion. We should be aware that a ministry that is apparently thriving today may suddenly fall tomorrow if it was founded as a result of defiance toward a former leader.

For example, suppose some members of a church are dissatisfied with their senior pastor. They talk badly about the pastor and sow discontent among the members of the congregation before leaving to start a new church. A rebellious spirit is destructive, and it will not allow the people who harbor it to sustain what they build. The destiny of those who have caused division in a church or another group is to similarly face disunity and division in their ministry, unless they ask for forgiveness, reconcile with those whom they have wronged, and resubmit themselves to proper authority. The only reasons God may bless such a work and keep it going for a period of time is for the sake of the believers' spiritual growth and for the purpose of protecting His people.

But the work born of rebellion will not last or remain strong. Sooner or later, the spirit of rebellion will be activated over the new congregation, meaning that the seed from which the ministry grew will bear its destructive fruit and end up poisoning it. For instance, a new leader who had rebelled against the authority of his former pastor will often find members of his own ministry rebelling against him, because everything reproduces according to its own seed. A rebellious person who never repented will give birth to other rebels. When the new church begins to grow, someone with a rebellious spirit will rise within the leadership, and many of those whom the new leader had trained may leave, taking a portion of the members with them. In this sense, a rebellious leader will inevitably raise up his own adversaries.

A work born of rebellion will never last
or remain strong. In time, it will be divided
and terminated from the inside.

Every family, church, business, nation, or other entity has its own character, which is established by the person or persons who lead it. For example, in King Jesus International Ministry, I have been delegated the responsibility of being the spiritual leader. Thus, the ministry has my "spiritual DNA," so that, when people see the church, they should see my character. Character is something I have to carefully monitor. Through regrettable experiences such as I described above, I learned that I must establish my ministry leaders according to their spiritual and personal character, and not only the basis of their gifts. Now, all our ministry leaders are appointed according to maturity of character. If our church were founded upon people's gifts alone, we never would have been able to endure the various crises we have faced or to retain what God has given us by His grace.

Every family, church, business, nation,
or other entity has its own character, which is
established by the person or persons who lead it.

Therefore, if you build solely upon a leader's gift when his character is weak, the work will crumble when that immature character comes to light. Sooner or later, a crisis will arise that demonstrates the immaturity of the character behind the talent. On the other hand, when an endeavor is established upon someone's mature personal character, the Holy Spirit will cause it to grow and to bear fruit. The character of God in the leader will maintain the work.

The spirit under which a work is born will determine its degree of purity and its duration.

If you have a rebellious spirit, and you fail to deal with it, it will harm you—and may even cause your utter downfall. For this reason, the only appropriate response to rebellion is to halt it, remove it, and destroy it. We must do to our rebellion exactly what God did to Satan when he rebelled: defeat it and cast it out.

God does not dwell where there is lawlessness and lack of order, where people are rebellious against the authorities whom He has put in place. His Spirit cannot be united with the iniquity that is released when rebellion takes the heart of a person, a church, or a nation. Ask yourself the following: "Am I in rebellion against any God-given authority?" "Is the church or ministry I lead the result of a rebellion?" If the answer to either question is yes, are you willing to repent and to be reconciled with those whom you have wronged? These steps are necessary to be free of the spirit of rebellion and its consequences.

The rebellion you do not deal with will destroy you.

Sedition

A second expression of the spirit of rebellion is sedition, which is always in a subtle manner, never direct. According to the dictionary, *sedition* is "incitement of resistance to or insurrection against lawful authority." Remember that Satan incited a third of God's angels to rebel with him against the Creator.

Another clear biblical example of sedition is the treasonous act of Absalom, the son of David. Absalom harbored anger and a desire for revenge in his heart following the tragic rape of his sister Tamar by their half-brother Amnon. For Absalom, there could be no other punishment for his brother than death, yet David spared his life. So, Absalom plotted in secret and had Amnon killed, after which he fled to another region for three years, before David allowed him to come home. (See 2 Samuel 13–14.)

Because of his response to the tragedy with Tamar, Absalom allowed iniquity to be planted in his heart, opening the door for a spirit of sedition against his father to take root over several years. Craftily, methodically, Absalom won over many of the people of Israel in preparation for an attempt to seize his father's throne. (See 2 Samuel 15:2–6.)

Neither rebellion nor sedition is tolerated in the kingdom of God. Spiritually speaking, these are criminal acts. What happened to Lucifer after he allowed pride and jealousy to grow in his heart until they manifested in sedition and defiance? Wanting to be equal with God, he rose up against his Creator and attempted to usurp His throne. So, God banished him and his angels from heaven. Lucifer lost his position in God's kingdom and forfeited the purpose for which he had been created. Sedition usually brings exile and death. For example, after Absalom tried to usurp David's throne, he was killed. (See 2 Samuel 18:14–15.)

A seditious person sets himself apart to create discord against his leader. He seeks out others who are discontented, who harbor the same rebellious spirit (or who can be incited to have it), as he plots to undermine legitimate authority. An individual who has a "spirit of Absalom" is full of anger, and he uses others to meet his own agenda.

He constantly thinks about his own rights while ignoring the rights and needs of others.

In contrast to this rebellious spirit is the heart of a "servant leader." Such a leader is always thinking about how he can assist others and help them to succeed. He even changes his own agenda to serve people. You know you are being influenced by rebellion when your heart is motivated by selfishness and you lack the desire to help meet the needs of others.

A seditious person also feels that the current leader "owes" him something. In the case of a ministry, he may feel that his spiritual father has not given him enough or promoted him as fast as he deserved; consequently, he is convinced that he has been treated unfairly. At times, such a person is not satisfied until he sees his spiritual father ruined and left with nothing. But remember that every time someone gives place to rebellion, he also gives place to his own undoing. Again, we must be discerning about those whom we place in leadership. It is bad enough when the people in a congregation are rebellious, but it is even more dangerous to have a rebellious team member who has clandestine plans to usurp authority.

As I wrote earlier, there have been leaders in my church who have caused dissension and then left the ministry. Fortunately, these have been only a small percentage of the total leadership. Some of them came to me with nothing, and I received them into my house, helped to restore their personal lives, families, and finances, and then empowered them for ministry. I believed in them and helped to lead them into their spiritual destiny. I sent them out in ministry with all of my backing and support. We shared a relationship of trust, and together we expanded the kingdom of God. Yet, after a time, they demonstrated a spirit of sedition and tried to recruit for their own ministry anyone from my congregation who crossed their path. Even after I had given them my heart, my resources, my time, and my energy, as well as impartation, revelation, and anointing, their hearts became corrupted.

Others rebelled within the church, even before they could be sent out. Recruiting others in secret, they left the ministry taking hundreds of members with them. One leader seduced most of the musicians to leave the church. At the time, I had five services every Sunday, so I was left without a worship team. But God was good, and He soon supplied excellent musicians who could take their place.

The following is an example of how sedition can develop in the heart of a leader-in-training. Suppose he is on the ministry team of a thriving church. He observes the church's numerical growth, outreaches, abundant finances, anointing, miracles, and signs, and he begins to desire to compete against or replace the senior pastor because he thinks he is ready to lead on his own now and could do things better than his mentor. Perhaps the senior pastor has recognized that this team member has not yet completed the necessary process of growth and maturity to begin his own ministry. The leader-in-training may interpret the senior pastor's rejection of his plans as a lack of vision, while failing to see the immaturity and rebellion in his own heart. If the team member cannot make the pastor either do what he says or surrender his leadership, he will begin to sow discontentment, division, and sedition among the members.

Sedition dishonors the established authority; it always has its own agenda, and it feels no gratitude toward the present leadership. That is why, when this ministry team member trusts in his own abilities rather than follow God's direction, he finds it very difficult to commit to the ministry's vision; instead, he remains on the sidelines, because he is devoted to his own way of thinking, doing, and leading. His next step is usually to open his own ministry so he can "do the will of God" his own way.

Sedition dishonors the established authority; it always has its own agenda, and it feels no gratitude toward the present leadership.

The leader-in-training has rebelled because he has become jealous of the grace that God has given the appointed leader to fulfill his calling. Additionally, the team member does not understand that, although his own gifts come from God, most of those gifts have been imparted or activated through the appointed leader, who has become his spiritual father. Even though the spiritual son may eventually have more success than the father, this does not mean that he is better than his mentor or that he can just discard him at will. If he does, he will have failed to recognize the spiritual "law of priority," meaning that a son should never have greater authority than his father. The father came first, and God respects that.

After more than a quarter of a century in ministry, I can say that the "Timothies" (the sons in the faith) that God has given me have been much more numerous than the "Absaloms" who have betrayed me. I was careful not to let my negative experiences cause me to close my heart against opportunities to train new leaders. In this way, I have been able to receive more sons and daughters in the faith from across the world whom I have formed, equipped, and given a spiritual inheritance to. Today, their ministries are some of the most powerful in their nations, and their families have been restored and strengthened. They honor me, and they work shoulder to shoulder with me to expand the kingdom.

Rebellion and sedition are
the root of all of mankind's problems.

Witchcraft

Let us now examine a third expression of the spirit of rebellion that leads people to defy authority—"witchcraft." Witchcraft seeks to rob glory from God and from the merits of His work and power. When something that has been accomplished through the power and grace of God begins to be attributed to human effort and merit, the spirit of witchcraft has begun to operate. This is what happened among the believers in Galatia, to whom Paul wrote, "*O foolish Galatians! Who has bewitched you that you should not obey the truth, before whose eyes Jesus Christ was clearly portrayed among you as crucified?...Are you so foolish? Having begun in the Spirit, are you now being made perfect by the flesh?*" (Galatians 3:1, 3).

There are two types of rebellion that I place under the heading of witchcraft. The first is demonic and is practiced by those outside the church who are influenced by or under the control of Satan. I call this "satanic witchcraft." The second is sometimes practiced by those within the church, so I have termed it "Christian witchcraft." Although I will explain both forms, I will focus on Christian witchcraft, since it is often so subtle and is a type of rebellion that we especially need to guard against.

Satanic Witchcraft

Satanic witchcraft is demonic power that manipulates and dominates people through the use of curses, hexes, spells, conjurations, music, drugs, blood or soul pacts, and various other aspects of occultism. This type of witchcraft is included in certain religions and is found in all parts of the world, taking a number of forms. The goal of this infernal spirit of witchcraft is to control either geographical areas, aspects of nature (such as the weather or harvests), or human beings for the purpose of accomplishing its dark will. Remember that evil spirits seek to possess or otherwise control human beings in order to operate on the physical earth. As spiritual entities, they can influence people and function in the world to a certain degree, but to exercise authority on earth, they need the will and the body of a human being.

Christian Witchcraft

When Satan is unable to divide or destroy a church through open rebellion or sedition, he tries a more subtle way to infiltrate the congregation. He often works through influential church members to control and manipulate the pastor and/or the congregation. This form of witchcraft can be hard to recognize because it does not come from a source that assaults the church from the outside but rather operates from within it—from Christians themselves.

Rebellion, sedition, and witchcraft all come from the same source—iniquity, particularly selfish motivations and defiance toward God. All power that is exercised outside of submission to God's authority is illegitimate. So, the leader or other believer who is influenced or controlled by the spirit of witchcraft rules with an unlawful power that comes from Satan. Due to Satan's ongoing activities, this is something to which we are all exposed at one time or another.

> *Witchcraft is a demonic means*
> *of making others do what one wants.*

Christian witchcraft is generally a work of the fleshly nature, even though it can also be the influence of a demonic spirit. If someone does "God's work" in his own way, primarily for his own personal benefit, the spirit under which he is operating is not the Holy Spirit but that of the corrupt soul. In chapter 3, we discussed the operation of a soul that is being controlled by the flesh, and we saw that the fleshly nature seeks to control others to achieve selfish ends. No desire that leads to controlling others comes from God. The Holy Spirit will not allow anyone to use Him for selfish purposes. If a cause or an endeavor does not originate in God, the Holy Spirit will not participate in its fulfillment. Jesus stated concerning those whose service was only superficial and whose hearts were not with Him, *"Then I will declare to them, 'I never knew you; depart from Me, you who practice lawlessness!'"* (Matthew 7:23).

Sometimes, an operation of witchcraft comes not only from a work of the flesh but also from a demonic spirit that has gained entrance to an individual through the rebellion of his fleshly nature. Such an evil spirit seeks, through manipulation and control, to usurp or replace an authority established by God. *"For rebellion is as the sin of witchcraft, and stubbornness* ["*insubordination*" NASB] *is as iniquity and idolatry"* (1 Samuel 15:23). In this Scripture, rebellion is equated to witchcraft, while stubbornness, which is also a work of the flesh, is put in the same category as iniquity and idolatry. We must be extremely careful in this regard. Those who practice idolatry and sorcery will not inherit the kingdom of God. (See, for example, Galatians 5:19–21.)

Rebellion says, "I will not do it." Sedition says, "I will do it better than you and take others with me." Stubbornness says, "I will do it—but in my own way." All stubbornness is based on egocentrism. So, every time you act stubbornly and wish to do things your own way, you expose yourself to demonic influences of rebellion.

> *A stubborn person often makes an idol out of his own opinions and ways of thinking, because all stubbornness is based on egocentrism.*

Some Manifestations of the Spirit of Witchcraft

As I said at the beginning of this chapter, we live in a rebellious society in which many people deliberately reject those in authority in order to do what their fleshly desires want, including controlling other people. Thus, our society has been invaded by the spirit of witchcraft. That is why, every time I deliver a person from rebellion, I also have to cast out the spirit of witchcraft. The following are some examples of how satanic witchcraft and Christian witchcraft are being practiced in our world.

Witchcraft in the media. In TV commercials and other advertisements, there is much hidden satanic witchcraft, because most ads appeal to two things in those who see and hear them: vanity and greed. Though they usually don't understand the spirit under which they are operating, media experts develop psychological plans and devise other strategies to attract people's attention, often with the purpose of manipulating them to desire what they do not need and to buy what they cannot afford.

Witchcraft in the home. Some husbands and fathers use intimidation, anger, and violence to control their families. If a father behaves in this way, the rest of the family usually thinks, *It is best do as he says.* They do not obey him out of love but out of fear of the consequences if they don't.

Some men manipulate their wives by expressing jealousy. For instance, if the wife goes beyond the limits the husband wishes for her— perhaps spending more time with her friends or other activities than he likes—the husband will become incensed at his wife, causing her to stop spending time with others outside the home out of fear that he will lose his temper and become violent.

Generally, wives who want to control their husbands or children do so through manipulation rather than intimidation. They will use emotions (including tears), self-pity, or feigned sickness or fatigue for the purpose of receiving attention and making others do what they want. Such manipulation can be overt or subtle, but behind it may be a demonic spirit inciting a compulsion for control. This spirit will inhibit the other family members from exercising their own free will and from growing beyond the shadow of the controlling person's personality.

Some people manipulate their spouses by denying them sexual relations. Trying to control one's mate in this way undermines the unity of the marriage, and it can backfire on the manipulator by driving the spouse away. The apostle Paul warned married couples about the dangers of withholding sexual relations, except for a short time for spiritual reasons. *"Let the husband render to his wife the affection due her, and likewise also the wife to her husband. Do not deprive one another...so that Satan does not tempt you because of your lack of self-control"* (1 Corinthians 7:3, 5).

People who seek to control their family members may also resort to using guilt. Perhaps a woman's husband has not been attentive or has spoken unkind words to her. Every time she wants to manipulate him, she just reminds him of the times when he has treated her poorly. These reminders do not even have to be spoken, because the spirit of guilt can be exercised in nonverbal ways. Whenever we force people to act in accordance to our own selfish will, we operate under a spirit of witchcraft, manifesting one type of manipulation or another. The Holy Spirit never makes us feel guilty. Instead, He convicts us of our sin and leads us to repentance, forgiveness, and transformation. Let me say that if you are struggling with guilt, that is not a work of the Holy Spirit; it is the work of an unclean spirit that seeks to oppress you and keep you separated from God.

Parents sometimes manipulate their children, pressuring them and making them overly dependent when they should be maturing and growing to manhood or womanhood. They place conditions on their love, saying things like the following: "If you love me, you won't do that," "...won't go there," "...won't pursue that vocation," "...won't move away," and so on. This makes the children believe that their parents' love for them is contingent on their behaving in a particular way, whether that behavior is beneficial or not. No son or daughter should be placed in a situation where he or she has to "earn" love from a parent. The love of the heavenly Father is unconditional, and it is from the demonstration of such love from parents that children feel secure and are enabled to develop confidence, self-discipline, and integrity.

It is not just adults who manipulate others. Children often manipulate their parents, siblings, or peers. With regard to their parents, they often manipulate through stubborn behavior and temper tantrums—throwing themselves on the ground and crying until they get what they want. Suppose a child wants to go to a friend's house, or to the movies, or outside to play, and his parents say no. He will often show his resistance by either yelling, crying, or getting very quiet and sullen. At these times, instead of correcting the child, many parents often give in, allowing the spirit of witchcraft to control their child and their home.

Witchcraft in the church. Christian witchcraft is used by some people to manipulate other believers. I have seen preachers lay guilt trips on Christians when asking them for money, saying things like, "If you don't send me an offering, children in Africa will starve." Others manipulate their members to give money by twisting the Scriptures, offering them things that God never promised, thereby using His name in vain. Still others use fear tactics, such as telling people, "If you leave this church, you will fall under a curse and never prosper." To "correct" or "direct" others, some pastors resort to using false prophetic words or fabricated visions, dreams, or messages that supposedly came from God.

Some pastors use prayer to manipulate people into places of leadership—or out of them. However, we should know that the purpose of prayer is not to control others but to manifest the kingdom on earth. Using prayer as a means of manipulation perverts its spirit, character, and power.

These four words describe the operation of witchcraft: manipulation, control, intimidation, and domination.

Signs of Rebellion, Sedition, and Witchcraft

Although some expressions of the spirit of rebellion can be subtle, there are also some clear indications that people are operating according to rebellion, sedition, or witchcraft:

- A spirit of independence, including the lack of a servant's heart.
- A strong ambition to receive personal recognition.

+ An attitude of criticism toward people who are in authority.

+ The sowing of discord among people for the purpose of damaging the image of the leader.

+ A gravitation toward those within a group who are discontented—particularly those who are also naïve, immature, and foolish, thus lacking in discernment—for the purpose of promoting rebellion against the leader.

+ A justification of divisive attitudes and actions in opposition to the leader.

+ An unsanctioned breaking away to start one's own group.

Consequences of Rebellion, Sedition, and Witchcraft

We find this pattern throughout the Scriptures: Every individual who has rebelled against God or the one whom He has placed in authority has suffered grave consequences. The following outcomes of the spirit of rebellion are a warning to us to renounce rebellion, to repent of idolatry and stubbornness toward God, and to submit our wills completely to the lordship of Jesus Christ.

1. Those Who Oppose God's Authority Are Under Judgment, or Condemnation

The apostle Paul wrote, "*Whoever resists the authority resists the ordinance of God, and those who resist will bring judgment* ["*condemnation*" NASB] *on themselves*" (Romans 13:2). Anyone who resists a human authority placed by God is not really resisting a person but rather God Himself. To resist authority is to bring judgment, or condemnation, on oneself. For example, when someone rejects the authority of a ministry leader in the church—an apostle, a prophet, an evangelist, a pastor, or a teacher—he resists Jesus, who set him in authority. (See Ephesians 4:11.) When a wife resists her husband's authority, she resists God, who placed her husband as the head of the home. (See Ephesians 5:23.) When an employee resists his supervisor's authority, he resists God, who placed that manager in his position. (See, for example, Colossians 3:22–23.) The same is true in other areas of life.

If you follow a rebellious person, the spirit of destruction will go with you. I have seen rebellious people fall back into the world, get divorced, and experience other consequences. One cannot play with God. When He chooses someone and places His mantle over him, that person cannot be touched without his adversaries suffering consequences. (See 1 Chronicles 16:22.) David honored this principle, and that is why he spared King Saul's life, even though Saul sought to kill him. (See, for example, 1 Samuel 26:6–9.)

> The origin of all authority is God.
> Whoever opposes authority
> resists God Himself.

2. The Rebellious Never Ultimately Prosper

"*God…brings out those who are bound into prosperity; but the rebellious dwell in a dry land*" (Psalm 68:6). I have observed people fail to prosper when they've refused to submit to God-given authority. They are sterile in their family life, their vocation, their ministry, and so forth. They are destined to fail because they lack favor from God.

It is impossible to live in rebellion against God and not experience consequences. Rebellious people always live in a "*dry land*" where there is no fruit or prosperity. When people speak against the mantle of anointing under which God has placed them, they are unable to bear fruit, because they cannot bring forth fruit from a mantle that they have offended. Everything we sow, we will reap. (See Galatians 6:7.)

3. God Resists, Brings Down, or Destroys Everything a Rebel Builds

"God resists the proud, but gives grace to the humble" (James 4:6). This means that God will resist the prideful heart of the rebellious person. Those who have such a heart cannot draw close to Him again until they repent.

God will also destroy what the rebellious attempt to establish. They may begin to build or to produce something at home, at work, or at church but, because they are living in a state of rebellion, everything they construct will be consumed; it will disappear as though it were part of the vanishing act of a magician. They may be about to finalize a contract but, at the last moment, it does not go through. They may be ready to start a business but, suddenly, everything stalls. All their work is in vain. When something like this happens to a rebellious person, it is most likely not an attack of the enemy; rather, it is God consuming what the rebel had planned to do.

All sin is based on pride.

In the Old Testament, the Israelites were constantly murmuring and complaining against God—the supreme Authority—and against Moses, the human authority He had appointed for them. (See, for example, Numbers 16.) Every time they rebelled against Moses, judgment was released upon them. In one instance, Moses' sister and brother, Miriam and Aaron, complained against him, thinking that they should receive equal honor. The result was that *"when the cloud departed from above the tabernacle, suddenly Miriam became leprous, as white as snow. Then Aaron turned toward Miriam, and there she was, a leper"* (Numbers 12:10). I believe that, in the same way, curses of sickness can come upon people today as a result of their rebellion. If you are sick, and people have prayed for you several times but you've seen no improvement, ask the Holy Spirit to reveal if you are under condemnation due to your own rebellion or that of your parents or ancestors. If that is the case, repent from this rebellion, and you will be set free.

Freedom from Rebellion, Sedition, and Witchcraft

I. Deliverance from Your Own Participation in Rebellion, Sedition, and Witchcraft

If you realize that you have been operating according to a spirit of rebellion, sedition, or witchcraft in your relationship with God or in your relationship with a family member, a boss, a fellow believer, or anyone else, you must be released from condemnation and restored to your heavenly Father, so that you can again receive the blessings of God. The first thing you must do to save yourself is to repent and ask for forgiveness. Make a firm decision that you want to live according to God's ways and not rebellious ways. It is through repentance that you can be free from your fleshly nature, as well as close the door to all unclean spirits, including the spirit of rebellion.

Next, you must renounce any involvement with the evil spirit of rebellion in order to remove it from your life and send it back to hell where it belongs. Then you must receive healing and deliverance in your soul and body, asking God to cleanse you and transform you into His likeness. Make it a priority to cultivate mature character in yourself, and continually renew your mind through the Word of God. In addition, voluntarily obey God and submit to his human authorities, so that the spirit of rebellion can no longer find any openings with which to influence or dominate your life.

2. Freedom from Public Rebellion

If you are a leader, and you are currently facing a rebellion against your authority, you must recognize that this rebellion cannot be "counseled" to behave better or just given a slap on the wrist; it must be eliminated. The best situation is for the rebellious person to repent and seek deliverance from the demonic spirit operating in him. Go to this person and appeal to him, following the guidelines of Matthew 18:15–17. If he will not listen, I have found that the only way to deal with stubborn rebellion in a leader is to expose the rebellion publicly, killing it at the roots. We cannot keep such rebellion private. A rebel usually does his work publicly in an attempt to usurp a leader or other legitimate authority. Accordingly, his rebellion must be publicly recognized and renounced. I have had to reveal the names of rebellious individuals in my church to the leadership team and sometimes to the congregation, as well as the cause of the rebellion, to avoid their dragging down more people with their selfish ambition and lies.

3. Deliverance from an Attack of Witchcraft

What should you do if someone is using satanic witchcraft against you? Reject and rebuke the power that the rebellious spirit may be wielding over you. A child of God must operate by faith, grace, and submission to the authorities delegated by God, and not be controlled, manipulated, or made to live in fear. Perhaps the family in which you were raised was involved in witchcraft. You need to renounce the root of rebellion in your bloodline and your family relationships in order to be delivered from any evil influence that might be operating today in your relationships, your health, your work, your finances, or any other area—and hindering your ability to submit to proper authority.

Furthermore, you must make a personal decision to submit only to healthy, God-given authority. People who are manipulated by others often fall into the trap of an emotional "soul tie." They have been seduced in their emotions, and this unhealthy bond must be broken. To be set free, recognize the destructive soul tie and renounce the spirit of rebellion that is behind it. Repent of allowing yourself to be manipulated or seduced, ask God for forgiveness, and cast off those soul ties by the power of the blood of Jesus.

Those who have been attacked through satanic witchcraft—and even those who have been deeply involved in the practices of witchcraft—can find freedom and new life, as the following testimony demonstrates.

"My name is Guerda, and I was delivered from a spirit of witchcraft when I came to Christ. I grew up in the Bahamas, where my sister and I were raised by our mother, a single parent, who was a voodoo witch. The spirit of witchcraft followed me so that I started to practice witchcraft, also. I would do rituals, channelings, curses, and hexes; I also worked for an evil spirit called 'Jezebel.' She would come in person and guide me regarding what I was supposed to do with men, and how I should seduce them to control them and make them do as I said. I would also make sacrifices to her, wearing certain garments and particular colors to honor her. My mom enslaved me to this spirit when she died, so that she would always serve me and teach me things.

"My assignment was to destroy marriages and to activate men to evil—I destroyed six major marriages. I was supposed to activate men into lust—including with little girls—building them up into witchcraft. Things got worse, and I started operating under unforgiveness and sexual immorality. There was one incident in which I was involved with a married man, and this led me to leave the island where I was born and move to Miami. This man's wife was involved in witchcraft, as well, so we would go back and forth with the witchcraft. She was trying to kill me, and I was trying to kill her. One evening, she sent out a spell on me, assigned a hex on me, and it was so strong that I got into a really bad car accident, so bad that I almost lost my daughter. That was too much for me; I no longer had the strength to continue fighting, so I ran away to Miami. In Miami, I met a new man, Denis, who is my husband today. I had run away from the Bahamas, but I was still practicing witchcraft, although no one else was aware of it. At that time, Denis and I were only dating.

"I ended up making a new friend who told me about King Jesus Ministry. I didn't visit the church right away, but one Thursday when I got off work, I went to a service. I will never forget the preaching. At the end of his message, the pastor said, "If you want to give your life to

Christ, run to the altar." I took what he said literally, and I stood up and ran to the altar, where I experienced the power of God. I learned about the conflict between the kingdom of darkness and the kingdom of heaven and about the battle that was being fought over my soul. My deliverance happened when I went to a retreat. I exposed all demons and fleshly works, confessed all the spells I had done and all the hurt and pain I had caused, and repented of my sin fully from my heart. I gave my life to Christ and was born again. I could not believe that I was able to be delivered and set free; witchcraft had always taught me that I could not leave it behind, because if I did, I would die. I had this paradigm in my mind, making me think it would be impossible to leave and making me believe the devil's lies. Today, I am a new woman, restored and complete. I no longer serve fear, hate, intimidation, or guilt. I am born again by the blood of Jesus Christ."

Prayer of Deliverance

To be set free from rebellion, sedition, and witchcraft, repeat the following prayer out loud:

Dear Lord Jesus,

I believe You are the Son of God, that You died on the cross for my sins, and that You rose victoriously from the dead. I repent of any sins of rebellion, sedition, and witchcraft that have governed my life—with or without my knowledge or willingness—particularly the sin of rebellion against God and His delegated authorities. I separate from them and reject them. I renounce any desire to control other people to do what I want them to do. I acknowledge that this is wrong, and I recognize it as a manifestation of the spirit of witchcraft. I ask You to forgive me, and, by faith, I receive that forgiveness now. I also rebuke every spirit of rebellion, sedition, and witchcraft and command them to leave my life right now. In the name of Jesus, I declare myself free. Now, Spirit of God, I ask You to fill the areas of my

life that these evil spirits have vacated. Give me the grace to submit to You and to the authorities You have appointed. Help me
to grow and mature in the character of Christ, so that the spirit
of rebellion can find no place in me. In the name of Jesus, amen.

5

ENTRY POINTS OF EVIL SPIRITS

While ministering deliverance to people, I have had experiences in which a demon has spoken through an afflicted person and said something along the lines of, "I am not leaving, because he gave me the legal right to be in his body." We have already discussed how a demon can enter someone only when it has been given access by the person's disobedience to God. And so it is easy to understand why removing the demon's permission to operate is the foundation for effective and lasting deliverance. To do this, we must first understand the "entry points," or areas of disobedience, in which demons can gain a foothold in our lives. If such entry points are not completely dealt with, deliverance cannot occur. Once a demonized person repents, however, the demon can be cast out. What follows in this chapter will not only enable believers to receive deliverance, but it will also help them to minister deliverance to others much more effectively.

The first entry point we will discuss is the habitual practice of sin. Most sins can be habitually practiced, and as the chapter progresses, we will look at some specific examples. But let us begin with an overall discussion of repeated sin so that we may understand how patterns and habits of sin make us vulnerable to the works of Satan.

I. The Habitual Practice of Sin

Sin is a violation or transgression of the laws and commandments of God. It is rebellion against Him, which can bring both earthly and eternal consequences. People commit sin in two ways: by doing what is wrong and incorrect, and by *not* doing what is right and correct. Committing a sin does not necessarily create an entry point for a demon. The Word says that all of us sin and that *"if we say that we have no sin, we deceive ourselves, and the truth is not in us. If we confess our sins, [God] is faithful and just to forgive us our sins and to cleanse us from all unrighteousness"* (1 John 1:8–9).

We must also realize, however, that if we commit a sin continuously or repeatedly, we give ourselves over to that sin, and we become a slave to it. (See Romans 6:16.) Whatever we yield to continuously, we will conform to. The sin that dominates us will shape our character; it will contribute to who we become. Moreover, the continuous practice of a sin that we have not repented of and confessed to God creates an opening through which a demon may enter our life. It gives demonic powers the legal right to control the area in which the disobedience occurred.

The habitual or continuous practice
of any sin is an entry point for demons.

Ask yourself: "What specific sin have I repeatedly committed? What wrongs do I continuously yield to? Do I regularly give in to worry, fear, phobias, anger, gossip, complaining, jealousy, unforgiveness, or some other sin?" If you are engaging in habitual or continuous sin, you have made yourself vulnerable to demonization. Once an evil spirit gains access to your life, it increases the pressure for you to keep on sinning, so that you experience the temptation from within. Previously, the temptation came from the outside, but now it lives inside you. Continued sin builds up and forms iniquity, which, like lust, demands to be fed with more sin. (See James 1:14–15.) It becomes a "Goliath" inside you! The attack of a demonic spirit is more powerful when it is inside you; therefore, it is more difficult to be delivered from. But be assured that you can be delivered.

After someone has repeatedly sinned in a particular area of his life, demons seem to choose that person's weakest moment to enter him and to control that area.

In some cases, a single, decisive sin will open the door for a demon to enter. That is what happened to Judas Iscariot. After he made the decision to betray Jesus, Satan entered him. (See Luke 22:1–6; John 13:2, 18–30.) From the biblical record of Judas' fate, we learn that we cannot play with sin, either carelessly or habitually, because it can cost us our physical life and our eternal salvation. (See Matthew 27:1–5.)

To close an entry point that we have opened to demons due to habitual sin, we need to humble ourselves before God, repent, confess and renounce the sin, ask for God's forgiveness, reject and rebuke the evil spirit in the name of Jesus, and then ask God to refill us with His Holy Spirit. The demon will be expelled and the entrance will be closed.

Thereafter, we need to live in continuous obedience to God, repenting of any subsequent sin immediately.

> *The keys to deliverance from demons that*
> *have entered due to our personal sin are always*
> *confession and repentance.*

Jesus came to set us free, but we must know the truth, or the root, of each problem in order to apply the power of the cross of Christ to it. (See John 8:31–32.) As we now look at some specific areas of repeated sin, as well as other entry points of demons, I want to share with you knowledge that God has revealed to me about how to close the doors through which demons gain access to our lives.

2. Jealousy

Jealousy is a work of the flesh—it can also be an evil spirit— that, when continuously indulged in, opens the door to a demon of murder. That was the case with Saul, who became jealous of David's success on the battlefield and his subsequent popularity. He thought that David would take away his kingdom. (See 1 Samuel 18:7–10.) The jealousy that was awakened in King Saul by the people's praise for David was so strong that, from that moment on, he dedicated himself to killing David. The king's envy gave place to a spirit of murder. A similar thing happened with Cain when God was displeased with his offering but accepted the offering of Cain's brother Abel. Filled with jealousy and anger, Cain killed his brother. (See Genesis 4:1–8.) In the end, jealousy always wants to kill the object of its anger.

So, the entry point for the spirit of murder in Saul was the sin of jealousy. Saul never repented of this sin, and he disobeyed God in other serious ways, as well, refusing to follow the specific instructions of the Lord through Samuel the prophet (see 1 Samuel 13:1–14; 15:1–22) and even consulting a medium (see 1 Samuel 28:3–19).

We must recognize that the spirit of murder includes not only a desire to extinguish the physical life of another person but also to destroy his character, reputation, and influence. When you feel jealous of someone, you may not necessarily want that person dead, but you may begin to defame him or to "kill" his influence and success, even in subtle ways. And the Bible says that when we hate someone or are angry with him without cause, this is the equivalent of murder. (See, for example, Matthew 5:21–22.)

> *Jealousy causes anger and is the seed of murder.*

Ask yourself: "Am I jealous of anyone? Am I envious of another person's gifts or of God's grace toward him or of God's blessings on him?" It could be that this person seems to be more successful, more anointed, or better looking than you are. If you are in a leadership position of any kind, are you envious of someone who is in authority over you, or someone who is under your authority and seems to be especially talented? If you are in ministry, do you feel jealous of another pastor who has a bigger church or organization? Could a demon of jealousy be influencing your life?

Regardless of the specific reason for your envy, let me warn you that recurrent jealousy will open a door to the spirit of murder. Repent and flee from being under a curse like Saul's! Make a decision to cast out the evil spirit this instant and to permanently block this point of access by being obedient to God and by developing the fruit of the Spirit in your life. (See Galatians 5:22–23.)

3. Unforgiveness and Taking Offense

Offenses come to all of us (see, for example, Matthew 18:7), but our response toward them is crucial. To take offense is to develop a negative attitude after being affronted by someone, so that we develop bitterness and resentment toward the person. I am not speaking about being briefly bothered by someone's remark or behavior, after which we immediately let it go or release it through prayer. I am referring to something that remains in our heart as we harbor unforgiveness.

Jesus said, *"For if you forgive men their trespasses, your heavenly Father will also forgive you. But if you do not forgive men their trespasses, neither will your Father forgive your trespasses"* (Matthew 6:14–15). Forgiving those who offend us is vital to maintaining a right relationship with God and being obedient to Him. And, harboring unforgiveness opens an entry point for demons to invade our life.

Earlier, we saw how Absalom held unforgiveness toward his father, King David, because David did not avenge the rape of Absalom's sister Tamar. So, Absalom took matters into his own hands. He had Amnon killed, and he later dedicated himself to usurping his father's kingdom. Unforgiveness opens an entry point for various negative spirits, including the spirit of sedition, which Absalom operated in. When acting according to a demon of sedition, a person will begin plotting against his leader to weaken his authority and to "murder" his character.

The testimony that follows demonstrates how destructive and broken we can become when we hold on to offenses and live in anger and unforgiveness. It also shows God's mercy and power to heal us spiritually, emotionally, and physically.

"My name is Barbara, and my husband, Roland, and I come from France. Our first seven years of marriage were terrible. We were Christians and knew God, but only in a religious way. We believed solely in a historic Christ who was crucified but was without power or authority, and especially without love. I did not love my family; there was no communication between us—not between my husband and me, and not with our children. When we spoke, we did so only with hatred and resentment; the atmosphere in our house was very negative and violent.

"My husband drank a lot and was completely irresponsible. My son suffered from such severe depression and autism that he would bite himself and hit himself against the wall. As for me, I had very low self-esteem and was depressed; all I wanted to do was commit suicide.

"One day, someone spoke to my husband about a new church, with a different pastor. This is how we met Pastor Jose Murillo, a spiritual son of Apostle Guillermo Maldonado. Pastor Murillo listened to us and ministered the love of God to us without judgment. He taught us to love each other as a family, and he taught us about the ministry of deliverance.

"A short time later, we traveled to meet the apostle, who was visiting Madrid. We brought him our autistic son, and he gave us anointing oil so we could put it on him and declare his healing. I did so, and today my child is completely normal. He speaks clearly, pays attention during services, and does not injure himself. His learning level in school is good.

"Similarly, God intervened in our marriage. His love restored us, transformed us, delivered us, and brought us peace. Jesus gave us identity and purpose. Now we are involved in the vision of King Jesus in France, and we attend Apostle Maldonado's events. We are very grateful to God because He showed us the root of our problems and revealed to us His power to deliver. Autism, depression, alcoholism, anger, hatred, and suicidal desires—all were removed by His great power!"

4. Sexual Immorality

Outside the context of marriage, any type of sexual relations is sin and is always an entry point for evil spirits. Sexual sin has been one of the greatest problems of society and of the church throughout the centuries. Today, there is statistical evidence that the practice of sexual immorality is very high in our society—not only outside the church but also inside it. As a pastor, this is the area in which I have most ministered deliverance.

The following sexual practices are entry points for demons.

Fornication: To commit fornication is to have illicit sexual relations with another single person, whether you live together or not. (See, for example, 1 Corinthians 6:18.) Today, having sexual relations outside of marriage is common and generally accepted by society. However, it has always been a sin in God's eyes because He considers the one-flesh relationship to be holy; it is appropriate only in the context of a marriage, because marriage represents the spiritual reality of our oneness with God and is a reflection of complete faithfulness to Him. To move outside this God-given boundary is to open an entry point for demons.

Sex was designed so that, within the marriage covenant, a husband and wife would become one in body and soul. (See, for example, Genesis 2:24.) This is known as a spiritual bond, so that everything that happens to one person affects the other. When that bond occurs outside of marriage, it is the same as fraud, and the souls of those involved are contaminated. When people have sex with multiple partners, the situation becomes even worse, because they leave a part of themselves with each person and take parts of those partners into themselves—and the "parts" they receive can include demonic spirits.

When you engage in illicit sexual relations, you give demons a right to operate within you, while you effect a dangerous, possibly fatal, disintegration of your very being. The more deeply you are involved in an illicit relationship, or the more sexual relationships you have, the greater the strength the demon or demons will have in your soul, ultimately leading you to a state of strong demonization.* You must deal with this sin by going to God in confession and repentance. If you don't, you will end up contending with demons who have found a legal right to operate in this area of your life.

---

*For more information on this topic, please refer to the book *Sexual Immorality* by Apostle Guillermo Maldonado.

> *Demonic spirits can be transferred through illicit sexual relations.*

Adultery: Adultery means having sexual relations with someone other than one's own spouse, or having sexual relations with someone who is married to another person. To commit adultery is to disrespect the covenant of marriage through faithlessness. (See Matthew 5:28; 19:17–18.) The consequences I stated above in the section on sex outside of marriage apply to adultery, as well. Furthermore, when a spouse commits adultery, he or she is violating a pact, sacred to God; this brings spiritual death and opens the door to Satan, giving him a legal right to destroy the marriage, the children, and the future generations. It can also bring sicknesses and evil spiritual forces that will ruin the family spiritually, emotionally, and even physically.

Homosexuality and lesbianism: The practice of having sexual relations with someone of the same gender is clearly prohibited by God, both in the Old Testament and in the New Testament. For example, Leviticus 18:22 says, *"You shall not lie with a male as with a woman."* (See also Romans 1:26–27.) Such a practice has a number of consequences. For example, statistics show that AIDS has been largely transmitted through sexual immorality, especially among members of the homosexual community. In addition to physical consequences, it also invites unclean spirits into our lives.

There are various reasons why a man may feel homosexual tendencies, including the following: rebellion against his parents, a rejection of his sexuality, a choice to be homosexual, emotional pain and psychological confusion from sexual abuse or paternal or maternal domination, a generational curse, or even a demonic attack while in the womb. Homosexuality often stems from a previous sin, whether committed by the person or by someone else, and it is a curse.

Many homosexuals feel that they were born that way. For instance, a three-year-old who has not been raped or otherwise sexually mistreated might still feel a sexual attraction toward someone of the same gender. But while he might have been *born* a homosexual, God did not *create* him as a homosexual. Most likely, it was the result of a spiritual attack that occurred during the time he was in his mother's womb. When pregnancy occurs outside of spiritual coverage in a marriage or outside of marriage itself, a door is open to this kind of attack. Additionally, as noted above, there are various other reasons why a person may fall into homosexual attraction.

God did not create people to be homosexual; homosexuality is a manifestation of man's fall. What is the solution for someone with homosexual inclinations? The solution is to be born again and delivered. The whole message of Christianity is based on the new birth in Christ. And being born again brings about not only a spiritual change but also a biological, physical change. The instant we are born again, God changes us completely, and we need to enter into the full deliverance He provided for us. Jesus died on the cross for our sins so that we could be cleansed, forgiven, and set free. We simply need to repent of our sins from our heart.

At King Jesus Ministry, we have seen hundreds of homosexual men and boys receive Jesus into their hearts and be completely set free from homosexuality; they have been reestablished in their masculinity after receiving inner healing and deliverance. Today, these men have been restored by God; they have happy marriages with women, and they have healthy children. Likewise, our ministry has seen hundreds of women who were in lesbian relationships for years receive deliverance. They have recovered their femininity and their attraction to men; additionally, their self-image, which Satan had distorted, has been restored.

The church must therefore use wisdom when dealing with this issue of homosexuality. We must consider it as being alongside all the other sins of sexual immorality. God is never against the sinner, so we should never attack the person. God hates sin, but He deeply loves the sinner. Jesus received all types of people, including prostitutes, and He rejected no one; He forgave them. We are to do the same.

Pornography: Pornography is the representation of sexual acts in videos, theatrical movies, magazines, books, the Internet, and live environments. People who participate in pornography can suffer profound consequences, especially in their relationships with their spouse and children. It can destroy their lives as it becomes an entry point for demons. I have ministered to both men and women who were addicted to pornography and have helped them to find deliverance. If you are involved in pornography, repent, confess your sin to God, receive His forgiveness, and seek the support of a trusted Christian leader or fellow believer who can help you to stay accountable so that you can resist temptation.

Oral and anal sex: God's intention and design is for men and women to have sexual relations with their genital organs. The anus and the mouth fulfill other functions in the body. When sex is practiced in these ways, it becomes perverted, opening the door to demons.

Masturbation: Generally, our educational system today teaches that the practice of masturbation is healthy and acceptable; but masturbation, manually exciting the genital organs, opens the door to the spirit of lust.

Sexual abuse and rape: In addition to enduring violence and humiliation, the victims of sexual abuse also suffer spiritual consequences. Many women and men who have been raped later deal with spirits of lust, lesbianism/homosexuality, and frigidity.

Sexual activity with demons: There are two types of spirits involved in this activity, whose names are "incubus" (an evil presence with a male appearance that stimulates a female and leads her to orgasm) and "succubus" (an evil presence with a female appearance that stimulates a male and leads him to ejaculation). These spirits come to people because they have obtained a legal right to do so through a sin committed by either the people or their ancestors. When that right is removed, the demons leave, and the person is delivered from attack.

Bestiality: This is a sexual act between a person and an animal. It is a very high level of degradation that leads to demonization. If a person has reached the stage where he commits this sin, he needs a great deliverance; sometimes, multiple deliverances are needed until the iniquity formed by that sin is finally uprooted.

> *All types of sexual relations that are outside the safe bounds of marriage are sin.*

5. Fears and Phobias

There is a proper fear of God, but that kind of fear is not terror; rather, it is reverence and respect for our almighty Lord, especially when we are in His presence. (See, for example, Deuteronomy 6:2.) However, there is another type of fear, or fright, that is not from God and that can open the door to demonic oppression. (See Matthew 14:26–27.) For example, when people encounter an attack from the devil, they often feel frightened, and this can become an entry point for a demon of fear. In contrast, note that, in both the Old and New Testaments, when the angel of the Lord or Jesus Christ appeared to a human being, the supernatural message that was communicated often included statements like, *"Do not be afraid"* (see, for example, Genesis 15:1) or *"Peace be with you"* (see, for example, Judges 6:22–23; John 20:19).

The Spirit of Fear

The apostle Paul spoke of a "spirit" of fear, saying, *"For God has not given us a spirit of fear..."* (2 Timothy 1:7). This fear is a perversion of the imagination, and it is induced by an evil spirit. Fear also unleashes the demonic supernatural. The spirit of fear is destructive; it feeds on anxiety, phobias, dread, panic, faithlessness, and a lack of love.

Effects of the Spirit of Fear

The spirit of fear produces the following:

+ Paralysis of the mind, will, or emotions; fear can terrorize people and prevent them from thinking correctly.

+ Spiritual, mental, or emotional bondage, including a dread of punishment. (See Romans 8:15; 1 John 4:18.)

+ Delusions or imagined dangers. Fear can cause our imagination to become distorted; for example, a person who has been in an accident may suddenly become continuously fearful of having another accident. Fear creates dire scenarios in our mind.

+ A blockage of the flow of the supernatural. When we yield to fear, the supernatural "turns off."

+ The contamination of one's faith and anointing.

+ The opening of a door to hell (just as faith opens a portal to heaven).

+ An attraction to what frightens you. (See, for example, Job 3:25.) For instance, it can bring depression, accidents, disease, neglect, family dissolution, and even death.

+ The "failing" of men's hearts. (See Luke 21:26.) This failing, or fainting, of hearts is a sign of the end times, when there will be much confusion and turmoil in the world. People will be overcome by fear, because there is no way out without Christ. There is no human solution for what is happening in these last days, because it is beyond the capacity of human knowledge, including such fields as science, philosophy, and education.

Fear is a perversion of our God-given imagination and is a magnet for demons.

Faith Versus Fear

In view of the above, fear leads a person to have:

+ Wrongful thoughts (that lack trust in God)
+ Wrong beliefs (that lack the truth concerning God)
+ A wrongful life (that does not reflect who God is and is unable to fulfill His purposes)

Faith is the opposite of fear; it builds us up and leads us to have:

+ The right thoughts (that trust in God)
+ The right beliefs (that include the truth concerning God)
+ A wholesome life (that reflects the nature of God and is able to fulfill His purposes)

Faith releases the divine supernatural in our lives.

How to Deal with Fear

1. Confront the root, or origin, of the fear. Determine how the fear entered. For example, you might ask yourself, "When did the panic attacks start?" Fear calls out to fear, similar to "deep calling to deep." (See Psalm 42:7.) This means that the fear within us calls to the fear outside of us (the demonic world and other negative influences), and we must discern between the two. We first deal with the cause of the inner fear. When we are free on the inside, we will stop calling out to external sources of fear. If you don't remember when you first began to fear, ask the heavenly Father to reveal it to you. You may also want to talk with a family member or friend who can help you to recognize the cause.

2. Deal with the thought that conceived the fear. Many times, as people grow up, they develop patterns of fear from their exposure to those around them; they often absorb the negative attitudes and beliefs of their parents and other influential adults. People can also develop wrong thoughts from negative personal experiences or from having demeaning comments directed toward them. Thus, we must cast down any thoughts or "arguments" that exalt themselves against the knowledge of God—that are not in line with the truth of His Word. (See 2 Corinthians 10:5.)

3. Repent for having opened the door to fear. Ask God to forgive you for succumbing to fear. Give all your concerns over to Him, and then receive His peace into your life. (See Philippians 4:6–7.)

4. Face the fear with boldness. Often, what we are required to do in life, including what we are especially called to do by God, is huge or difficult, and we fear failure. This can cause emotional and mental paralysis, such as we discussed above. When this is the case, we must rise up and do what we are meant to do, even if we are scared. This is one way in which we overcome fear. We must act with spiritual courage, remembering that our heavenly Father is with us wherever we go. (See, for example, Joshua 1:9; Isaiah 41:10.)

5. Guard the mind. To protect our mind against thoughts of fear, we need to occupy it with thoughts of faith, grace, and victory, based on the Word of God. (See Philippians 4:8; 1 Peter 4:1.)

6. Perfect yourself in the love of God. When true love—the love of the Father—is revealed to us and established in us, fear will leave. (See 1 John 4:18.)

7. Resist fear with power and authority. As a child of God, you can order the spirit of fear to leave your life this instant so that you can live according to the peace and power of the Holy Spirit. (See, for example, Psalm 118:5–6.)

8. Do not allow the spirit of fear to return. Close the door to fear! Do not play with thoughts of fear or entertain unwholesome ideas. Reject them! Repeat Scriptures such as Psalm 46 to fill your mind with God's outlook.

> *We choose to live either by faith,*
> *which is the life of God in the now,*
> *or by fear, which is a state of oppression.*

6. Self-Pity

Indulging in self-pity is a work of the flesh, a demand of the ego that always feels the need to be at the center of everything. It can also be the influence of an evil spirit. Those who give in to self-pity are focused on themselves, rather than on God or others. When people remain in this frame of mind, they open the door to demonic spirits of victimization or manipulation.

People can develop an attitude of self-pity when they have experienced offenses, rejection, and abandonment, because a wounded heart dwells on itself and how much it has suffered. Often, people's habit of self-pity begins during childhood as a behavior pattern that has proven effective in keeping people's attention and making sure everything revolves around them.

Characteristics of Self-Pity

The following are some identifying characteristics of self-pity:

+ *People with self-pity resist change.* It is human nature for us to defend a wrongful condition when we don't want to change, or to want to keep the status quo if it allows us to indulge in self-absorption. We will use self-pity to justify our current state. We think we want a quick solution, but we don't want to do anything differently in order to arrive at a remedy.

* *People with self-pity feed on sympathy.* We indulge in self-pity because we want people to feel sorry for us and to commiserate with us, thus extending our sense of victimization and the length of time attention is paid to us. For this reason, it's important to remember that if we try to help someone merely out of sympathy or pity, we will likely leave them in the same condition in which they started; no permanent change will be made to their situation. However, if we seek to help others out of true compassion, we will lovingly place a demand on them to deal with their issues, including self-pity, leading them to repentance and transformation.

> **Pity is controlled by need, while compassion is directed by love. Jesus Christ healed people out of compassion, not pity.**

* *People with self-pity lack initiative.* When we are indulging in self-pity, we live in the past, regretting all the bad things we have done or placing blame on those who have hurt us or mistreated us. As a result, we cannot look to the future or build anything constructive for our lives. We need someone to push us to do anything.
* *People with self-pity are often jealous, as well.* Self-pity stems from a sense of loss or lack. Thus, when we are in this state of mind, it is easy to become envious of what other people have or what they have accomplished. Yet harboring envy is perilous due to the demonic influences it attracts, as we saw in the section on jealousy, above.

How to Deal with Self-Pity

Self-pity is a continuous cycle that must be broken by deliverance, by learning new behavior patterns based on a knowledge of who we are in Christ, and by learning how to thwart the enemy's schemes to destroy us. Here are some keys for dealing with the destructive cycle of self-pity:

+ Refuse to give in to feelings of self-pity.

+ If you find yourself in self-pity, do not indulge in it or sympathize with it but rather "kill" it. This involves dying to self, a process we discussed earlier.

+ Break free from a spirit of self-pity by taking authority over it. Cast it out and refuse to submit to it, so that it does not nullify the anointing that God has given you.

It is possible to be free from self-pity! Refuse it, reject it, and rebuke it.

If we attempt to use our God-given gifts
from a mind-set of self-pity,
our anointing is ineffective.

7. A Soul Tie, or Bond

A soul tie is a connection or union between the souls of two people. Some soul ties come from God, and others do not, but what they all have in common is that the people involved have a powerful bond. Soul ties that do not come from God restrain the free will of one or both parties in the relationship and are contrary to the divine plan for healthy relationships between human beings.

Soul ties can be established with:

+ People

+ Animals

+ Groups or organizations

+ Places

+ Things or activities

+ Demons (by allowing an entry point through disobedience)

Some examples of the above categories of soul ties are the following: a mentor relationship between an individual and his teacher or pastor; a sexual relationship (whether in the covenant of marriage or not); the manipulation of one person by another; a close attachment to a pet; a bond with an organization, a company, a church, a denomination, or another group; a connection to a family home or to a city one has lived in or visited; a material object, such as an heirloom; a hobby; a game; or an occult practice.

Biblical Examples of Healthy Soul Ties

One example of a healthy soul tie in the Old Testament is the bond that was formed between David and Jonathan, the son of Saul. This was a godly relationship of friendship that clearly blessed both parties. *"The soul of Jonathan was knit to the soul of David, and Jonathan loved him as his own soul"* (1 Samuel 18:1). Another example is the close relationship between Naomi and her daughter-in-law Ruth, who told her, *"Wherever you go, I will go; and wherever you lodge, I will lodge; your people shall be my people, and your God, my God"* (Ruth 1:16). In the New Testament, an example of a healthy soul tie is the relationship between Jesus and His disciples (which Judas Iscariot forfeited). Another is the spiritual father-son relationship of Paul and Timothy. Paul wrote that Timothy was his *"beloved and faithful son in the Lord"* (1 Corinthians 4:17).

Biblical Examples of Unhealthy Soul Ties

One example of an unhealthy soul tie in the Old Testament is the relationship between Israel's King Ahab and his wife, Queen Jezebel, who were united in their evil purposes to worship the false god Baal and to kill all of God's prophets. (See, for example, 1 Kings 16:30–33; 17:4, 16–18; 19:1–2.) Another example may be the tie that Lot, the nephew of Abraham, seemed to have to a place—the city of Sodom—imperiling his own life and that of his family. Lot's wife had a strong soul tie with Sodom. Even when she was pulled from the city after being warned of its impending doom due to its wickedness, she didn't want to leave. She disobeyed God's command not to look back at the city as it burned, and thus died. (See Genesis 19:1–29.) One additional illustration is the soul tie that Samson, the judge and warrior of Israel, had with Delilah. Due to this unhealthy alliance, Samson revealed to Delilah the secrets of the anointing on his life, which she then reported to his enemies, to his destruction.

In the New Testament, an illustration of a negative soul tie is the association between Herod and Pilate, who became friends due to their joint abuse of Jesus. (See Luke 23:1–12.) Another is that between Ananias and his wife, Sapphira, who agreed together to lie and to deceive the apostles and the church over their donation to the poor. (See Acts 5:1–11.)

These examples demonstrate the two sides of the soul tie, or bond—those that are from God and those that are not.

Even good soul ties may be intended for only a specific period of time, and then they must be released with thanksgiving. This may happen with friendships and other associations, including that of a church member to a pastor. Many church members have a spiritual bond, or covenantal relationship, with their pastor, in which the pastor helps them to cultivate their spiritual life, bring them to maturity, and apply their gifts to extending the kingdom. This is a godly soul tie; however, after being in such a relationship, a believer may find that it is necessary to adapt to a change, such as a move to another state. The believer may begin attending a new church where God has planted him to grow. Yet, if he still has a soul tie with his former pastor, that bond may now prevent him from progressing in his spiritual life by becoming a barrier to receiving from the new pastor. The believer might make comparisons between the two leaders and believe that the new pastor can't help him to grow effectively. He may be unable to establish a new covenantal relationship because he is always looking back at the past. So, we must recognize our soul ties and how they may be affecting our lives.

Consequences of Negative Soul Ties

When you retain a soul tie that is not from God, or that was meant for only a certain period of time, you will often experience:

+ Depression
+ Obstacles to transformation
+ Stagnancy in fulfilling your purpose
+ A slowdown in your spiritual growth
+ An inability to enjoy other relationships

Regarding the last point, when you form a wrong tie with someone (or something), you are often unable to enjoy other relationships and to develop healthy soul ties. That is why many men and women who have acquired countless soul ties from sleeping with different people now seem incapable of establishing a good relationship and making it last.

> *When you surrender yourself to someone,*
> *you establish a soul tie that becomes*
> *a form of pact.*

Freedom from Wrong Soul Ties

To be set free from a soul tie that is not in accordance with God's will, the following steps are essential:

+ Repent of any sin that led you to this tie.

- Receive God's forgiveness.

- Renounce the tie.

- Die to the desires of your carnal self related to the soul tie.

- Correct any wrong thinking that led to the tie. For example, you may have been deceived into thinking that another person should control you, usurping your free will.

- Let go of any shame and guilt you developed over the wrong soul tie. (See 1 John 1:9.)

- Stand firm and resist the devil's attacks. (See, for example, Ephesians 6:10–17.) For instance, after you have renounced a soul tie in a particular area, such as an illicit relationship, and you start doing well and obeying God in that area, you may suddenly be tempted to again open a door to that old soul tie; perhaps you receive a phone call from someone connected with your past who encourages you to renew that illicit relationship. Be alert for such temptations, reject them, and ask mature fellow believers to pray with you for continued spiritual strength to resist.

- Bind your soul to the Lord. Revelation 12:11 says, *"They overcame [Satan] by the blood of the Lamb and by the word of their testimony, and they did not love their lives to the death."* On behalf of Christ, the believers referred to in the above verse were willing to give up their very lives. This is an illustration of a right relationship and soul tie with Jesus and reflects total devotion to Him.

8. An Emotional or Mental Trauma

I have seen (and also experienced) situations in which, in a moment of crisis—perhaps a great trauma or a terrible accident involving injuries—people become emotionally or mentally vulnerable, so that they open up entry points for demons to attack them. Generally, when people have dominion and authority over themselves through Christ, no demon can enter. But when they are weakened due to a crisis such as I described above, they can inadvertently relinquish their dominion and authority. Their soul becomes "fragmented," so that they lose their former stability. Demons then take advantage of their weakness.

For example, receiving an unexpected diagnosis of a terminal disease can produce a traumatic effect on a person and/or his family. In one day, a sense of perfect health may be replaced by a fear of suffering, loss, and death that allows a spirit of fear to enter. Likewise, a sudden car accident can produce intense emotional stress that becomes an entry point for a spirit of fear or a spirit of phobias. The death of a loved one can create an emotional blow that leads a person to become afflicted by a spirit of mourning or loneliness. When a normal feeling of grief or loneliness becomes intense and prolonged, a demon can use that emotion to begin to control the person. A child whose parent has died may come to feel, in his heart or subconscious mind, that his parent has abandoned him, and he leaves himself open to a spirit of rejection. As believers, we must trust the Lord to guard and protect us; if a crisis occurs, we need to stand strong and give no place to the enemy.

9. An Attack in the Womb

I believe that demons can attack an unborn child in its mother's womb, and that this is the cause of some birth defects and childhood illnesses, emotional and mental weaknesses, and abnormal traits (all of which may follow a person into adulthood). A baby may be developing normally until an opening is created for a demon to enter the womb and mar his development.

In the New Testament, Jesus sometimes asked a person questions about his ailment or the ailment of a loved one. I believe this was because He wanted to show the person (and teach His disciples) where the entry point for the demon had occurred. In Mark 9, when Jesus encountered the father who had brought his mute son to be healed, *"He asked his father, 'How long has this been happening to him?' And he said: From childhood"* (Mark 9:21).

There is a difference between being
born with an issue and falling into it.

All of us were either born with some negative trait or fell into wrong thinking or sinful behavior during the course of our lives, but the key we need to remember is this: We don't have to live with it as part of an unavoidable destiny. Yes, it is true that we were all "conceived in sin" (see Psalm 51:5), because the sinful nature is passed down from one generation to another without our being able to do anything about it, at least in our own strength. But Jesus, the Son of God, came to deliver us from the enslavement of sin and its effects. The solution to our being born with a sinful nature is to be *born again* in Christ. (See, for example, John 3:3–5.) If you were born with a mental disability, a physical deformity, or another problem, or if you have a negative trait whose cause seems unexplainable, it may be that a demon found an entry point to attack you in your mother's womb. Deal with it in a similar way to any other point of entry, by acknowledging the sin connected with it (known or unknown), renouncing it, and receiving God's forgiveness and cleansing; rebuking and casting out the demon in the name of Jesus; and then standing firm in the wholeness and righteousness that Christ has provided by His death and resurrection.

8. Addictions

Many people struggle with addictions to drugs, alcohol, food, tobacco, or other substances. Some people are hooked on chemicals, while others are slaves to destructive behaviors, obsessions, or compulsions. I have found that demonic control is a factor in all addictions. This makes it very difficult for a person to let go of an addiction in his own strength. Once a person's use of a substance or practice of a certain behavior becomes a lifestyle, the enemy will do everything he can to bind that person to be controlled by demons and to lead him to destruction. The good news is that Jesus bore all our addictions on the cross, and He can set us free if we make the decision to renounce the addiction, receive forgiveness and cleansing, and take hold of the power of Christ for deliverance and for withstanding temptation.

Sometimes, an addiction or a destructive behavior itself is not the actual entry point for a demon. Instead, the opening is created through the person's recurrent emotional issue, such as loneliness, low self-esteem, or feelings of rejection and abandonment; or, it may come through the person's desire to escape reality. In this case, to be free of the addiction, the original entry point that led to the substance abuse or compulsive behavior must be dealt with through inner healing and deliverance in Jesus.

9. Witchcraft and the Occult

Any form of participation in the occult will always open a door for demons to oppress you. I recommend to every believer who comes from a background in the occult or witchcraft to go through personal deliverance. Jesus defeated the enemy, but again, we have to apply that victory specifically to our lives. The following is a powerful testimony of a man who was delivered from the occult and the control of Satan.

"My name is Heriberto. I lived in Cuba, and for thirty-two years, I dedicated myself to witchcraft and Santeria. I was an alcoholic and a smoker. I also stole money from people. I would even deceive women and take advantage of them and their situation in order to steal from them. When I came to the United States, I raised a great altar to the saints, where I worshipped them and made animal sacrifices. I knew that many of those practices were a lie. However, because I earned a lot of money and had women, I, too, fell into deception; I felt protected by the saints and spirits.

"A short time later, I opened a large company with many employees; I lived in a mansion with servants, traveled, and stayed at luxurious hotels. I had a great life. I saw Apostle Maldonado on television many times, but I thought he was a crazy liar. Suddenly, my life went downhill, and I lost absolutely everything (money, women, and friends); I was left on the street, living in a car and having many debts. I owed so much money that I started thinking about committing suicide.

"Some Christians found me on the street and invited me to church. I was desperate and truly needed the help of God. When I entered the church, I saw Apostle Maldonado and said, 'Oh no, they brought me to the crazy one's house!' I was upset, doubting that I could find anything good there. But then the apostle said that there was a man who was in Santeria and had lost everything, and who had come because God wanted to save him. He invited that man to go to the front so he could pray for him. I knew he was speaking to me, so I went to the front.

"Previously, I had always said that people would fall down at the altar only as part of the 'show,' but when the apostle touched me, I felt the power of the Holy Spirit and, without wanting to, I fell to the floor. I had no strength; it was as if my body was boneless. Immediately, I felt that I had been delivered from Santeria and forgiven from all evil. It was as though a blindfold had been removed from my eyes, and I was shown the truth.

"Today, I am ashamed of having served the devil and of the other wrongs I have committed. Satan will always demand payment for everything; nothing that he supposedly gives you is yours. Everything is an illusion, a lie, to trap you, to separate you from God, and to lead you to hell. Now I am truly free. I am free from sacrificing animals, free from being afraid of saints and the devil, free from lies and deceit, free from fornication, free from alcohol and drugs, and free from debt. Now I know a true and living God who speaks to me and guides me, who does not allow me to do bad things to people, and who saved me out of His great love and mercy and gave me eternal life."

Steps to Freedom

Throughout this chapter, we have discussed various entry points of demons and how to be free from them. In this section, I want to review the steps to freedom so that you can apply them to your specific situation. From my experience of ministering deliverance for over twenty-five years, I have learned that the key to deliverance is to meet God's requirements. Once you understand His conditions, you must obey them. When you do, you can remove any demon, demonic oppression, or negative soul tie. About 75 percent of all deliverance is founded upon that key.

> *One key to effective deliverance is to fulfill God's prerequisites.*

Here, then, are God's conditions.

1. Humble Yourself Before God

"Therefore humble yourselves under the mighty hand of God, that He may exalt you in due time" (1 Peter 5:6). Make the decision to humble yourself, as an act of your own free will, in order to be delivered. There comes a moment where you must choose between your "dignity" (the ego, or flesh) and your deliverance. If you keep your pride and don't humble yourself, you may maintain your dignity but retain the demon, and the oppression will continue. There are people who don't want to receive deliverance in public because they are afraid of being embarrassed if a demon would manifest in their body when it is being cast out. We must remember that *"God resists the proud, but gives grace to the humble"* (James 4:6). The decision to be humble cannot be made by anyone other than you. It is your choice! It is you who must recognize your condition and your need to be free; otherwise, deliverance will be very difficult.

2. Repent and Confess Your Sin

Repentance

To repent is to turn your back on sin, to recognize it as an enemy, and to renounce it. You cannot repent of something if you do not acknowledge that it is evil and that it offends God. When someone enjoys practicing a particular form of evil, he usually will not repent because he thinks there is some positive element in what he is doing. He needs the conviction of the Holy Spirit, who convinces the soul of sin. (See John 16:7–8.) If God calls something sin, there is no reason for us to consider it good; we must be aligned with His outlook and commandments.

A repentant heart hates everything evil and demonic, and separates itself from such things. We always have the choice of whether or not to sin. No matter how demonized we are, Satan cannot remove or violate our will; however, the more we yield to sin, the more power we give to demons to take our will captive. Eventually, we may not be able to say no even if we want to.

Sincere repentance, with a complete confession of sin, always weakens or removes the rights of demons to access our lives.

Our sin opens the door for demons to oppress us in various areas of our lives, but repentance will expel those demons; it will also shut the door to them and prevent them from reentering. Remember that demons gain a foothold when we do not repent of our sin but instead continue to commit it. Recurrent sin molds our character in negative ways. It hardens our heart and separates us from God. One form of continuous sin is unforgiveness, which is also a manifestation of a lack of reverent fear for God. When we refuse to forgive, we give birth to an uninterrupted cycle of sin, opening an entry point for demons.

Here are some key points to remember regarding repentance:

+ Everything in the kingdom of God begins with repentance. In other words, it is how the fullness of the kingdom opens up to us in *"righteousness and peace and joy"* (Romans 14:17).

+ It is difficult to repent when you don't want to die to the carnal self. Yet if the "old man" lives, the "new man" cannot take full control. These "selves" are incompatible. Either one or the other will rule your life.

+ When we find ourselves in sin, our natural reaction is to hide from God, just as Adam and Eve did. However, the solution is not to hide but to reject the sin, go to God, and ask for forgiveness.

+ Repentance is the fastest way of returning to the presence of God.

+ Sin closes God's ear to our cries (see Isaiah 59:2), but repentance turns His ear toward our prayers (see, for example, 2 Chronicles 7:14). You may cry, scream, beg, and have great faith, but if you do not repent, God will not hear your prayers.

+ The best defense against demonization that originated in personal sin is to repent and confess the sin.

Confession of Sin

When we confess our wrongdoing, we are not telling God something He doesn't know. We cannot surprise Him. Confession of sin is mainly for *our* good—so we can get it off our chest, expose it to the light of God, take responsibility for it, and be forgiven. *"If we confess our sins, He is faithful and just to forgive us our sins and to cleanse us from all unrighteousness"* (1 John 1:9).

3. Forgive Others Wholeheartedly

We cannot hold on to bitterness and resentment, because they open the door to demons. When we do not forgive the offenses of others, God Himself will turn us over to demons who will torture us.

(See Matthew 18:34–35.) Therefore, when we harbor anger, resentment, and bitterness, forgiveness is the only thing that can deliver us. Forgiveness is a decision of the will and not of the emotions. Right now, you can forgive someone who has wronged you, if you ask the Holy Spirit for grace to do so.

4. Surrender Yourself to the Deliverance of God and to the Operation of the Holy Spirit

The agent that ministers deliverance is the Holy Spirit. If you resist Him, you are opposing your deliverance. Allow the Spirit of God to freely operate in you. Come into agreement with Him so that every demon will know that it must flee.

The word "spirit" means breath. We know that the Holy Spirit is the breath of the Almighty, the Most High. (See, for example, John 20:21–22.) But an evil spirit is a "breath" from hell. Consequently, I believe that an important step to activating deliverance is to exhale through your mouth. This physical action by your body indicates the decision of your will. Exhaling is the opposite of inhaling or of drinking. You do not receive the baptism with the Holy Spirit by the act of prayer but by "drinking" of Him in faith. In a related way, you do not remove demons by praying but by casting them out (exhaling the demons, drinking in the Spirit so that you are refilled with Him, and operating in faith, believing that you are free). From where do you cast out a demon that has gained legal entrance to you? From yourself, from your soul. Deliverance comes by your decision to reject and evict the demons, followed by the physical action of breathing out. So again, the casting out of demons is a spiritual activity that is reaffirmed by the prophetic act of exhaling. (See Mark 16:17.)

Prayer of Deliverance

Heavenly Father, I believe that Jesus is the Son of God, the Messiah, who came to earth as a human being and died for my sins.

I also believe that He rose from the dead to give me a new life in Him and to fill me with His power. Now, I repent of all my sins, recognizing that I have opened entry points to demons. I confess my sins, which stagnate my purpose in You and prevent me from serving You. [Name your sins, including any habitual sin, such as jealousy, unforgiveness, sexual immorality, fears, phobias, self-pity, addictions, or compulsive behaviors; as well as improper and demonic ties to people, animals, groups, places, things, or demons; witchcraft or other satanic practices; or anything else.] I ask Your forgiveness through Jesus Christ for these sins. I also cast out any spirit that entered my life through an emotional or mental trauma. I cast out any spirit that entered and attacked me when I was in my mother's womb. I renounce any involvement in the occult. I repent of all these things, and I bind every evil spirit. I cry out for the protection of the blood of Jesus over my life. I am free now, in the name of Jesus!

By faith, exhale every spirit from hell that is being expelled due to your repentance, renunciation of evil, and declaration of deliverance. Just exhale the demons and then inhale, or drink in, the Spirit of God. The prayer of faith will set you free.

6

HOW TO BE FREE
OF UNFORGIVENESS

My experience of ministering inner healing and deliverance for more than two and a half decades has shown me that a large majority of Christians live with unforgiveness in their hearts. I often wonder about this state of affairs, because forgiveness is essentially the center of Christianity. Our new life in Christ can begin only as we receive forgiveness for our sins through Jesus' sacrifice on the cross. And Jesus' teachings are filled with references and commandments to forgive others as God has forgiven us. How it is possible, therefore, that for many believers, forgiveness is not a high priority?

Unforgiveness is one of the most frequent causes of mental and emotional oppression and even physical illness. This fact urges me to bring the subject of forgiveness to light in the church. Moreover, many people in the world need mental, emotional, and physical healing, and Jesus calls us to help them. But how we can minister healing to others if we ourselves have mental and emotional wounds that we have not allowed to heal through forgiveness?

Countless blessings flow from forgiveness, such as reconciliation, peace, harmony, and companionship, as well as spiritual, mental, physical, and financial health. Both the world and the church desperately need these blessings. In contrast, multiple consequences spring from unforgiveness—often due to associated demonic oppression—like anxiety, bitterness, resentment, hatred, restlessness, division, disease, war, and death. All human beings are at risk of suffering consequences such as these due to their own lack of forgiveness or the unforgiveness of others. The only way of escape is for us to practice forgiveness as a lifestyle.

The Power of Forgiveness

I've heard many testimonies about the power of forgiveness, but it always touches my heart when I hear about someone forgiving a parent, because I understand how much damage resentment against a parent can do to the heart of a son or a daughter. The following is just such a testimony from a young woman of Hispanic heritage named Johanna Parra.

"For ten years, I dealt with issues of abandonment, unforgiveness, anger, rejection, and hatred toward my father. Previous to those years, up to the age of ten, I'd had a very good relationship with my dad; but one day, he just left. He didn't say good-bye, and he never came back.

"About a year before that, my father had talked to me about a girlfriend of his who had Christian kids. He told me he would give anything for me to be like them. Those words broke my heart. For many years, I tried to be like them, but instead I fell into a lack of identity.

"I was very sad and depressed for a long time after my father left. I failed fifth grade, and I started doing bad things. I even hated looking at myself in the mirror because I have my dad's eyes, and I didn't want to be reminded of him. In time, my mother remarried, but I couldn't accept my stepdad; I neither needed him nor wanted him. In fact, I rejected every father figure who came into my life.

"One day, I decided to really give my life to Christ. Immediately, the hatred and the feelings of rejection left, but the unforgiveness remained. Then, during a service in which Apostle Maldonado was preaching about unforgiveness, I was convicted by the Holy Spirit that the Lord had forgiven me and therefore I had to forgive my father. So I made the decision to forgive. I don't know where my dad is right now; I don't even know if he is alive because I have never seen him again, but through the grace of God, I was able to forgive him. When I went up to the altar and was prayed for, it felt as if a weight was lifted off of my shoulders. I felt peaceful in my heart, free and happy. Accepting Jesus into my life had given me the peace and love I needed to forgive my father. Now I know that God is my heavenly Father and that He loves me, and I don't need anything else. I love Him and He loves me!"

Vertical and Horizontal Forgiveness

There are two directions in which forgiveness must be extended. These directions are represented by the cross, which is made up of two lengths of wood—one vertical and the other horizontal. The vertical represents the fact that we all need forgiveness from God, which we can obtain only by receiving the finished work of Christ on the cross to forgive and save us. The horizontal represents the fact that forgiveness is necessary between and among human beings. There are two aspects to horizontal forgiveness: giving it and receiving it. Although people must offer forgiveness to one another, ultimate forgiveness comes from God through Jesus' sacrifice on the cross for the sins of the world. (See 1 John 2:2.)

What Are Forgiveness and Unforgiveness?

Forgiveness is the voluntary act of spiritually freeing someone who has offended us or hurt us. It means to no longer hold anything against the person—to cancel, or pardon, any outstanding spiritual, mental, emotional, or physical debt the individual owes us.

Unforgiveness is a stance of resentment or bitterness toward someone due to a wrong the person committed against us. When we harbor unforgiveness, it is as if we have in our possession a written statement of debt against the offending person, an account we refuse to close until that obligation has been paid in some way. If we don't immediately deal with a lack of forgiveness, it can become a spiritual stronghold from which we will need deliverance.

Unforgiveness is rebellion against God, because it is a transgression against the laws of His kingdom. All such transgressions bring negative consequences. Even if God were to ignore our violation of His laws, that would not stop the course of the consequences brought about by our wrong decisions and actions. Our transgressions can't just be ignored; they must be forgiven, and then God will use all things in our life—even the negative things—for our good. (See Romans 8:28.)

In the natural world, prosecutors compile evidence against alleged offenders of the law that can be used against them in court. And when we have been hurt by someone, we often act like a prosecutor, compiling mental "evidence" against the person as we dwell on his infractions against us. However, we are so focused on the person's offense toward us that we don't realize that our unforgiveness becomes spiritual evidence of our own sinfulness before almighty God, who is the ultimate Judge and who has commanded us to forgive.

Forgiveness allows the life of God to flow to us, while unforgiveness restrains it. Accordingly, to refuse to forgive is to be spiritually isolated and imprisoned. When this is the case, we often become stuck in a religious mind-set that focuses on the letter of the law rather than on the spirit of it. (See, for example, Romans 7:6.) Our heart hardens, our faith is no longer alive and flowing, and we have merely a superficial relationship with God. We may have an external formality of religion, but our heart is empty. This explains why so many believers struggle year after year with a vicious cycle of frustration and disappointment in regard to their spiritual life, their family life, their vocations, and other areas of life, seeing few positive changes.

Moreover, by our unforgiveness, we allow Satan to take advantage of us; we leave the door open for him to come in and push us around, steal from us, and perhaps destroy us. Paul wrote to the Corinthians, *"Now whom you forgive anything, I also forgive. For if indeed I have forgiven anything, I have forgiven that one for your sakes in the presence of Christ, lest Satan should take advantage of us"* (2 Corinthians 2:10–11).

> *Unforgiveness is sin, rebellion, transgression.*
> *It is one of the greatest offenses in God's kingdom.*

When they have been hurt, people often keep that information to themselves, burying it deep in their heart. This is the response of many individuals who have been physically or emotionally abused by a parent, a grandparent, a sibling, a child, a friend, or anyone else. They never talk about their pain to anyone, and their silence prevents them from obtaining help and healing. To be set free, they need to talk to a trusted Christian leader, counselor, or friend who will keep their situation confidential but also help them to release the situation to God, find healing, and forgive the offender. In cases where a crime has been committed against us, and we are involved in legal proceedings against the perpetrator, forgiveness may be extremely difficult. But when the victim of a crime chooses not to forgive his offender, it keeps the victim in a spiritual and emotional prison of his own.

A similar consequence occurs with any form of hurt we experience that remains unexpressed and is not given over to God. If we silently harbor resentment and unforgiveness, we won't be able to receive the emotional, mental, and physical healing we need.

Unfortunately, there are many opportunities for us to become hurt due to a wrong committed against us. We might become offended by someone at home, in the workplace, in the church, or in another realm of life. As I have mentioned previously, in my experience, most people who leave a church do so because they were offended by someone or something and held on to hurts that they never told anyone about. But secretly holding on to our hurts and offenses will slowly kill us spiritually—just as any other hidden sin will.

> *Unforgiveness is often a silent sin.*

Causes, or Roots, of Unforgiveness

Let's now discuss three related causes of unforgiveness—(1) refusing to release an offense, (2) being spiritually immature, and (3) being selfish or self-centered.

1. Refusing to Release an Offense

Not letting go of an offense is the main root of unforgiveness. The unforgiving person operates from a spiritual stronghold, so that almost everything he does becomes tainted by the offense or is cultivated by it. It is from such a stance that the individual chooses his responses and actions toward other people. Some people say things like, "I once was betrayed, so I will never give my heart to another person as long as I live."

When someone is affronted, whether by something small or great—a coworker's insult, a parent's failure to provide attention, a spouse's betrayal, or anything else—that individual may come to view every subsequent relationship with bitterness and suspicion. The person may close himself off from other people, not feeling that it is worth the risk to give of himself to others. Sadly, offenses produce many such walled-off hearts. The Scriptures say, *"A brother offended is harder to win than a strong city, and contentions are like the bars of a castle"* (Proverbs 18:19).

2. Being Spiritually Immature

A degree of spiritual maturity is needed to truly forgive another person, especially when the offense is real and the anger is justified. In his famous chapter on love, which is a picture of the love of the heavenly Father, the apostle Paul wrote, *"Love...is not provoked, thinks no evil; does not rejoice in iniquity, but rejoices in the truth; bears all things, believes all things, hopes all things, endures all things"* (1 Corinthians 13:4–7). Consequently, when we refuse to forgive, we demonstrate our own spiritual and emotional immaturity rather than the love of God. (See Ephesians 5:1.)

3. Being Selfish or Self-centered

Every sin stems from the egocentric self, and unforgiveness is clear evidence of the dominance of our fleshly nature. The "old man" always demands its rights and insists on being first in importance. It loves to complain, saying things like "You hurt me!" or "I don't deserve this" or "This isn't fair." In fact, most of the people whom I have delivered from evil spirits have had selfishness in common. We must be careful about falling into egocentrism, because Satan spiritually imprisons those who walk according to their fleshly desires.

A primary cause of unforgiveness
is a refusal to die to the carnal self.

Our Need to Be Forgiven

Every Person Must Be Forgiven for Sin

Generally, unless we truly understand our own need for forgiveness, we cannot forgive others. The Bible says, *"All we like sheep have gone astray; we have turned, every one, to his own way"* (Isaiah 53:6). We were not given a choice about whether we would be born with a sinful nature; we inherited that nature. However, we still need to be cleansed from our sinful nature, as well as forgiven for our particular sins, and that is why *"the Lord has laid on* [Jesus] *the iniquity of us all"* (Isaiah 53:6). Even if we have never committed any "terrible" sins, all of us have sinned in some way, thus cutting ourselves off from God's holy presence. (See Romans 3:23.) Yet God has made complete provision for us to be forgiven and restored to Him. We must receive Jesus' sacrifice on the cross on our behalf. This is the only way we can be sanctified and made righteous so that we can return to our heavenly Father and develop a relationship of love and truth with Him.

Jesus Paid Our Debt of Sin

Keep in mind that God cannot compromise His righteousness for anyone; to do so would be to relinquish His own integrity. On the cross, as our Substitute, Jesus took upon Himself all of our rebelliousness, sins, transgressions, and iniquities—past, present, and future—so that the debt of our sin could be completely paid. And we receive this work of forgiveness by faith. (See Romans 4:20–25.)

The basis by which we can receive God's forgiveness is Christ's sacrifice on the cross.

God Forgives Us Completely

When God forgives us, He does not do so partially but *completely.* *"Who is a God like You, pardoning iniquity and passing over the transgression of the remnant of His heritage?…He will again have compassion on us, and will subdue our iniquities. You will cast all our sins into the depths of the sea"* (Micah 7:18–19). Any wrong we have done, and any accusation the enemy has made against us, God has thrown into *"the depths of the sea."* The Lord says, *"I, even I, am He who blots out your transgressions for My own sake; and I will not remember your sins"* (Isaiah 43:25). When God forgives, He erases all records of our debts as though they had never existed. Not only does He delete them, but He also forgets them. It is not that God has a poor memory but that He chooses not to remember our sins; He does not hold them against us. When He forgives, He forgets.

Because God Forgives Us, We Can Forgive Ourselves and Others

Judas, the disciple of Jesus who surrendered the Messiah to be murdered, could not forgive himself or accept God's forgiveness. He felt condemned and thought there was no way out for him; thus, he killed himself. In contrast, Peter, the disciple who denied Jesus at a critical time during His trial and suffering, received Jesus' forgiveness, was restored, and became one of the greatest apostles of history.

Feelings of shame, and their accompanying pain, often grow within people when they cannot forgive themselves. Frequently, when someone does not forgive himself for making a mistake or sinning, he begins to conform to a kind of legalism in which he condemns himself whenever he makes any additional mistakes or commits any further sins. He essentially becomes his own judge and jury. Yet consider this: If the Lord has forgiven you, but you do not forgive yourself or others, it is as if you are saying that you are greater than He is, that your word is truer than His.

When you do not forgive yourself or others,
you make yourself greater than God.

Forgiveness Brings Blessings

As I wrote earlier, many blessings come with forgiveness. To receive forgiveness from God, we need to be sincere and honest with Him about our sins rather than try to cover them up, to make excuses for them, or to hide from them. Only God can cover our sins; He does so by the blood of Jesus, sacrificed on our behalf. King David wrote, *"Blessed is he whose transgression is forgiven, whose sin is covered. Blessed is the man to whom the LORD does not impute iniquity, and in whose spirit there is no deceit"* (Psalm 32:1–2).

Psalm 32 is believed to have been written by David in response to his sins of committing adultery with Bathsheba and murdering her husband, Uriah. At first, David had refused to face these grave sins. He tried to ignore them, to pretend that nothing had really happened. While his sins remained unconfessed, his bones *"wasted away"* (Psalm 32:3 NIV) and his *"strength was sapped"* (verse 4 NIV). (The mention of his bones wasting away may be a reference to sickness.) Yet, when he humbled himself before God, he was forgiven and restored. (See verse 5.) The book of James makes a similar connection between confession of sin, forgiveness, and healing. (See James 5:14–16.)

If you have sinned, do not delay in asking God for forgiveness. There is a period of grace for you to seek Him and for Him to give you the opportunity to repent. (See Isaiah 55:6–7.) During this time, the Holy Spirit brings conviction of sin. This is an urgent matter! You might defend yourself and say, "I didn't commit a 'big' sin, so I'm okay." But the magnitude of a particular transgression is not the issue. All sin separates us from the glory of God and therefore needs to be forgiven. We should never take sin lightly.

Malena is a young, African-American woman who attends our church. Hurts from her past, unforgiveness toward others, and her own need for forgiveness were leading her in a downward spiral toward death. She felt brokenhearted and trapped, and she knew something had to change. Here is her testimony.

"I was adopted when I was four, but the extended family on my adoptive father's side (which practiced witchcraft) never accepted me; I suffered a lot from their rejection. When I was nineteen, I had a relationship with a man who also rejected me and even tried to kill me. I felt great shame over this situation. Because I was depressed, I turned to alcohol and drugs. I smoked marijuana every morning to escape reality, and I also used cocaine. I did not want to look at myself in the mirror; I felt rejected, dirty, and ugly.

"After that relationship, I met another man and got married. We were together for five years until, one morning, I woke up and found that my husband had written a good-bye note. He did not care about me at all. He had abandoned me and our two-year-old son, taking everything of material value with him. I did not want to live anymore! I attempted suicide on the highway with my little one. I felt alone and ashamed, drank alcohol daily, and hated men and everyone else. I no longer cared about anything.

"One day, I visited King Jesus Ministry and felt the immense love of God, a love I had never experienced before. Neither men nor drugs had made me feel as loved as the heavenly Father did. I was able to forgive my parents and my adoptive father's family, the men who had mistreated and abandoned me, and men overall. God forgave me and removed my guilt and desire to die. His love delivered me from depression, loneliness, and pain. Since that time, nothing in this world has been able to make me feel like I did before. Now I feel happy, peaceful, safe, loved, and filled with the desire to live, both for myself and for my little one. God's love and forgiveness have healed me and taught me that He is the only One I need."

Whenever the power of God heals somebody, it is a manifestation of forgiveness.

We Must Forgive as We Have Been Forgiven

When Jesus provided His disciples with an example of how to pray to their heavenly Father, He included a reference to forgiveness that held this clear and unavoidable condition: *"And forgive us our debts, as we forgive our debtors"* (Matthew 6:12). He emphasized the principle that receiving God's forgiveness depends on our forgiving other people. If we deny forgiveness to others, it will be denied to us, as well.

Additionally, Jesus' parable of the unmerciful servant yields powerful revelation truths about forgiveness. (See Matthew 18:21–35.) In the parable, the first servant of the king, who owed his sovereign the huge amount of ten thousand talents, represents you and me. This debt, which the servant found impossible to repay, denotes the incalculable cost of our sin against a holy God. The second servant represents our fellow human beings, perhaps our fellow believers especially. That servant owed a much smaller debt to the first servant. In other words, our debt of sin toward God is infinitely greater than the debt of any transgressions that others commit against us.

Let us examine more closely some truths this parable illustrates.

Unforgiveness Is a Form of Wickedness

In this parable, the king (representing God) called the first servant *"wicked"* (Matthew 18:32) because he did not forgive his fellow servant. From a legal standpoint on earth, the first servant had not committed a crime but had simply failed to forgive. But the heavenly standpoint is much different from our earthly one.

A Lack of Forgiveness Provokes God's Anger

The king told the first servant, "*I forgave you all that debt because you begged me. Should you not also have had compassion on your fellow servant, just as I had pity on you?*" (Matthew 18:32–33). It's important to understand the difference between the two debts described in this parable; in today's currency, ten thousand talents would be approximately 425 million dollars, while a hundred denarii would be about 74 dollars. So, the king was essentially saying, "I forgave you 425 million dollars, yet you couldn't forgive 74 dollars?" The forgiven servant's merciless act stirred the king's anger.

When you compare the two debts, it seems ridiculous that the first servant did not forgive the small amount his fellow servant owed him. Yet we do basically the same thing whenever we refuse to forgive a wrong committed against us by a fellow human being. Jesus forgave us an incalculable debt of sin that we could not have paid with all the gold in the world, but then we turn around and harden our hearts against someone who offended us. Our unforgiveness grieves God and may even provoke Him to anger, bringing serious consequences.

A Lack of Forgiveness Delivers Us to the "Torturers"

"*And his master was angry, and delivered him to the torturers until he should pay all that was due to him*" (Matthew 18:34). With this statement, I believe Jesus was saying, in effect, "In the same way that the king dealt with the wicked servant, My heavenly Father will deal with anyone who does not forgive. He will deliver him to the demons (torturers)." It is not that God sends evil spirits to torture a person; rather, He withdraws from the person so that the demons that the person himself has allowed into his life will torture him. God permits the demons to oppress that person in the hopes that he will repent, return to God, forgive the one who offended him, and receive forgiveness from the Lord. The apostle Paul discussed a similar scenario with Timothy regarding two members of the early church. (See 1 Timothy 1:18–20.) Today, countless people are in the hands of demonic torturers because they have refused to forgive others.

What type of torments do these demons inflict? Mental and emotional torments, such as fear, confusion, depression, grief, loneliness, resentment, anger, bitterness, and guilt; and physical torments, like arthritis and cancer. Demons will often taunt people, reminding them that they haven't been forgiven for their sins because they haven't forgiven others and are still in debt to the Lord. This awareness adds to people's feelings of fear and guilt until they choose to be obedient to God and forgive those who have wronged them.

Our Intellect, or Reason, Believes Unforgiveness Is Justified

In our minds, we tend to justify our unforgiveness. We may think, *God wants me to forgive that person for what he did? He doesn't deserve it!* The unmerciful servant believed he was justified in trying to collect the small debt that his fellow servant owed him, even though he himself had been forgiven a huge amount. It somehow didn't occur to him that because he had received mercy, he should extend mercy to others.

Unforgiveness is always trying to prove that it is right.

Many Christians reason in much the same way. Even though God has forgiven them for all their sins and given them the gift of the Holy Spirit and the promise of eternal life, they refuse to forgive those who have sinned against them. If someone abuses us or treats us unjustly, we have a legitimate right to be angry or hurt because that person has wronged us. Even so, our anger or hurt doesn't give us the right to not forgive.

We can't fully focus on God and grow in our faith unhindered while we harbor unforgiveness, because we are occupied with trying to excuse our resentment, anger, and hatred. This merely caters to our carnal self. Let us stop justifying our unforgiveness! Instead, let us release our hurts and offenses and thereby release those who have offended us.

Consequences of Unforgiveness

The violation of God's laws brings consequences, and the sin of unforgiveness is no exception, as we saw in the parable of the unmerciful servant. Let us now examine some specific consequences of unforgiveness.

1. Unforgiveness perverts and contaminates the flow of God's anointing in our life. For instance, a pastor who harbors bitterness will sooner or later contaminate the members of his church because he ministers from a place of hurt. (See, for example, Hebrews 12:15.) It is as though his "deposit" of anointing has been cracked or broken so that it leaks and cannot retain a full impartation, activation, or blessing. As a result, most of the ministry that the church members receive from him during a worship service will soon evaporate, and what remains will probably be tainted. This explains why many people go to church but never change for the better, even though they participate in worship and listen to teaching from the Word of God.

A hurt or offense

drains away the anointing.

2. Unforgiveness leaves us in a virtual prison until we forgive those who have offended us. Jesus gave the following warning, which is similar to the king's judgment in the parable of the unmerciful servant:

Agree with your adversary quickly, while you are on the way with him, lest your adversary deliver you to the judge, the judge hand you over to the officer, and you be thrown into prison. Assuredly, I say to you, you will by no means get out of there till you have paid the last penny. (Matthew 5:25–26; see also verses 21–24)

In the Old Testament, the life of Joseph is a remarkable example of the power of forgiveness, even when we have been greatly wronged. Joseph's brothers envied him, rejected him, and finally sold him into slavery to get rid of him! But Joseph was apparently able to forgive his brothers and let go of his resentment against them, because even while he was a slave in Egypt in the house of Potiphar, *"the LORD was with Joseph, and he was a successful man"* (Genesis 39:2), and even after he was unjustly accused by Potiphar's wife and thrown into prison, *"the LORD was with him; and whatever he did, the LORD made it prosper"* (Genesis 39:23). Eventually, Joseph was elevated to a position in which he ruled over all Egypt, second only to Pharaoh. (See Genesis 41.)

However, it is obvious from the biblical account that Joseph's heart was still wounded. We aren't told Joseph's innermost thoughts, but I imagine that his pain over the way he had been treated by his brothers was deep and tormenting. Genesis 45:2 says that when the time came for Joseph to reveal his identity to his brothers and be reconciled to them, he wept aloud. Not only had Joseph endured physical enslavement and imprisonment, but his heart was still being held captive to his pain. After Joseph reconciled with his brothers, his heart was healed. Note that he was able to comfort his brothers and urge them to forgive themselves for what they had done. (See Genesis 45:4–15.)

If a person has been offended, he will remain in a prison of emotional pain, depression, alcoholism, sickness, or another form of oppression until he forgives the wrong committed against him and is reconciled to the offender, as far as he is able to. (See Romans 12:17–21.) What prison are you confined in right now? Is it a prison of sadness, fear, confusion, resentment, addiction, poverty, or disease? Make a decision right now to forgive every offense committed against you. Give all your hurts to God and ask Him to heal your mind, your emotions, and your body.

> *Forgiveness grants us the power to release a wrong committed against us; unforgiveness doesn't allow us to release an offense.*

3. *Unforgiveness makes us insensitive to the presence of God.* Anger and bitterness will not only deaden a person emotionally but also stifle his spiritual sensitivity; in this state, the individual finds it difficult to feel the presence of God. This explains why an unforgiving person is often unable to sense the heavenly Father's presence even when he is in a worship service in which God's glory is strong and the majority of the participants are experiencing His manifestation, receiving spiritual, emotional, or physical healing.

> *When you lose your sensitivity toward God, you lose your sensitivity toward other people, and vice versa.*

4. *Unforgiveness usurps the place of faith in our life.* God designed the heart to be the dwelling place of faith. (See Romans 10:9–10.) People who harbor unforgiveness are unable to live by faith because their pain, bitterness, and anger have essentially overridden their belief. Such attitudes block the avenue through which faith works. As a result, their spiritual discernment may become cloudy, as well. So, if you have surrendered your heart to anger and bitterness, then your pain is sitting in

the seat that was designed for your faith. And we know that without faith, it is impossible to please God. (See Hebrews 11:6.)

Forgiveness is greater

than unforgiveness.

5. *Unforgiveness can block the hand of God from bringing about justice and/or reconciliation in a situation.* Until we forgive and release the person who has offended us, it may be difficult for our circumstances to be resolved. Unforgiveness affects not only our own spiritual condition but also the spiritual state of the offender. When we forgive those who have wronged us, we release them and their debt, thus setting them free. This opens the way for God to deal with their hearts; it may lead them to repent and be reconciled. Furthermore, I have seen God give favor to a forgiving person by bestowing on him a new circle of positive friendships and other blessings.

Forgiveness frees both

the offender and the offended.

6. *Unforgiveness hardens our heart.* The unforgiving heart develops a hardness, like a callus, so that the person's capacity for compassion is diminished. Instead, he feels that the world is indebted to him. This is the underlying reason why many people who harbor unforgiveness find it difficult to give and receive love. Their emotions become stifled. It is usually very easy for them to function mentally or to converse with other people on an intellectual level, but they lack true companionship with others on the heart level.

Sometimes, bitterness can cause a heart to harden instantly; the heart becomes walled-off and darkened. This sets in motion a downward slide into perversion: bitterness leads to hatred, and hatred leads to a seared conscience. Someone with a seared conscience will frequently employ intimidation, manipulation, and other forms of control in his personal relationships.

> *If you cannot forgive,*
> *you will never grow*
> *in your relationships.*

7. *Unforgiveness closes the heavens to us.* Jesus taught us, *"If you do not forgive, neither will your Father in heaven forgive your trespasses"* (Mark 11:26). As we have noted, unforgiveness can impede every area of our life—our relationships, our finances, our job/business, our ministry, and our mental, emotional, and spiritual health, even to the point of blocking our prayers. (See, for example, 1 Peter 3:12.) Thus, unforgiveness builds a spiritual barrier, creating limits to what we can receive from God.

When a relationship has been broken, on whom did Jesus place the responsibility to forgive or to ask for forgiveness first? On *us*. We are not to wait for the person who offended us to come and ask for forgiveness, and we are not to wait for the one whom we have offended to approach us seeking reconciliation. Sometimes, it is not possible for us to be reconciled to someone personally or face-to-face, due to physical distance, the death of the other person, the other party's refusal to cooperate, or some other reason; regardless, we must let go of any hurt, anger, and bitterness, and forgive the offender from our heart. God's kingdom and His will for our lives cannot come to us while we hold on to unforgiveness. We cannot progress spiritually beyond our level of repentance and forgiveness.

Jesus placed the responsibility on us

to forgive and to ask for forgiveness first.

8. Unforgiveness can lead us to reproduce the same offense. There is a consequence of unforgiveness that many people don't foresee: They often become just like the person whom they refuse to forgive. (See, for example, Luke 6:37.) For instance, a person who was abused may become an abuser. Someone who was unjustly judged may become judgmental. Therefore, the person who does not forgive the pain inflicted upon him will frequently end up hurting others.

When we refuse to forgive an offense,

we are at risk of becoming like our offender.

9. Unforgiveness attracts demonic powers. If you do not allow your offended heart to heal, it will "bleed," figuratively speaking, making you vulnerable to demonic attack. Like vicious sharks, Satan and his demons are attracted by the blood of unresolved hurts, especially when that blood emits a cry for revenge. The Scriptures tell us that we are not to take revenge—either for ourselves or for others—but to leave justice to God. (See Romans 12:19.) Entrenched hurts and a desire for revenge usually lead a person to suffer oppression and other afflictions from the enemy.

Unforgiveness is an

entry point for demons.

10. Unforgiveness can be the source of physical illness. For example, from my experience in ministering healing, I have found that many people who are ill from cancer are harboring bitterness and resentment in their hearts. When a person's unresolved offenses manifest as physical illness, the sickness is merely the symptom. The real source of the problem, the foundational cause of the pain, is unforgiveness. Every hurt that the person holds within him will feed that illness until it reaps its destructive harvest. But if the person repents, forgiving his offenders, the Lord will rip out the root of that illness in an instant. When that happens, the door to healing is opened. As I wrote earlier with regard to the sin of rebellion, if you are sick and have been prayed for without results, check your heart to see if there is anything for which you need to repent and be forgiven (or any generational sin that needs to be renounced). If you are harboring any unforgiveness, repent immediately and be delivered.

> **While you hold on to unforgiveness, sickness has a legal right to develop in your body.**

11. Unforgiveness brings judgment and eternal condemnation.

[Jesus said,] *But I say to you that whoever is angry with his brother without a cause shall be in danger of the judgment. And whoever says to his brother, "Raca!" shall be in danger of the council. But whoever says, "You fool!" shall be in danger of hell fire.*

(Matthew 5:22)

Unforgiveness is a sin; as such, it can lead people to hell. How many people have refused to forgive an offense and have stubbornly carried their unforgiveness to the grave! Some people have preferred to die from a disease whose root is bitterness rather than forgive their offender. Certain people have even committed suicide in order to use their death as a form of punishment against the one who wronged them, instead of living to forgive and be forgiven.

A lack of forgiveness brings spiritual condemnation while functioning as a death sentence because it binds people to past hurts, to sickness, and—ultimately, perhaps—to hell. Unforgiveness often represents the death of a relationship—a marriage, a friendship, a ministry partnership, a business association, or another relationship. Wherever there is unforgiveness, sickness and death follow. You cannot harbor unforgiveness and be spiritually alive. Unforgiveness is therefore a silent assassin that can lead you to an early grave and to eternal punishment.

> *Unforgiveness is a sin; as such, it can lead people to hell.*

12. *Unforgiveness causes us to conform to evil, producing negative behaviors.* Our character is continually built and refined by our personal choices. We develop good character when we conform to the image of Jesus Christ (see, for example, Romans 8:29); thus, forgiveness leads to the development of Christlike character in us. The opposite is also true. When we conform to our fleshly nature, becoming bitter and refusing to forgive, we develop adverse character qualities that lead to negative behaviors that are aligned with the kingdom of darkness rather than the kingdom of God.

> *Unforgiveness promotes the character of Satan in a person's life.*

13. Unforgiveness has no present and no future, causing us to live primarily in the past. While faith leads us to live in the present and to design a future, unforgiveness won't allow us to let go of the past. It replays offenses and insults in our mind as though they were occurring right now. Consequently, unforgiveness chains our heart to former (usually negative) times, which Satan likes to use against us. The devil cannot affect the future; in fact, he does not even know the future, beyond his own inevitable destruction. But one of his primary means of ruining people's destiny is to cause them to dwell on their past. That is why he deceives us into reliving situations over and over—including events that happened to us ten, twenty, or thirty years ago.

Demonic forces will cause us to remember hurts due to thoughtless comments or insults; the pain of a relationship in which we were rejected or abandoned; physical, emotional, or verbal abuse; and other causes of emotional or mental distress. The more we relive an offense, the deeper the roots of pain and bitterness will extend into our heart. Those who focus on the past will never be able to live fully in the present or plan a meaningful future.

> *The more we relive an offense,*
> *the deeper the roots of*
> *our pain and bitterness.*

14. Unforgiveness suppresses our purpose and calling in God. In accordance with the previous point, someone who lives in the past has an inactive purpose in life, because purpose generally involves an expectation for the future. Remember that the unmerciful servant in Jesus' parable was incarcerated and placed at the mercy of the "torturers" due to his lack of forgiveness. Similarly, people who harbor unforgiveness often find themselves imprisoned by circumstances that always seem to block their goals. For example, they may attempt to complete a project that should take only a short while to accomplish but instead takes years to finish—or never gets done.

Some adults function emotionally at the level of a child because twenty years ago, they suffered the shock of some offense, and their subsequent unforgiveness has caused them to remain stuck at that point. Their emotional stagnancy keeps them from progressing to maturity. When we are unable to mature, we can't receive our full spiritual inheritance; consequently, our God-given purpose may never be manifested or fulfilled in this world.

When you forgive, you do yourself a favor:
you loosen the blessings of God on your behalf.

Transformed Through Forgiveness

Many of the consequences of unforgiveness described above were manifested in the life of Justin Schopp, a young Caucasian man from North America who attends our ministry. The following is his testimony.

"My parents divorced when I was three years old, and my mother and I moved halfway across the country. Growing up, I didn't understand why my dad wasn't there and why he didn't come to visit me or want to be with me. I grew up hurt, lost, angry, and bitter. I was full of hatred, rebellion, rage, depression, confusion, and pain. I would act out at school, getting into fights. I couldn't forgive my father.

"I started smoking and drinking at thirteen, progressing into a lifestyle of heavy drug use, along with alcohol abuse and promiscuity. With all of that, I was trying to fill the hole in my heart, trying to medicate the pain and the unforgiveness. I worked full-time but in dead-end jobs. I was unable to have successful relationships with my father and my uncle, and with bosses and others in authority.

"I lived in multiple bondages, including fear. I was fearful of rejection, failure, success, and taking risks; I was afraid to open my heart. I didn't believe in myself enough to do anything big with my life. I would often stay in relationships for fear of being alone, and I was dominated by manipulative women. Because I had taken so many drugs into my system, I developed paranoia and heard voices that tormented me. I couldn't sleep at night. I was miserable in every area of my life. For twenty-seven years, I was bound and living in hell.

"Then, one day, the Holy Spirit came upon me when I was in my bathroom, and He convicted me. At that moment, the fear of God entered my life. I had been living with my girlfriend, but I abruptly moved out and distanced myself from her. I began praying, seeking God, and looking for a church. I tried many churches around Miami Beach until I finally found King Jesus Ministry and began the discipleship process there. The Holy Spirit ministered to me every step of the way. By His grace, I have been able to forgive my father, my mother, and everyone else who hurt me. When I made the decision to forgive, I was delivered from fear and feelings of rejection!

"When I forgave myself for all my mistakes and for the years of bondage, God started revealing to me my true identity. I was no longer bound to drugs, illicit sex, alcohol, or fights. I became more intimate with God, and He filled me with His love. I had an encounter with Him as my heavenly Father that changed me. For the first time in my life, I knew who I was. I was satisfied, secure, and bold.

"Since that experience, I have been empowered to move in the supernatural power of God. I also serve the apostle, something that previously would have been unimaginable to me because I hadn't been able to receive correction; I hadn't been able to truly serve anyone else or be a real son. When I was delivered from unforgiveness, I became free in every other area of my life. Today, I'm married and am the priest of my home. I am also a leader at church. I'm now endeavoring to be closer to God, pushing for more encounters with Him and walking in my purpose."

Important Truths About Forgiveness

People often tell me that it is hard for them to forgive. My response is that their willingness *not* to forgive, then, must be greater than their willingness to let go of the offense. Their unforgiveness tells me that they prefer to remain oppressed, estranged from other people, financially unstable, sick, and even vulnerable to an early death rather than forgive. When we are hurt or offended, we need to immediately ask God for His supernatural grace to forgive the perpetrator.

Our most difficult struggles with unforgiveness usually involve people who are closest to us. It is those with whom we live—spending a large portion of our time together, eating meals together, sleeping under the same roof, sharing our dreams—who can hurt us the most. No one can provoke greater feelings of betrayal and resentment than a loved one who has wronged us.

Before we discuss the steps that can lead us to complete freedom from unforgiveness, let's review these truths:

- Forgiveness is not an emotion but rather a decision we make. We cannot force a negative emotion to change, but we can make a decision with our will to release an offense committed against us. This means that we can forgive if we know how.

- If we want to bring about real change in our life, our wounded heart must be restored and made whole. Jesus Christ went to the cross so that we could be healed. Quoting Isaiah, Jesus said about Himself, *"The Spirit of the LORD is upon Me, because He has anointed Me to preach the gospel to the poor; He has sent Me to heal the brokenhearted, to proclaim liberty to the captives and recovery of sight to the blind, to set at liberty those who are oppressed"* (Luke 4:18). Among other things, Jesus was anointed to heal the brokenhearted and to release those who are oppressed, and He can make your heart whole again. Do your part today by surrendering your unforgiveness to Him and allowing Him to heal all your hurts.

Steps to Forgiving from the Heart

Here, then, are five essential steps by which you can forgive those who have wronged you.

1. Recognize Your Need to Forgive

Inevitably, you have been hurt, betrayed, unjustly judged, rejected, or abandoned at some time in your life. Here are some points that will enable you to recognize your need to forgive:

+ Don't deceive yourself or others by pretending that you don't feel pain over the incident or incidents in which you were wronged. If you continue to assert that nothing happened, you will remain trapped in that initial place of offense.

+ Don't fool yourself into thinking you have already forgiven the offender if, when someone talks about that person, you still feel the same pain and cannot stand to hear the individual's name mentioned.

+ Don't wait for "time" to heal the hurt, because it won't happen.

+ Do acknowledge how you feel—hurt, resentful, bitter, scared, and so forth. Rather than try to hide those feelings, be willing to speak to God the names of those who have caused you pain so that you can release them and deliver them from their spiritual debt.

2. Submit to God and His Word

"Therefore submit to God. Resist the devil and he will flee from you" (James 4:7). Instead of resisting God by holding on to unforgiveness, submit to Him and obey His Word. (The devil is the one we are to resist!) Again, the person who wronged you owes very little in comparison to what you owed God when you first came to Him for the forgiveness of your sins. As in the parable of the unmerciful servant, your debt was enormous in contrast!

3. Make a Specific Decision to Forgive

Don't wait for your feelings to be ready to forgive. Until you make a decision to release the offender, your emotions will never want to completely let go of the offense. Furthermore, emotions are ever-changing. You may feel peace toward the person one day, and anger the next. If you try to forgive someone on the basis of your emotions alone, you will likely feel anger and hurt all over again whenever the memory of the offense returns.

Some people say, "If I don't feel it, I don't do it." But we may never "feel" it. We don't have full control over our emotions, and they can become imprisoned by our fleshly responses. So, if you wait for your emotions to cooperate, you are relying on the wrong source. Instead, as we discussed earlier, make the decision to forgive the wrong out of a will submitted to God. Tell the Lord that you desire to forgive those who have offended you and that you *do* forgive them as an act of your will.

4. Verbally Affirm the Pardon

The Scriptures say, "*Confess your trespasses to one another, and pray for one another, that you may be healed*" (James 5:16). Therefore, do not allow your forgiveness to be merely a thought in your mind. Confess it in a strong, clear voice, saying, "I forgive _____." Speak the person's name out loud, whether it is your husband, wife, child, father, mother, brother, sister, cousin, friend, pastor, mentor, business partner, coworker, or anyone else, including a thief or another criminal who has harmed you in some way. If your declaration does not sound right or sincere the first time, do it again, over and over, until your heart obeys. Often, when we do not verbalize our pain, it becomes entrenched within us and ultimately manifests in sin.

5. Ask God to Give You Supernatural Grace

The Holy Spirit is waiting for you to say, "Yes, I forgive." That is your part, which you carry out in the natural realm. But choosing to forgive opens up to you the spiritual realm, where God gives you His supernatural grace to completely let go of the offense committed against you. The Holy Spirit will "circumcise" your pained and offended heart and remove any hardness that has caused you to become insensitive to His presence. (See, for example, Deuteronomy 30:6.) This will release you to love God and to recognize that He is near. Then, your personal relationships—both vertical and horizontal—can be healed, enabling you to have fellowship with God and with other people, and to have the freedom to serve others in Jesus' name.

Prayer of Deliverance

Pray this prayer to be a forgiver:

Heavenly Father, I come before Your presence recognizing my need to forgive. With all my heart, I repent for harboring unforgiveness toward other people—and myself—thus breaking Your law. I freely submit to You and Your Word. I believe You are willing to forgive me for my bitterness and unforgiveness, and that Jesus Christ made this possible through His death on the cross. I receive His work on my behalf, which has loosed me not only to be forgiven but also to forgive others. Jesus carried my sins so I could be forgiven; and, right now, I make a decision to forgive these people: _____
(identify them by name and specifically mention their offense). Lord, right now, I forgive all who have hurt me, just as You have forgiven me for my sins and continue to forgive me when I sin against You. I trust in Your supernatural grace to enable me to fully forgive and release all who have offended me. I affirm that I have forgiven them and that I have been forgiven. Thank You, Lord. In Jesus' name, amen.

Let me now pray for you:

Father, in the name of Jesus, I tear out all roots of unforgiveness from the heart of this reader. I deliver him/her from any spirit of hatred, resentment, bitterness, hurt, anger, fear, suffering, or disease. I bind these spirits and cast them out in the name of Jesus, never to return. I cancel all demonic assignments, bonds, oppression, spiritual influences, and power right now, in the name of Jesus. The "tree" of unforgiveness is dead and can never again bear fruit. I now release the power of Christ's blood over His child. I declare that he/she is healthy and free, having supernatural grace to fully forgive and to live the life You intended. In Jesus' name, amen.

7

THE SPIRITUAL BATTLE
OF THE MIND

We are living in the end times, and the return of our Lord Jesus Christ is near. The enemy knows this and has therefore intensified his spiritual warfare over the dominion of the earth and its inhabitants. There are multiple spiritual battles being fought right now, and there are many battlefields. One of the major battlefields is the mind of man, and the battle begins in our thoughts. As we discussed earlier, because Jesus defeated Satan at the cross, the enemy no longer has any authority on earth, but he does retain power. With that power, he tempts and attacks believers in order to usurp their

God-given authority. He tries to seduce their wills by planting wrong thoughts in their minds and urging them to act in disobedience to God, committing works of evil.

> *The enemy wants to steal your mind,*
> *your focus—and your authority.*

We must recognize that our mind is a "territory" and that our spirit—our very essence—is always open to whatever occupies that territory. Our thoughts direct our life; it is through them that we ally ourselves with either the kingdom of God or the kingdom of darkness. The enemy fights to have his thoughts inhabit our mind because, from there, he can attack our spirit. A single thought can positively or negatively affect our soul, our body, and our spirit, and thus our destiny. Accordingly, the devil wants to infiltrate our mind with wrong thoughts because he knows that if we accept a wrong thought, we will likely act in a wrong way; and if we continually repeat a wrong action, we will form a wrong habit; and a negative habit will produce faulty character within us. Ultimately, our character forges our destiny—one that is blessed or cursed, one that is of heaven or of hell.

> *The first thing we must understand*
> *about spiritual warfare is that*
> *the mind is a "territory."*

Satanic Weapons in the Spiritual Battle of the Mind

In the battle of the mind, Satan often uses the defective thinking of our fallen human nature as an "advance guard" or a "sniper unit" in order to make way for greater attacks. Thoughts that are contrary to the mind, the character, and the plan of God often originate in human reason and facts that are based on the natural world rather than on the supernatural realm of God's kingdom. But God's truth is higher than human reason and facts. A fact is a temporary earthly reality, but truth is eternal; truth is the highest level of reality. Thus, the battle of the mind is largely fought over earthly facts versus eternal truth. God tells us that we can win this very personal battle being waged in our own minds. Jesus said, *"You shall know the truth, and the truth shall make you free"* (John 8:32).

Faith operates in a realm above and beyond reason.

The natural mind uses reason alone to assess the reality and viability of the supernatural. Consequently, its faulty conclusions limit what is possible in God. The Lord calls us to wholeheartedly believe in Him, in His promises, and in His supernatural power, but human reason doesn't understand how faith works, and therefore it shuts down such belief. We all have "reasons" for why we haven't done what God has asked and commanded us to do; we place limitations on His power and make excuses for why we remain captive to our circumstances. But since when does human reason tell God what He can and cannot do? Since when does reason tell God what is and isn't possible? God is almighty; He lacks nothing. He is merely waiting for us to shift our thoughts from a dependence on human reason, which understands the world and makes decisions according to the natural realm, to faith, which understands the world and makes decisions according to the supernatural realm.

For example, many believers have arguments for why they do not tithe or give offerings to the Lord. Others have reasons not to serve God, not to commit to His vision, not to evangelize, not to prosper, not to receive healing, not to submit to God-given authority, not to forgive and love other people, and so forth. Some Christians think they're not intelligent, anointed, or prepared enough to obey God. Whatever their reason for not believing God and obeying Him, it will always keep them in a state of spiritual weakness and in a condition of lack.

> *Human reason that is controlled by the fallen nature goes against God's truth, conforming us to a lie.*

How dependent are you on human reason? Could an earthly perspective be generating feelings of fear or inadequacy in you? Could it be stopping you from fulfilling your destiny? The apostle Paul knew how reason operates when it is not submitted to God, and how the enemy uses reason against us. He wrote,

> *For though we walk in the flesh, we do not war according to the flesh. For the weapons of our warfare are not carnal but mighty in God for pulling down strongholds, casting down arguments and every high thing that exalts itself against the knowledge of God, bringing every thought into captivity to the obedience of Christ.*
> (2 Corinthians 10:3–5)

This Scripture tells us that, although we live in a physical body and function in a material world, the war we are engaged in with the enemy is not a physical one. Our battles are waged in the spiritual realm. Thus, the weapons that Jesus gives us are not *"carnal"* or material but spiritual, *"mighty in God."* When we are confronted with spiritual battle, it is futile to fight back according to the natural realm. We will never have the victory by fighting in the wrong arena and with the wrong weapons.

> *The natural mind uses reason*
> *to evaluate the supernatural,*
> *thus limiting what is possible in God.*

The Greek word translated as *"arguments"* in the above passage is *logismos.* Its literal meaning is "computation," and it can signify "reasoning," "imagination," or "thought." Thus, in some Bible versions, the word for *"arguments"* has been translated as *"reasonings"* (for example, Young's Literal Translation) or *"imaginations"* (for example, the King James Version). I would like to elaborate on each of these three words chosen by the Bible translators—*arguments, reasonings,* and *imaginations*—because it will help us to glean insights about the demonic works that assail us. Then we will examine the concept of *"strongholds,"* also found in the above passage.

1. Arguments

An *argument* is an attempt to prove, or demonstrate, a proposed idea or perspective; it seeks to convince us of something. Arguments based on knowledge and mind-sets derived from the fallen human nature are flawed. They are mental constructs founded on natural knowledge, and the enemy uses such arguments—as well as demonic deceptions—to distract us from spiritual truths.

The goal of many satanic "arguments" is to keep people thinking outside the realm of the eternal, or spiritual, so that they will be confined to the realm of the physical world, with its limited ideas and resources. The arguments that Satan brings to people's minds are not truths but corrupt opinions. When these arguments are accepted and begin to accumulate, they can become thought patterns, or structures, that are contrary to God. Such thought patterns resist and dispute the supernatural, including the principles of God's kingdom; they depend on philosophical, psychological, and "religious" arguments to support their propositions. Sometimes, Christians try to use natural arguments to convince people to accept Jesus Christ as the Truth. However, we know that human arguments can't draw people to God or change them spiritually. Only the Holy Spirit can do this, and He operates in the supernatural realm. (See, for example, 1 Corinthians 2:4–5.)

> *Most arguments employed by the demonic realm are aligned with fallen human reason.*

2. Reasonings

Next, I want to point out that the term *reasoning* refers to a series of concepts that have been compiled or arranged in order to prove something or to persuade others. Reasoning endeavors to put ideas in a logical order and thereby reach an accurate and useful conclusion.

However, human reasoning has taken the place of reasoning according to God's Word and character and is therefore deficient; this is especially the case in many of the educational institutions and much of the academic scholarship found in Western nations. In essence, people have made reason their god and, in so doing, have placed limits on what the Lord and Creator of the universe can do in people's lives. Our capacity for reason was given to us by God, but it was meant to be exercised in accordance with His Spirit. When human reason encounters God's promises and His supernatural power, it usually places them in the realm of "impossibility." This is because it is trapped in mental patterns that do not acknowledge the wisdom and knowledge of God.

3. Imaginations

Imagination is the ability to form an image of something in one's mind without seeing it with the physical eye. An image of the future can have such a powerful impact on a person that he lives as if it is already a reality for him. The imagination can be activated in us by words, either spoken or written. To use a simple example, suppose someone suggests a word to you, such as "fruit." When you hear that word, you begin seeing something specific in your head—an image that reflects that particular category of food.

Let's apply the above illustration to faith so that we can understand why we often fail to exercise it in our lives. In a previous chapter, we saw that fear can be a significant entry point for demons, and that fear contrasts with faith. Our imagination plays an essential role in our lives because it can produce thoughts of either faith or fear. And the mind-set that rules the imagination will determine which one of those responses it produces.

First, let's consider the following points:

+ Faith and fear are both derived from what the imagination projects.

+ The imagination is the part of the mind in which faith operates, because in the realm of the imagination there are no mental confines, physical restrictions, or limitations of time.

+ Faith activates the imagination of God in us, or the vision of what He can do; fear paralyzes the imagination of God in us.

+ Every fearful thought comes from an imagination corrupted by the sinful nature.

In light of the above, we must be careful about the words we receive from those around us. If people speak words of fear, confusion, doubt, and unbelief to us, those words can disturb the focus of our imagination, throwing it into disorder. They can create a mental state in which we expect the worst in any given situation. The imagination is amazing! It has eyes through which we see the possibilities of God, or through which we see disappointment, failure, poverty, accidents, sickness, tragedy, or even death before it manifests. When you project something in your imagination, that idea has the power to create itself in the physical world, so you must pay attention to what you are envisioning.

"For the thing I greatly feared has come upon me, and what I dreaded has happened to me" (Job 3:25). Whenever someone is fearful, that person is operating from a distorted imagination that lacks faith, because the fear, in itself, is not real. There are times when danger and abuse are real, and these situations can prompt a natural reaction of fear that leads us to take action for self-preservation. Faith is essential in those situations, as well. But here I'm referring to fears that control our everyday lives, limiting them and crippling them so that we don't become and accomplish what God intended. Those whose imaginations dwell on the negative will always remain in the same place in life—or will end up in a worse situation. They never try anything different, and they live without expectation of receiving something better.

A person whose imagination is based on faith lives each day with a new expectation.

4. Strongholds

The dictionary defines a *stronghold* as "a fortified place," "a place of security or survival." A stronghold is a place where someone who is in danger or under the threat of danger can rest in safety, such as a walled castle or a strong tower. A stronghold is a difficult place to penetrate because it is guarded and is not easily accessible. *"When a strong man, fully armed, guards his own palace, his goods are in peace"* (Luke 11:21).

Mental strongholds are formed when we accept, and come into one accord with, false and negative arguments, reasonings, and imaginations. Satan's plan is to provide us with enough destructive thoughts to build those strongholds, because then he will have a safe place from which he can rule our life and steal our destiny in God. He will have a secure fortification from which he can operate in us, a fortification he has constructed from the building materials of our own erroneous ways of thinking.

False and distorted thoughts

open the door to demonic

activity in your life.

How can we prevent this from happening to us? By fighting *"the good fight of faith"* (1 Timothy 6:12). This involves not allowing our mind to become abandoned territory—a place devoid of God's thoughts, truths, and principles—in which the enemy can construct anything he desires. We must be good stewards and guardians of our minds. We must wage war to preserve the integrity of our thoughts! To accomplish this, we need to understand more about the process by which mental strongholds develop in the mind. We know that they are built by a progressive reinforcement of wrong thinking, but if we understand the mechanism by which strongholds are constructed, we can also learn how to dismantle them.

Most strongholds are

rooted in selfish desire.

First, as an introduction to our exploration of this process, let's look at the testimony of a man named Orlando from Puerto Rico, a soldier whose traumatic injuries threatened not only his physical future but his mental, emotional, and spiritual future, as well. His story describes the change that had to take place in his mind to allow him to activate the supernatural power of God in his life.

"I was involved in the war in Afghanistan for sixteen months until, one day, during an ambush, a bomb exploded near me and left me unconscious. I was injured so badly that the army sent me home, and I retired from the service as a war veteran. I suffered a brain injury, a stroke, acute headaches (so strong that not even morphine relieved the pain), six herniated discs, and deafness. I had two operations on one of my feet, and another operation on my knee. Additionally, my brain's cognitive area was damaged. I was told that I would be able to use only 10 percent of my brain and that I could not learn anything new because my short-term memory had been affected.

"This stressful situation—all the sicknesses and the treatments with their secondary effects—provoked great anxiety and aggression in me. I was extremely irritable, to the point that everything put me in a bad mood. I couldn't look at fire, and I was very sensitive to the smell of smoke. One day, my blood pressure started climbing, resulting in a heart attack and respiratory arrest. I survived, but I knew I couldn't keep living this way.

"One night, I dreamed that I was fighting an animal, and I heard someone crying. When I woke up, I realized that it was actually my wife who was crying because, while I was dreaming, I was hitting her. That made me feel miserable! For years, I took countless medicines without seeing any improvement, and the doctors gave me no hope. I knew I had no cure, and believed that I would have to live that way forever.

"But then my wife and I started to follow Apostle Maldonado of King Jesus Ministry (KJM) via the Internet and television. We moved to Florida and began attending his church. Every time I went to a service, his preaching increased my faith in God, and my mind began to change. So, despite the medical diagnosis concerning the cognitive ability of my brain, I decided to register for the University of the Supernatural Ministry at KJM. In one of the classes, Apostle Maldonado said that he did not understand Christians who couldn't rebuke even a headache and who spent their lives taking pills. Those words were a challenge to my natural mind, and I was dared to believe in what God could do.

"I went to the front, where I was prayed for, and God did what my mind had believed was impossible. From that day, I have not taken any more medicine because all the pain and symptoms of sickness disappeared. I was also freed from anger, anxiety, and uncontrollable irritation. In addition, thanks to God, my marriage was restored. My brain was healed and, to prove it, I took the university exams. To the glory of the Father, I passed them with very good grades. Furthermore, despite having gone through surgeries on my foot and knee, I can now bend down, stretch, and even dance with no problem.

"The power of God is available, but I had to take a step of faith and change my mind in order to access it. I could not conform to what the doctors said. While sickness was a reality in my body, the Bible says that Jesus carried our sicknesses. I had to grab hold of that truth and make it a tangible reality in my life."

Mental strongholds are formed when we accept, and come into one accord with, false and negative arguments, reasonings, and imaginations.

The Cycle of Thought Patterns

God is not so much interested in every thought that goes through our head as He is with the thought patterns we allow to develop in our mind. We all have wrong thoughts from time to time, but they don't have to influence our lives. We can quickly reject such thoughts and move on. But our thought *patterns* become our established ways of thinking; that is why they are so powerful. Thought patterns can be either positive or negative, so we need to carefully consider what ideas we accept into our mind and what thought patterns we develop.

Whether positive or negative, each idea we allow into our mind travels a route of progressive stages. At almost any point in the process, we have a choice of either continuing on that path or diverging from it. Often, the route has a cyclical element, as well. This happens when we apply the same mind-set to each new circumstance and end up with a similar result. In a case where we travel the path of a negative thought, we inevitably conform to a natural reality rather than to a supernatural one; thus, we never discover real solutions for the problems and issues we face. The reverse is true when we travel the path of a biblical, Spirit-led thought. We enter into the realm of the supernatural in which we can receive God's power and blessings in the midst of our circumstances.

> *A mind that has not been renewed will repeat negative cycles of thinking.*

It is spiritually dangerous to follow a negative thought pathway, because Satan can use it to progressively lead us to ruin. Let's examine how a negative thought path begins and develops, as well as the disastrous consequences that can occur if it is allowed to follow its course. This path begins with a mere suggestion to our mind.

1. A Thought Is Suggested

The first step is that a thought is introduced to our mind. Remember that God gives us positive thoughts and that we can receive positive ideas from a number of sources, including the Bible, our pastor, our Christian friends, biblically based literature, and so forth. Negative thoughts or ideas come from our fleshly nature, from demonic spirits, from worldly sources, or from a combination of them. The devil will always try to tempt our minds with the power of suggestion as he seeks a place to enter our lives by appealing to a desire of our heart. His advantage is that we usually think we have generated the thought ourselves. If we have a desire for money, he may present a suggestion about how we can make quick money in an unethical way. If we have a desire for illicit sex, he may plant a corresponding suggestion that we have a right to satisfy the desires of our flesh. Similarly, he may plant thoughts leading to fear, jealousy, loneliness, low self-esteem, sadness, or death. Satan wants us to accept and dwell on ideas that are outside of God's counsel. He wants us to cooperate with his suggestions and entertain them in our mind so that we will take action on them. When such thoughts come into our life, we have two options: *approve them* or *reject them*. Often, we have little time to choose our response before our mind accepts them and we are negatively affected, so we must learn to reject them quickly.

Satan's thoughts will usually come to us in the first person, as if they were our own. When such thoughts come into our life, we have two options: approve them or reject them.

I hope you are beginning to recognize how Satan uses our minds as a battlefield. The enemy plants thoughts to tempt us, and his highest platform of temptation is our desires. Knowing this, he gathers the necessary arguments to present to our thoughts in the form of suggestions, and then he proceeds to provide the "reasonings" and the "imaginations" that will feed them. (You may already have recognized that much of the entertainment industry that rules our society today is geared toward nurturing negative suggestions that appeal to our fleshly desires.)

The enemy observes and tests what stimuli you respond to so that he can learn your weak points. Sometimes, he appeals to lawful desires, but in a corrupt way. For example, when Jesus was in the wilderness, having fasted for forty days, He was justifiably in need of food. Satan came and tempted Him, appealing to His legitimate desire to eat but in a way that was contrary to Jesus' relationship with the Father. What did Jesus do when faced with temptation? He rebuked Satan with the Word of God. He did not allow His mind to entertain the rebellious thought or give place to the devil, which would have provided the enemy the opportunity to present more arguments and reasonings in his attempts to entrap the Messiah. (See Matthew 4:1–4.)

The battle over mental strongholds begins with arguments and reasonings.

While the devil and his demons often suggest wrong thoughts to us directly, they may also use various people with whom we are in contact to achieve this purpose. They might use those who have already yielded to temptation in the same area in which we are tempted, or those who live in ignorance of their fleshly nature and are unaware of the reality of the spiritual realm. Whatever source the negative thoughts come from, you must not allow those thoughts to remain in your mind. There is no way to completely prevent such thoughts from coming, because our minds are battlefields in our spiritual warfare with the enemy. However, again, this does not mean that you have to put up with those thoughts. In the natural world, you cannot stop termites from trying to enter your home, but you can take steps to remove their nests and to eliminate them, thus preventing them from consuming your house. Similarly, you must prevent all negative, destructive thoughts from controlling the atmosphere or dominion of your life—or they will consume you.

When we have wrong or evil thoughts, we attract demons, but when our thoughts are centered on God, we draw Him to us. Thoughts are like signals that alert the spiritual realm—evil thoughts draw evil powers to us, while godly thoughts draw God's Spirit to us. Every time I think about and reflect upon the purposes of God, His kingdom, and His glory, His presence comes upon me. It is essential for us to immediately put a halt to satanic suggestions that come to our minds and to replace those suggestions with thoughts of God.

> *As flies are attracted to garbage, demons are attracted to wicked, carnal thoughts.*

What thoughts are you struggling with right now? Are they thoughts of insecurity, of loneliness, of anxiety over the future, of never being able to succeed in life? Do you have thoughts that accuse you of the wrongs you have committed in the past? Are you daydreaming about homosexuality, lesbianism, or illicit sex? Do you have thoughts of revenge due to an offense or betrayal you experienced?

You can learn to deal with satanic thoughts just as Jesus did. For example, when Satan tried to use Peter, one of Jesus's closest disciples, to tempt Him not to go to the cross, "[Jesus] *turned and said to Peter, 'Get behind Me, Satan! You are an offense to Me, for you are not mindful of the things of God, but the things of men'*" (Matthew 16:23). It seems that the enemy had discovered Peter's thought processes by observing him. He knew what kind of man Peter was, and he understood his weaknesses, so he sent him the corresponding suggestions in an attempt to accomplish his goal of derailing Jesus. Satan does not know everything; he is not omniscient, and he is not aware of all our innermost thoughts. But he does observe people's behavior patterns, as if he were a psychologist, to see how they react to various situations. That enables him to make educated guesses about how they think.

What Peter was thinking—that he did not want Jesus to suffer and to die—was in alignment with Satan's suggestions, and Jesus recognized that fact through Peter's words. That is why He rebuked him. Just prior to this, Jesus had spoken about fulfilling His purpose on the cross (see Matthew 16:21), but Peter had opposed that suggestion and talked about preserving Jesus' life. He did not want to lose his Master. Peter did not comprehend what Jesus' death would accomplish for humanity. Jesus was ultimately rebuking Satan, rather than Peter, because the enemy was using Peter's weakness to tempt Him. Likewise, we must quickly reject any thoughts that aren't in accordance with God and His purposes. If we don't, we risk progressing to the next step.

2. A Thought Is Established, Becoming a Mind-set

When we reflect on positive thoughts, they serve as a platform for developing a positive mind-set. This is actually part of the process by which we renew our minds according to God's thoughts, words, and commands. It enables us to apply His truths to all areas of our life. However, if our mind becomes established in certain negative thoughts or opinions, it will thereby develop a wrong pattern of thinking that we will apply to our life situations. This becomes a real problem because wherever our mind goes, our life will follow.

Once a negative thought is fixed in our mind, the following consequences are set in motion:

+ Our attitudes become un-Christlike.

+ Our behavior is adversely modified.

+ We develop bad habits.

+ We "become" our negative thoughts, being yoked to them.

+ We conform to the natural realm and to negative circumstances.

+ Our negative way of thinking becomes our reality.

> *When you cooperate with a thought*
> *and establish it in your mind,*
> *you "become" that thought.*

Once a negative mentality is established in our mind, we begin seeking opportunities to share that mentality with others and to cultivate it. Satan's suggestions are accelerated in sinful atmospheres. Thus, we start meeting with people who have the same negative outlook. We seek an environment that feeds our thoughts, providing additional arguments and reasoning to justify them so that we can appease our guilty conscience for our disobedience toward God. We essentially become trapped in this negative environment. We continue to be occupied with the negative thoughts, and we start forming bad habits in relation to them.

At this point, the mind urgently needs to be set free in order to prevent it from progressing to the next level, where demonic strongholds can be built in it. The devil is a liar, and his lies have a concrete objective—our spiritual death and destruction. He desires to separate us from God for all eternity.

> *Your thought patterns create*
> *your world, and the condition of*
> *your life reveals your mental state.*

When the enemy sees that the thought he suggested has become established in your mind, you stop being a problem for him in that area of your life because you now think like he does. He knows that your mind is set on sickness, unemployment, fear of the future, family or marriage problems, death, or another negative reality, and that your heart will be occupied by this. He can just sit back and wait for you to crash—for your life to stray from the purpose of God and be destroyed. This is a deep revelation! It means that your circumstances, your problems, and your crises may directly correspond to your mind-set.

Generally, if the ongoing condition of your life is poverty, it is because your mentality is set on thoughts of lack. If you continually battle depression, it is because your mind has entered a cycle of negative thoughts that are contrary to the mind of God. Again, wherever your thoughts go, your life will follow.

When we cooperate with thoughts suggested to us by Satan, it grieves the Holy Spirit.

3. An Established Thought Builds a Stronghold

Once a thought becomes established, a stronghold can be built in relation to it. Satan's goal in attacking our thoughts is to build negative strongholds in our minds. By this third stage, Satan has made many destructive suggestions to us in various areas of our life, and these have become set in our mind. With that foundation, the enemy builds a mental stronghold from which he operates and feels safe. He can exercise control because *"his goods are in peace"* (Luke 11:21). This stronghold, which is like a fortress in our mind, will impede us from making progress in life, will damage our relationships, and will become an obstacle to receiving God's blessings. It will make us stagnant, preventing us from advancing, because it was built to separate us from God and to destroy us from the inside; it is especially designed to keep the truth from penetrating our minds. There is no other answer to this condition but deliverance in Jesus.

The following testimony demonstrates the lengths that Satan is willing to go to in order to oppress people's minds. He attacks not only adults but also children who are vulnerable to his schemes. At the age of seven, Alexander was diagnosed with bipolar disorder, attention deficit hyperactivity disorder (ADHD), and chronic depression. His mother, Claudia, explains the tormented life he led until God delivered his mind.

"My son Alexander began having severe behavior problems when he started elementary school. His teachers would frequently call me about his conduct. It didn't matter what I said to Alex, he continued to grow worse. After he entered second grade, he began to be treated by a psychiatrist who prescribed every type of medicine to control the oppression in his mind. Nothing worked. Alex was periodically admitted to psychiatric hospitals for months at a time. When he was released, it wasn't because he had recovered but because the insurance would no longer cover the costs involved.

"Alex would have violent attacks, during which he would do the following: curse at people; spit on us; threaten us with sticks and knives; hit us; break and throw everything around him; and run away from the house. We couldn't control him—he was too strong! In fact, we had to call the police more than fifteen times due to his behavior.

"Alex constantly hurt himself. One day, we were driving in the car and he threw himself from the vehicle because I wouldn't give him what he wanted. Fortunately, he survived. On one occasion, he tried to commit suicide by taking pills, and he stopped breathing. The paramedics came, and Alex was in intensive care for five days before being admitted to Miami Children's Hospital for three more weeks. By that time, I was already desperate; I did not know what to do with him. I was sad because I knew that my son was very sick, but no doctor would give me any hope, and no hospital would take him in. Neither psychiatrists, psychologists, nor any other specialist knew what to do with him. The psychiatrist told me there was no way to help him and that if he survived, he'd end up imprisoned for life.

"Then I began seeking God, and we went to King Jesus Ministry. During a service, Alex willingly went to the altar to receive Christ. There, I came to understand that my son's mind was being taken over by spirits from hell that wanted to end his life. He needed to be set free! We took him to a deliverance retreat sponsored by the church; as a family, we refused to let Satan take our son from us.

"When Alex stepped on the bus to go to the retreat, he became very violent. People from the church immediately began to minister to him. At the retreat, many strong deliverances took place. Since that day, Alex has not been violent; he has recovered his mind and his conscience. He is doing well in school, takes regular classes, and gets good grades. This radical transformation is due to the supernatural power of God to deliver an oppressed mind."

4. A Negative Stronghold Leads to a Reprobate Mind

This stage can follow if a negative stronghold is not broken but continues in a downward direction. With every negative thought that has come to our mind, we have had an opportunity to stand upon the Word of God and to cast out that thought; we have had a chance to repent. Yet what happens when we don't take that opportunity to reject the thought, and we fail to repent? Perhaps many people have tried to encourage us to do so, but we have hidden behind our pride and stubbornly maintained our negative mind-set. There will come a time when God says, "Enough!"

This is an alarming consequence. Paul wrote, *"And even as they did not like to retain God in their knowledge, God gave them over to a debased ["reprobate"* KJV] *mind, to do those things which are not fitting"* (Romans 1:28). The dictionary defines *reprobate* as "morally corrupt" or "depraved." When people hold on to a mental stronghold for a long time, they can develop a reprobate mind. They begin to lose their identity in God and may experience depression. The demons that they have been listening to and that have nurtured their thoughts now oppress their minds, and they become demonized. All this happens because they accepted wrong thoughts suggested by Satan and allowed them to become established in their minds.

> *Depression is nothing more than mental death.*

5. A Reprobate Mind Can Lead to Apostasy of Faith

For someone who has belonged to God, apostasy is a deadly sin. Someone can have been saved, filled with the Holy Spirit, experienced God's supernatural power, and tasted His good Word; however, after hearing demonic suggestions, he has the capacity to return to sin to the point of denying Christ, the Savior of his soul. (See Hebrews 6:4–6.) Is it possible for apostasy to begin with a single wrong thought? Of course! That is why we cannot treat our thoughts casually but must take all negative thoughts captive to the obedience of Christ.

At each stage outlined above, we determine whether we are going to live by the principles of the kingdom or adopt the mentality of the world. As I write this, I am reminded of the ministry of Scott and Fiona, pastors from Yorkshire, England, who serve in an area where many Christians are yielding to the world's mentality. However, a small remnant of believers there is committed to renewing their minds. The following is their testimony, as told by Scott.

"My wife and I came across Apostle Maldonado's book *How to Walk in the Supernatural Power of God* when we were still new pastors in ministry. We watched the apostle on TV while he was on a trip to Africa a couple of years ago, and we began to receive the impartation of the supernatural. Our minds began to be renewed. Many people assume or believe that demons do not manifest in the United Kingdom, but they do! You just have to get the 'Englishness' mentality out of you and let the kingdom mind-set in.

"We are manifesting the supernatural, and we are seeing it go against the flow of the other religious churches in our city and against what is considered 'normal.' Many people have compromised and are accepting liberalism, conformism, homosexuality, and same-gender relationships. But as a ministry, we are going against that flow and toward the kingdom and toward seeking a manifestation of the power of God. We are seeing miracles, signs, and wonders that can be explained only as interventions of God.

"In one situation, we met a man who had been tortured in a prison in Iran for being a Christian, and he had come to the United Kingdom as a refugee. He had been crippled for twenty-one years; his pelvis was damaged, and he couldn't sit normally. He lived in the UK on disability benefits, was depressed, and had lost all hope. Through a divine encounter, God brought him to our church. From what we had learned about renewing our minds and not accepting the "usual order of things," we aligned with the mind-set of God, made a decision to act accordingly, and said, 'That man walks now!' After we prayed for him, he was instantly healed; as evidence, he was able to sit in a chair normally and walk without difficulty for the first time in twenty-one years! Now he is a brand-new man; he loves Jesus so much, and he is being trained to be an evangelist. The supernatural transformation of his mind set him free and propelled him into his purpose!"

How to Win the Spiritual Battle of the Mind

Even if you have a reprobate mind, you still have an opportunity to repent and be forgiven. Let us explore the steps to freedom from mental oppression, so that you can overthrow the wrong thoughts, mind-sets, and strongholds that have been raised in your mind.

1. Discern the Wrong Thought

Before you can establish a new mind-set and be set free, you need to recognize your condition. You must identify the wrong thought or thoughts that you have made room for in your mind.

Only when the truth is known can one argue with the enemy.

2. Confess the Wrong Thought Before God

Confess the wrong thought as sin—as an offense against the truth of God, as something that separates you from God, His reality, and His promises.

3. Repent

The enemy can raise up a stronghold in relation to any wrong thought that is not rejected and confessed to God. To repent is to make a 180-degree turn, to move in the opposite direction from which you were going. If you do not repent, God cannot destroy the strongholds that have been constructed in your mind, and the "strong man"—the devil—cannot be defeated.

4. Come into Agreement with the Word of God

God's Word is the final authority, and final authority will always be challenged. That is the reason why arguments continuously rise up against the knowledge of God. The Word of God is the highest level of reality, and it has the last word. If your way of thinking is not in agreement with biblical principles, there is error in your mind-set. When a thought has been established in your mind that goes against the truth, you must break any agreement with that false idea and come into alignment with God's Word and principles.

5. Renounce Erroneous Thoughts and Mind-sets

It is important to specifically renounce false thoughts and erroneous mind-sets, even if you have already made a decision to reject them and have repented. Everything that you do not renounce has the potential to remain within you. To renounce means to leave, to remove, or to cut ties with someone or something. The longer you remain in a false mind-set, the stronger it becomes within you. Therefore, renounce every thought of poverty, fear, unbelief, confusion, discouragement, depression, rebellion, and any other wrong idea. Decisively—and out loud—say, "I renounce lack, I renounce poverty, I renounce mediocrity, I renounce sickness, I renounce low self-esteem, I renounce self-pity, and I renounce any other thought that does not come from God." (Be as specific as you can.)

6. From Now on, Immediately Bring Every Thought Captive to Christ

"Casting down arguments and every high thing that exalts itself against the knowledge of God, bringing every thought into captivity to the obedience of Christ" (2 Corinthians 10:5). Note that this Scripture does not say God will do the *"casting down"* for you. As soon as a wrong thought comes to your mind, you must take authority over it. You must not entertain it, cooperate with it, or meditate upon it. Don't think about it for even a second. It is a poisonous dart from the enemy, and if you are not immunized with the Word and if you allow yourself to dwell on it, it will take hold in your mind.

After a stronghold has been built and your mind has become demonized, then your will, your repentance, and your renouncing may not be enough. You need the power of the One who is stronger than the *"strong man"* who has turned your mind into a fortified place that he can live in, operate out of, and use to destroy your life. You need Jesus to win the battle in your mind! Let's review the following verse once more, so that it fully sinks in: *"When a strong man, fully armed, guards his own palace, his goods are in peace. But when a stronger than he comes upon him and overcomes him, he takes from him all his armor in which he trusted, and divides his spoils"* (Luke 11:21–22). Ask Jesus to break down the stronghold and set you free in His name.

7. Renew Your Mind

"And be renewed in the spirit of your mind."   (Ephesians 4:23)

God has given us defenses for all the attacks of the enemy, and His chief defense mechanism consists in our continuously renewing our minds. Breaking and removing old thought patterns is the beginning of transformation, but we must also constantly renew our mind according to God's Word and Spirit. When we do this, the enemy will not be able to guess our thoughts or anticipate our reactions because our behavior will no longer be based on the desires of the flesh. It will no longer fit into patterns of sin. If the enemy does anticipate our thoughts, he will expect that we will think and subsequently act exactly as Jesus does.

Therefore, stay in permanent communion with Jesus and continually renew your mind. Seek supernatural encounters with His presence, which will bring transformation to your mind and heart. As soon as your mind begins to be transformed, the devil has lost that "territory" to God, because the enemy lives in our ignorance and rebellion. Be careful not to become spiritually lazy or apathetic. If you stop learning about God and His kingdom, or if you neglect the spiritual knowledge you have gained, your mind will cease to be renewed, and you will start to regress to old thought patterns and old habits. The renewal of our mind is not a choice but a requirement; it is a necessity. Renewal always establishes or reestablishes our spiritual clarity and focus.

Moreover, you can exercise faith only when your mind is established in God and His Word. Exercising one's faith is an ability that comes from having a lucid and renewed mind. Only then can we begin to operate in the supernatural.

> When we take our wrong thoughts captive
> and renew our mind, we break any agreement or
> contract we have made with the enemy of God.

8. Set Your Mind on What Is Above

"Set your mind on things above, not on things on the earth."
(Colossians 3:2)

When we are spiritually weak, it is a sign that we lack faith and commitment. This is because whenever we believe in something, we commit to it. However, if we doubt something, we do not fully believe it; and if we do not fully believe it, our mind is divided and our direction is uncertain. *"A double-minded man* [is] *unstable in all his ways"* (James 1:8).

> An indecisive mind is a sign
> of spiritual immaturity.

A divided mind leaves itself open to receive demonic suggestions because it remains undecided about whether it truly believes God's Word. Often, the reason why certain blessings come to some believers rather than to others is that those who receive the blessings have made a conscious decision to believe what God has said. Likewise, the reason certain negative things happen to some believers is that they have allowed demons an entrance into their lives through their spiritual indecisiveness or indifference.

> *The enemy seeks to infiltrate*
> *a mind that has not yet decided to*
> *believe or commit itself to what God has said.*

Setting our mind on things above (the spiritual realm) is like programming the navigation system of a ship to a specific course, because whatever we constantly think about is the destiny that we will move toward and eventually reach. We will arrive at the purpose for which our mind has been set. Similarly, when a pilot flies a plane, he needs a definite flight plan; otherwise, he will not have a safe flight or reach his destination. If the pilot just wanders through the sky with no objective, his plane will eventually run out of fuel, and he will be forced to land anywhere he can or lose altitude and crash. If you have not established your mind in God, if you have not made a "flight plan" in regard to the destiny of your life and the direction in which you will go, then the enemy will set your direction for you. Children of God know that their destiny is in Christ and that the Holy Spirit and the Word will provide them with the direction and the plan that will enable them to arrive safely at their destination.

> *The indecisive mind*
> *lacks direction.*

When we are not occupied with spiritual things, what direction does our mind automatically take? There are people whose minds are constantly fixed on their careers; their families; their education; their rights; their worries; their hurts; their fears; or their desire for money, sexual satisfaction, or revenge. They "*set* [their] *minds on...things on the earth*" (Colossians 3:2). When people set their minds on the flesh, they allow themselves to be led by its demands, by the mentality and priorities of the world, and by Satan's suggestions. Again, to "set your mind on" means to establish a specific direction. We are to direct our mind toward the right destiny. The mind that is not set on God and "*things above*" will be at war with Him. "*For those who live according to the flesh set their minds on the things of the flesh, but those who live according to the Spirit, the things of the Spirit*" (Romans 8:5).

To win the spiritual battle of the mind, start by praying the following prayer of deliverance.

Prayer of Deliverance

Heavenly Father, I come before Your presence on the merits of Your Son, Jesus Christ. I thank You for the finished work of Christ on the cross, which I take hold of now for my deliverance. Lord, I recognize that I have given place to worldly and evil thoughts that go against Your Word. Today, I repent with all my heart, and I confess every one of those thoughts by name. [Name each one.] I break any agreement with them, and I come into agreement with You and with the mind of Christ. I renounce every wrong thought, argument, reasoning, and imagination. I renounce every mind-set that conforms to worldly thinking, unbelief, lack, sexual immorality, fear, rebellion, stubbornness, and anything else that is opposed to You, and I cast them out of my mind. Right now, I break all agreements, or pacts, with the enemy, and I take every thought captive to the lordship of Christ. I renew my mind and declare myself free now, in Jesus' name! Amen.

8

FREEDOM FROM
GENERATIONAL CURSES

At the beginning of my ministry, I could not understand why so many Christians seem to live under a curse. These believers love God and are committed to Christ, but they experience problems that are frequent or cyclical, such as recurring sicknesses or persistent financial crises. I knew that Jesus Christ had redeemed us from the curse of sin, sickness, and death when He died on the cross; therefore, I could not explain why they remained in these negative circumstances without being set free. Then I began seeking revelation from God about this matter. I eventually came to understand that although many Christians know in theory that Jesus has redeemed them, they lack a practical knowledge of what Jesus has actually accomplished for them. Accordingly, they have not discovered how Jesus' death and resurrection apply to breaking generational curses in their lives.

Cycles of Defeat

We have seen that a generational curse is a recurring or persistent bondage, such as an illness or an addiction, that is passed down to us from our parents, grandparents, and other ancestors. After I received the above revelation, I faced a personal spiritual battle with a generational curse of heart disease and premature death. My father and my grandfather had both died of a heart attack, and I was beginning to experience some early symptoms of heart trouble. Since God had already shown me how to be set free from generational curses, I rose up in spiritual warfare against that curse, breaking its power, and I live free from it today. My heart is completely healthy.

Even if you are born again, redeemed by the blood of Jesus, you may be plagued by a generational curse. Many believers repeat the oppressive pattern of sickness, sin, or poverty experienced by their parents and other preceding generations. Such curses are like an invisible hand that holds them back from health and prosperity; it pushes them in the wrong direction, even though they do not want to go there. As much as they try to avoid it, a dark shadow always returns to them; the cycle of defeat generates enormous frustration for them.

For example, when a generational curse is operating in someone's finances, that person is able to reach a certain level of success but then can never advance any further. He may meet all the qualifications to receive a promotion in his job, or he may have all the elements lined up to sign a profitable business contract, when everything suddenly falls apart, and he is unable to enter into abundance. When a generational curse is operating in someone's health, that person begins to suffer the same sickness or the same addiction from which his parents or grandparents suffered. When a generational curse is operating in someone's marriage, that person will experience the same tendency toward divorce that previous generations did.

Every Curse Has an Inciting Cause

Generational curses are demonic. If you are afflicted by such a curse, it is because somewhere in your family history, the sin of one of your ancestors opened a door for it to enter. The Bible says, *"Like a flitting sparrow, like a flying swallow, so a curse without cause shall not alight"* (Proverbs 26:2). A curse does not *"alight"* in our lives unless it has been given a reason to.

The testimony of Victor and Jacqueline, a married couple who attend our church, reveals the potency of generational curses, as well as the power of Christ to break them. Victor and Jacqueline endured many financial difficulties due to generational curses of poverty that were operating in their lives. Victor's grandfather had been a wealthy landowner who had engaged in an illicit affair, resulting in the birth of two children—Victor's mother and uncle. Because the children were illegitimate, they were put to work as slaves by their own father when they were very young. Years later, at the age of twenty-seven, Victor's mother married one of her cousins, and they were subsequently disowned. The couple moved to another state, had children, and found themselves dealing with financial problems their entire lives. Moreover, when the grandfather died, Victor's mother and uncle received no inheritance from him. Victor's mother was authoritative and controlling with her children. When Victor grew up and decided to marry Jacqueline, his mother was opposed to the union and swore that she would never accept it. For her part, Jacqueline had been only seventeen years old when her father had died of a stroke. Her father's mistress, who had also been the secretary and bookkeeper for his business, quickly sold off all the company's assets and kept the money for herself; consequently, the family received no inheritance.

Victor and Jacqueline began to see their respective generational curses manifesting in their finances and in their relationship. There were times when they made a lot of money, but, for some reason, their financial situation would always crash, and they would have to start over from scratch. At one point, they moved to Miami. Victor, Jacqueline, and their oldest son all got jobs, and they started making good money. They bought a house and brand-new cars, but Victor was negligent; he was not aware of biblical principles concerning his role as the head of the family; he did not know how to function as God's priest in his home in order to bring security and peace to his loved ones. Subsequently, Victor and Jacqueline's marriage deteriorated, almost to the point of no return; they could not agree on anything. Moreover, their business went bankrupt, and they lost their house, their cars, and almost everything else of material value.

By this point, Jacqueline hated her husband and wanted a divorce. Victor asked to speak with her one last time, and they went out for coffee. At the coffee shop, they saw an acquaintance of Victor's who shared his testimony about how Jesus had transformed his life. He told them that he attended King Jesus Ministry, where he had learned to receive and maintain God's blessings. Victor asked Jacqueline if she would go with him to a service at KJM, and she agreed. The next Sunday, they visited the church, and at the end of the service, I had the opportunity to talk with them. When Victor presented Jacqueline to me as his wife, she immediately replied that they were getting a divorce and that she wasn't his wife any longer. However, I told them they would not get divorced and gave them a word of knowledge from God that in the next week, they would find a house to move into. By the following Wednesday, they had the house; the grace of God had prompted the owner of that home to help them. They also were ministered to by the staff at our church, and the generational curses over their finances and marriage were broken. After that, their lives began to change for the better. Victor became a stockbroker and soon had many clients. Their daughter received a scholarship to study in Rome. And Jacqueline is now a real estate agent with her own office. Victor and Jacqueline's marriage, home, and finances were restored due to the intervention of Jesus Christ, who broke all the curses that had been strongholds in their lives.

The Origin of Curses

What is the origin of generational curses? They began with the fall of humanity in the garden of Eden.

Then to Adam [God] said, "Because you have heeded the voice of your wife, and have eaten from the tree of which I commanded you, saying, 'You shall not eat of it': Cursed is the ground for your sake; in toil you shall eat of it all the days of your life....In the sweat of your face you shall eat bread till you return to the ground."   (Genesis 3:17, 19)

As a result of humanity's disobedience, God cursed the ground; from that moment on, human beings experienced hardship. Humanity and the earth itself were sentenced to frustration, failure, and corruption. (See Romans 8:21–22.) When God told Adam that the ground was cursed due to his rebellion, He was saying that the world would no longer respond to him in a supernatural way. Now it would respond to him in only a natural way; additionally, the earth would be subject to time and decay. Functions and actions that formerly had been instantaneous now required a process; for example, there was now an interval of time between sowing and reaping to allow for incremental growth, something that I believe hadn't been the case before the fall.

The origin of curses is the fall of mankind.

Generational curses are therefore a product of two things: (1) the wider curse to which human beings were sentenced due to the rebellion of the first man and woman, and (2) the resulting sinful nature and sinful actions that became the controlling factor of people's lives after humanity's disobedience. Essentially, we inherit our spiritual legacy in much the same way that we inherit our natural one. We all know that we receive certain natural traits from the genes that are passed along to us by our parents and other preceding generations. The dictionary defines a gene as "the functional unit of inheritance controlling the transmission and expression of one or more traits." In the physical realm, the human race is a phenomenon influenced by genes; genes are what cause a child to look like his parents and even to behave like them. As a race, human beings were created in the image of God our heavenly Father, and we were originally designed to have His "DNA," reflecting His traits and characteristics. But when human beings fell from glory due to sin, a genetic alteration took place, and that spiritual DNA became corrupted. As a result, our generational inheritance also changed—from receiving God's blessings to being cursed. This is the root of many of the problems and issues that human beings deal with to this day.

The genes we receive from our parents at conception include traits from some of our natural ancestors—and those traits can reflect generational curses. Just as we inherit physical traits, characteristics, and tastes, we also inherit tendencies toward certain transgressions and forms of iniquity. Cain apparently inherited a tendency for needing to prove himself and to justify his actions; disastrously, he allowed that tendency to take over his life to the point that he killed his own brother out of jealousy. (See Genesis 4:1–15.)

> *The curse resulting from the fall of mankind includes sin, sickness, and poverty. Poverty, lack, and hardship are all signs of a curse.*

The Nature of Curses

Let's look a little more closely at the nature of curses. First, what is a curse? A curse can be either a pronouncement of judgment, a statement of condemnation, or an evil that is spoken or activated over a person. The first type come from God and from those with delegated authority to represent Him. The other two come from Satan and his demonic forces. A curse's manifestation can be spiritual, emotional, mental, and/or physical. The remedy for a curse from either source is the power of the blood of Jesus, which releases us from the curse and cleanses us from all unrighteousness. (See, for example, 1 John 1:7–9.)

We must understand that God and Satan have very different purposes and motivations for the bestowal of curses. God uses our human limitations and weaknesses—brought about by the curse of the fall—to reveal to us our need for Him; to lead us to Christ so that we can be free from sin, sickness, and death; and to teach us how to live according to the supernatural in the midst of the natural world. In contrast, Satan and his accomplices (both demonic and human) use curses to inflict evil and distress on people, bringing on them as much condemnation and as many consequences related to the fall as possible.

When a person is under a curse, he is in effect "empowered" to fail. He is vulnerable to evils that come his way because he cannot defend himself against them. His hands are tied, and he is able to succeed only at attracting bad circumstances to his life. Everything he does seems to fall apart, while others who have less talent than he has and who seem to exert less effort than he does are somehow successful. Consider your own circumstances. Do you work hard but never really prosper? Do all your undertakings seem to fail? When you start to make a certain amount of progress, does something always happen to halt you? If you are under a curse, it won't matter if you do everything right and work diligently, you will usually be left empty-handed; you will end up in some sort of discouraging failure or problem, such as a financial crisis, a divorce, an addiction, a sickness, an emotional issue, or a physical disaster. This occurs because the spiritual DNA that we receive from our bloodline emits a type of "sound" that can be detected in the spiritual realm. If our spiritual DNA has inherited a blessing, its sound will attract the presence of God. But the opposite is also true. If our spiritual DNA has inherited a curse, its sound will attract demonic powers to us.

*To be under a curse
is to be supernaturally
empowered to fail.*

Concepts and Characteristics Related to Curses

Let's examine some concepts and characteristics related to curses to better understand how they function.

1. A Curse Is of Supernatural Origin

Both blessings and curses are of supernatural origin. This means that a curse cannot be eliminated using natural means. The power behind a curse is demonic. We can therefore conclude that to be demonized is to be cursed, and to be cursed is to be afflicted by a demon. If you are battling sickness, addiction, poverty, or another generational curse, you are dealing with the demonic realm of the supernatural. Therefore, the solution is to be delivered by the supernatural power of God.

2. A Curse Must Be Activated

Whether it is of divine or demonic origin, a supernatural manifestation must first be activated in order to operate. We have noted that curses are often activated through people's sin and disobedience to God. If you think you haven't done anything "bad" enough to activate a curse, remember that sin is not limited to doing something explicitly evil, like committing murder. To sin means "to miss the mark." It means to do something wrong, whether out of wickedness, rebellion, recklessness, or ignorance. You might light a match near a barrel without knowing that the barrel contained gasoline, but your ignorance would not prevent the fuel from exploding upon contact with the flame. In a similar way, although you may be activating curses unknowingly, your ignorance of them will not prevent them from operating in your life and producing negative circumstances.

In 2011, I traveled to East London, South Africa, and held a conference called "Days of Glory." Many supernatural manifestations took place there, such as deliverances, salvations, and transformations of the heart. A South African businessman named Lawrence gave the following testimony about how he experienced a curse of lack and stagnation in his finances when he fell away from God. However, after he surrendered his life to the Lord, things turned around dramatically.

"For the past ten-plus years, I have been in business, having started my own appliance installation company. From the beginning, we had always been a Christian company, but as the years went by, I drifted away from the things of God and grew to have a love of money and success. I got caught up in competing for contracts, taking advantage of those around me and trying to become the 'best.' The last thing I wanted to do was give money to the kingdom of God; instead, I invested it in other resources that would make me money.

"After about five years, the business hit a wall, and we could not progress beyond a specific point of sales and revenue. Then, one day in July 2011, my business partner called me up and said, 'Turn on your TV. There's a man preaching, and you have to watch him!' Reluctantly, I turned on my TV and was introduced to the ministry of Apostle Guillermo Maldonado as he preached in my country of South Africa. I began to encounter God there in my office. Something happened to my heart that I can only explain as supernatural. My eyes were opened to my wicked ways, my deceit, and my love of money.

"After I watched the program, God broke the curse operating in me, and I was set free in my mind! I did something I hadn't done in a long time—I gave money to God! I sowed a seed offering into the ministry. That Sunday, I went back to my local church in Johannesburg and gave my heart to Jesus. I got baptized immediately, and God started to supernaturally transform my life. I broke away from 'Babylon principles'—the principles of the world—and turned the business into a *kingdom* business. Soon afterward, the Spirit of God directed me and eighteen other leaders from South Africa to go on a trip to Israel and be baptized in the Jordan River. At the moment of my baptism, I finally identified with Jesus' death and resurrection. In that water, I left behind my 'old man'—my old, worldly mammon mentality—and became a son of God. I learned that as true sons of God, we are kings in a marketplace we are called to dominate and to rule. Our God walks on gold. [See Revelation 21:21.] He is a King, and we must put a 'demand' on the supernatural to see it manifest in the natural.

"After I returned to South Africa, I began to experience abundant provision. The provision had always been there, but it was not mine to possess until I turned from worldly desires and aligned myself with God's priorities. My business partner and I now preach the Word daily in the office. I have seen the fruit of change in my staff members, who are now all devout Christians. Additionally, in the last two years since that encounter, we have been able to expand our staff from one hundred employees to four hundred.

"Another evidence of the change in my life was that the business began to receive contracts that would have been impossible to obtain under natural conditions. On one occasion, we were in competition to sign a contract, and other companies that were more experienced and had more money also made bids on the job. According to the world's standards, those other companies were more qualified than we were. But God raised a standard in us, and we were awarded the contract. In the last year alone, our business has earned thirty-eight million dollars in revenue! This is the most we have ever seen, enabling us to give a higher amount than ever before as an offering to the kingdom! Nothing is impossible to God, but one thing that God requires of us as sons is to leave our 'old man' behind and let go of worldly mind-sets—to deny ourselves and to follow Him. I made that decision and have seen nothing but blessings after turning away from the world. The battle for my finances was won!"

3. Curses Can Be Transferred from Generation to Generation

"For I, the LORD your God, am a jealous God, visiting the iniquity of the fathers upon the children to the third and fourth generations of those who hate Me, but showing mercy to thousands, to those who love Me and keep My commandments" (Exodus 20:5–6). Once a curse has been activated, it usually continues from generation to generation until it is either revoked or canceled.

In the above verse, God limited the reach of a curse to the fourth generation. However, a curse can be extended, because each generation creates its own cycles of iniquity or blessing. This is why some curses appear to be perpetual through many generations of a family. If the children commit the same sins as their parents, they will attract additional curses to their bloodline. Likewise, when we continue to function according to destructive forces, such as unforgiveness, poverty, or disease, we maintain an open channel for curses to inflict damage in our lives and in the lives of our descendants. In this way, the cycles continue and the sins accumulate. Thus, we may find ourselves experiencing the consequences of someone else's sin by suffering from a curse we did not personally invoke.

But blessings, as well as curses, can be generational. In contrast to curses, which may last until the third or fourth generation, the Scriptures tell us that God gives blessings for a thousand generations to those who love Him and keep His commandments. (See Deuteronomy 7:9.) God is merciful, and He desires to bless people, not curse them. He does not want them to live under generational curses, and He will cancel the curses of all who repent and turn to Him through Christ. Note that the blessing God promised Abraham in Genesis 22:17–18 was given more than six thousand years ago, but we can still receive it today. Because of that blessing, Christ came to earth as our Messiah, and the blessings of salvation and redemption continue from generation to generation among those who love God.

4. Curses Can Be Released by Words

"I will bless those who bless you, and I will curse him who curses you; and in you all the families of the earth shall be blessed" (Genesis 12:3). Blessings and curses alike can be released in our lives by the spoken word. Words are therefore instruments of supernatural power. Whatever words we speak with intent—whether for good or for evil—are charged with power. For example, in the promise God made to Abraham in Genesis 12:3, I believe we can see His divine protection against anti-Semitism. Whenever someone speaks against Israel and the Jews, that person is exposed to the curse spoken by God more than six thousand years ago. Throughout history, you will find that nations and people who have risen up against Israel have subsequently fallen into a curse.

5. Curses Come Through Iniquity

The word that is most often translated as *"iniquity"* in the Old Testament (more than two hundred times) is *awon*, which means "perversity," or "moral evil." *Awon* was the word used by David in Psalm 51:5: *"Behold, I was brought forth in **iniquity**, and in sin my mother conceived me."* The term comes from a root word meaning "to crook," which has both literal and figurative connotations, such as "do amiss," "make crooked," "commit iniquity," "pervert," "do perversely," "do wickedly," and "do wrong." It can also mean "twisted" or "to twist, pervert." It is these connotations of iniquity that I want to emphasize in relation to generational sins, because through them, our moral and spiritual values become "twisted" away from God's truth, whether intentionally or not.

When Adam disobeyed his Creator, the same hatred for God that Satan has became embedded in humanity's DNA; consequently, our rejection of God and our rebellion against Him are at the genetic level, spiritually speaking. (See, for example, Romans 3:10–13.) The sin and rebellion that accumulate in people's spiritual DNA from generation to generation are "iniquity"; they are the wickedness of a perverted heart, ensuing from the genetic alteration that occurred in Eden. Iniquity feeds on itself, spreading its roots according to the sins people commit the most, activating new generational curses—and so the cycle continues.

That is why the deliverance that Jesus provided for us by bringing God's kingdom to earth and by His sacrifice on the cross is so essential. Iniquities are the carriers of curses. If there are no iniquities, there are no curses. Thus, if the iniquities are taken away, the curses are taken away, as well. Jesus died on the cross for our iniquities, thereby removing them from us.

We should understand that iniquity includes any hidden sin that we have not dealt with. Sometimes, people think that if they move to a different location, they will be free from a generational curse, but this isn't the case, because the curse lies within them—they carry it with them wherever they go, because it is implanted in their genes. The "sound" it emits remains the same, attracting the same demonic powers of failure and destruction. The spiritual signal isn't affected by distance or borders, since there is no time or space in the spiritual world. (However, there are certain places that are especially oppressed by demonic activity, as I explain in the next section.) Accordingly, you can't run away from a curse; you must be released from it.

> *Spiritual DNA, which is genetically inherited, is a "territory" in the supernatural realm, meaning that it is an area over which spiritual battles take place.*

6. Curses Operate on Places and Things, as well as People

There are geographic locations in the world in which strong demonic activity can be perceived; this happens where physical territories and areas have been handed over to Satan by people who have dedicated themselves to witchcraft or idolatry. Satan's representatives on earth also use amulets and other objects that are employed in occult practices to operate curses against others or to incite demonic activity of other kinds.

Additionally, as we have seen throughout this chapter, curses operate in people's bloodlines, affecting their health, their relationships, their finances, and other areas of life. For example, a generational curse that afflicts many women is the ailment of varicose veins. Medically speaking, this condition is caused by congenital, or inherited, vascular problems. When I am ministering deliverance in a service and call to the front anyone who suffers from varicose veins, 99 percent of those who come forward are women. Their testimonies always start in the same way—their mothers, grandmothers, aunts, or other female relatives have suffered from the same problem. Sometimes, the condition manifests at a very early age. Not only are varicose veins aesthetically displeasing, but they are also often very painful. Sometimes, the afflicted person is able to stand up for only short periods of time.

That was the case for two women whose testimonies I would like to share with you. Amy is thirty-six and was born in the United States. Yolanda is sixty-five and comes from Colombia. They both suffered for many years with vascular problems inherited from their ancestors. Amy ended up being hospitalized for over two weeks when the veins in her left leg became clogged and infected; Yolanda's legs turned purple, and she developed thrombosis in her right leg. Both these women had seen the best vascular specialists, but they were told there was no cure; they would have to live with their disease. Desperate, they sought the supernatural power of God for deliverance. As they were ministered to, the curses in their lives were broken, and they received healing from varicose veins and vascular disease, as well as from the accompanying feelings of rejection, low self-esteem, and shame! Above all, they know that their daughters will not have to suffer as they did.

Causes of Curses

We must keep in mind the principle that was stated earlier: Wherever there is a curse, there is a cause behind it. If we are to deal effectively with a curse, we must know its origin. The following are the most common causes of curses:

+ Practicing idolatry or the occult. (See Deuteronomy 27:15.)

+ Dishonoring or disobeying one's parents. (See Deuteronomy 5:16, 31–33.)

+ Stealing tithes and offerings that belong to God. (See Malachi 3:8–12.)

+ Participating in illicit or perverted sex. (See Romans 1:18–32; Colossians 3:5–6.)

+ Committing injustice against the weak or helpless. (See Zechariah 7:8–12.)

+ Trusting more in man than in God. (See Jeremiah 17:5–6.)

+ Making a vow to God but not fulfilling it. (See Ecclesiastes 5:4–6.)

+ Not listening to the voice of God, or disobeying His voice. (See Deuteronomy 28:15–46.)

+ Making a negative proclamation against oneself (a self-imposed curse). (See, for example, Matthew 27:25.) Some common negative proclamations that people make are "I will never forgive myself for..." or "I will never be a success in life."

+ Receiving negative words from people who are in authority over you. (See, for example, Colossians 3:21.) I would like to expand on this point because although it is very important, it is often overlooked. God designed His kingdom with a structure based on various levels of authority. Accordingly, He has established an authority for every realm of life on earth. (See, for example, Romans 13:1–2.) Those who have been given authority have the potential to use their authority to either bless others or curse them. As we have discussed, within the realm of marriage, the husband is the ultimate authority. He is called by God to love his wife as Christ loves the church. (See Ephesians 5:25.) Yet, if he disparages her, saying something such as "You're worthless," he is in effect cursing his wife, and his words will have a detrimental effect on her life. Likewise, in the realm of the family, the parents have authority over their children, and they are meant to love, affirm, nurture, and discipline them. But if they abuse that authority and tell their children things like "You're never going to change," "You're stupid," or "You'll never outgrow your stubbornness," the children will grow up with a curse that their own parents have placed upon them. In the realm of business, the boss is meant to oversee his employees and to cultivate their gifts. Yet if a boss tells an employee, "You're never going to do this job right," he is abusing his authority by cursing the employee. In the realm of the church, the pastor has spiritual authority over those in his congregation. He is called to shepherd them and to build them up in the Lord. But if he tells a member of his church, in effect, "You're not needed," or "You're ignorant," he is using his authority to curse. One time, a family that was new to our ministry asked me for prayer in regard to a curse that had been placed on them by a former pastor. They had felt they should begin attending our church, but when they informed their pastor of this, he cursed them by telling them that nothing would go well for them if they left. God delegates authority to his ministers for the purpose of edifying and blessing people, not tearing them down and cursing them. When I prayed over these family members to remove the curse, all four of them fell to the floor under the anointing of God; they coughed as they were freed from the demonic operation that had been activated in their lives. Similarly, when I pray for people who are suffering from a disease, such as cancer, I always curse the seed, or root, of the illness and command it to dry up and die. In other words, I use my spiritual authority to curse the destructive works of the devil and to bless people with God's favor. (See Matthew 16:19; 18:18.)

- Being cursed by a human representative of Satan, such as a witch, a sorcerer, or a false prophet. I want to expand on this point, as well. These representatives of Satan are individuals who have been granted demonic power to use against the lives of others through spells, curses, and other avenues, including false and negative prayers. Believers who live in obedience to God cannot be affected by these curses, but those who live in disobedience are vulnerable to them. We must be careful not to allow other people's words against us to make us fearful, or we may become susceptible to them. First Kings 19 describes what happened to the prophet Elijah after he had been involved in a great spiritual victory by destroying the prophets of the false god Baal. Jezebel—the malicious queen who was a Baal-worshipper—threatened Elijah's life saying, "So let the gods do to me, and more also, if I do not make your life as the life of one of them by tomorrow about this time" (1 Kings 19:2). Elijah then "ran for his life" (verse 3) but then asked God to take his life (see verse 4). Elijah seems to have been overcome with fear and to have received Jezebel's words into his heart. But God reassured the prophet of His presence and power (see verses 9–18), and thereby restored him.

Let us turn now to the testimony of a young woman who was born under a curse due to her mother's ignorance and sin. Jenny is a high school senior of Angolan-Cuban descent who attends our church. She describes what her life was like before Jesus set her free. "In the late 1990s, my mother was living in Angola, Africa. Unable to conceive, she sought help from a woman who used a witchcraft spell on her as a 'spiritual remedy.' A couple of months later, I was conceived. When I was fourteen, I went to the doctor because I was experiencing pain in my abdominal area, and I was diagnosed with chronic ulcerative colitis [a disease in which the lining of the colon becomes inflamed and develops tiny open sores, or ulcers, that produce pus and mucous]. The organ that connects my esophagus with my stomach was enlarged three times the normal size and was about to burst. As a result, I bled continuously. The doctors couldn't control the bleeding, so they prescribed that I take eight pills every four hours on a daily basis. My mom didn't understand why I had this disease because it didn't seem to be a condition that ran in my family. So, she went to a witchdoctor to see if he could help. He told her that he needed to sacrifice some animals and that he wanted me to cleanse myself for twenty-four hours in a mixture of blood, meats, legumes, and other ingredients. I knew in my heart that there was something abnormal and evil about those rituals. My mother and I were desperate for other answers.

"By that time, I was fifteen, and we were living in Miami. A friend of ours invited us to King Jesus Ministry, and I attended a Thursday night service. During the altar call, I raised my hand, went to the front, and received Jesus as my Savior. I realized then that I needed the supernatural power of God to break the curse that was operating in my life. During a ministry conference, I was prayed for and was immediately healed! The pain went away, and the bleeding completely stopped. To this day, I have not taken another pill, and I have not bled at all. I can truly say that I was delivered from death; I was released from the curse that had been placed on me before I had even come into this world. When my mother sought the help of witchcraft, it became an open door through which Satan was able to attack my life, but Jesus set me free!"

Unless you get to the root of something,
you cannot truly change it.

Common Manifestations of Curses

From my experience in ministering deliverance, I have learned to recognize signs that a curse is working in someone's life; moreover, certain effects indicate what type of curse is operating. Here are various negative manifestations and the curses related to them:

+ Hereditary diseases (the curse of whatever sickness is being manifested, such as heart disease).

+ Barrenness in all areas of life (the curse of unfruitfulness).

+ Stagnation (the curse of unfruitfulness). With this curse, there is a hindrance to personal growth and development, so that the person never makes any progress. He may maintain the status quo, but he cannot expand or multiply. Even though he does the right things to move forward in life, nothing works out for him, and he remains in the same place. We may wonder, "How is it possible that someone who works hard, makes every effort, and does everything right cannot reach his purpose?" This is the sign of a curse.

+ Poverty or recurring financial crises (the curse of lack and deficiency).

+ Failure, defeat, and humiliation (the curse of shame and dishonor).

+ Emotional trauma, mental confusion, or insanity (the curse of instability and lack of peace).

+ The disintegration/destruction of a marriage or a family (the curse of discord, disunity, lust, or adultery).

+ A history of unusual accidents, of suicides, or of premature death from other causes (the curse of violence or death).

We must make a choice to receive God's blessings and be freed from all curses. Moses told the Israelites, *"I call heaven and earth as witnesses today against you, that I have set before you life and death, blessing and cursing; therefore choose life, that both you and your descendants may live"* (Deuteronomy 30:19). To choose blessing, the Israelites needed to live in obedience to God. In the same way, when we choose to love God and to obey His Word—relying on Jesus' righteousness and walking according to the Spirit—we activate His blessings. But when we choose to disobey God and to rebel against Him, we activate curses, and the effects on our lives can be catastrophic.

How to Be Free from Curses

Paul wrote, "*Christ has redeemed us from the curse of the law, having become a curse for us (for it is written, 'Cursed is everyone who hangs on a tree')*" (Galatians 3:13). Thus, we can say with certainty that the basis on which we are delivered from any curse is the sacrifice of Jesus on the cross as our Representative. Because He was cursed for the sins of the world—including our own iniquities—we have been freed from the curse and can now receive blessings in accordance with His righteousness, which has been credited to us. (See 2 Corinthians 5:21.) "*But [Jesus] was pierced for our transgressions, he was crushed for our iniquities; the punishment that brought us peace was on him, and by his wounds we are healed*" (Isaiah 53:5 NIV).

Again, when Christ paid the price for our iniquities, He also paid for the consequences of our transgressions; He nullified the curses that come as a result of our disobedience to God and His Word. Jesus took our curse so that we could receive His blessing! This work has already been accomplished. (See, for example, John 19:30.) Jesus Christ satisfied the legal issue of our guilt, which was pending against us; He paid the price and settled the entire debt. Now we must take hold of the provision He has made on our behalf. We need to have a personal experience with the results of the cross.

How can we do this? First, by identifying the cause, or entry point, of the curse that is hindering us. If it is a generational curse, you could try to find out when your ancestors were first exposed to it; this information might be obtained by learning the history of your family. However, I believe the best course is to ask the Holy Spirit for revelation regarding the origin of the curse, especially when your family history is sketchy.

Steps to Freedom from Curses

1. Repent of, confess, and renounce all sin committed by you and your ancestors.

2. Renounce the following: all involvement with the occult, witchcraft, and idolatry; all negative proclamations you have made against yourself; all negative words spoken against you from those in authority over you; all negative statements you have proclaimed against yourself; and all curses that have been directed against you by representatives of Satan.

3. Repent for not having honored your parents, for having stolen tithes and offerings from God, for having engaged in any form of illicit sex, for having committed any injustice against the weak or helpless, for having trusted in man more than in God, for having made a vow to God that you did not fulfill, and for not listening to or obeying God's commands.

4. Forgive everyone who has hurt you.

5. Reject your old "DNA," or natural lineage—the iniquity of your bloodline—and declare that the blood of Jesus now enters and cleanses your bloodline. Receive a supernatural blood transfusion through the power of the Holy Spirit.

In order to obtain full healing, deliverance, and transformation, including the redemption of our spiritual DNA, we must apply the work of the cross to our spiritual genes. We must renounce all Satan-incited hatred against the Creator that we inherited due to the perversion of our spiritual DNA after the fall of humanity, with its generational transfer of sin. Through His sacrifice on the cross and His resurrection, Christ put to death the DNA of fallen Adam and enabled us to receive His DNA, one that is holy and pure, having no sin or curse of any kind. Jesus' DNA has a natural love for God and is in right standing with the Father. Everything that humanity lost in Eden in terms of spiritual genetics, Jesus has restored to us.

Prayer of Deliverance

Please pray this prayer out loud for deliverance from generational curses:

Heavenly Father, I praise and adore You. Thank You for Jesus Christ and for the finished work of the cross. I recognize that Jesus paid the price for my rebellion and my transgressions so that I could be free from the curse of iniquity. Today, I go to the cross to take hold of all the blessings that Christ legally won.

Lord Jesus, I believe You are the Son of God and the only way to heaven. I believe that You died for my sins and rose from the dead. As it says in Galatians, You "became a curse" on the cross so that I might be redeemed from the curse of the fall and all its ramifications. I receive my blessing, and from now on I commit to obey Your Word and to follow You all the days of my life, according to the power of the Holy Spirit. I ask for forgiveness for every sin committed by my ancestors that has led to a generational curse. I also release all who have wronged me or committed evil against me. I forgive them as You have forgiven me.

Heavenly Father, I renounce any participation I have had in the practice of witchcraft, the occult, and idolatry, as well as any soul ties or spiritual links with others who have practiced these things. If I own any objects that are connected with these practices, I promise to destroy them right away. Now Lord, I take the authority and power that You have given me as Your child, and I release myself from every curse that has ever come to me. I rebuke and cast out every demon behind any of those curses. I remove all iniquity from within me. I declare myself free. Today, by the blood of Jesus, I am released from all generational curses. In Jesus' name, amen.

9

HOW TO POSSESS
GENERATIONAL BLESSINGS

The term "blessings" is used very lightly by many people today, having become a simple greeting. However, from God's standpoint, a blessing is something very powerful. In the Scriptures, both God and human beings give blessings to reveal, to define, and to establish people's destinies. In fact, the Lord considers blessings to be so important that He called the Israelites—and us—to choose between blessing and cursing, between life and death, depending upon our obedience and relationship to Him. (See Deuteronomy 30:15–19.)

As we have seen, just as curses can be transferred to subsequent generations, blessings can be passed to succeeding generations, as well. In the previous chapter, we examined the definition, reach, and ramifications of generational curses. We learned that we inherit these curses through our bloodline, and that we need a "transfusion" with the blood of Christ to erase inheritances of iniquity so that we can begin to enjoy an inheritance of blessing from God. Generational curses resulting from rebellion and disobedience against God can reach to the fourth generation, but blessings due to love and obedience toward God can last for a thousand generations for those who live according to the principles and laws of His kingdom.

The Nature of God's Blessing

God's blessing is essential for our well-being. One dictionary definition of the word *bless* is "to speak well of." The first thing God did after creating Adam and Eve was to bless them as He revealed their purpose and directed them toward their destiny. *"Then God blessed them, and God said to them, 'Be fruitful and multiply; fill the earth and subdue it; have dominion over the fish of the sea, over the birds of the air, and over every living thing that moves on the earth'"* (Genesis 1:28).

God does the same thing when blessing us: He reveals our purpose and directs us in how to fulfill our destiny. I don't believe we can have a true revelation of our deliverance in Christ if we don't understand the blessing of God. Whomever God calls, He first blesses; and whatever He calls them to do, He blesses so that they can accomplish it. Thus, if we want to enter into His blessings, we must do what He tells us to do; we must fulfill the purpose for which we were created.

Against All Odds

We must realize that the act of blessing someone carries supernatural power. The blessing is a mystery of God, and we need His revelation in regard to our particular situation in order to activate His blessing in our life. For the person who is blessed, even when his circumstances seem primed for things to go badly, they will ultimately go well for him. For example, even if someone lives in a poor country in the midst of a global economic recession; even if there is widespread unemployment and hunger; his success is assured in advance, regardless of his background, culture, nationality, or race.

The best gift or power we can receive is for God to speak well of us, because only under His words of blessing will we prosper and have success in all things. Remember that Joseph endured many trials when he was sold as a slave in Egypt and then unjustly accused and imprisoned; but *"the LORD was with Joseph, and he was a successful man"* (Genesis 39:2), essentially becoming the prime minister of Egypt under Pharaoh.

> *To be blessed is to be supernaturally empowered,*
> *or anointed, to prosper and to have*
> *success against all odds and adversity.*

Are you in a situation where the odds are stacked against your health, your family, your business, or your ministry? What are those odds, specifically? In other words, what are your "impossibilities"? Do you think you are deficient in intelligence or skills? Do you come from a background of poverty or from a single-parent family that didn't have access to the advantages others had? Do you lack the standard qualifications for ministry? Is your business in serious financial trouble? Are you suffering from a terminal disease?

I know what it's like to have all the odds stacked against you. I was born in a small town in the poor country of Honduras, Central America, where opportunities for improvement were practically nonexistent. When I was young, no one believed in me, and I did not have the conventional qualifications for advancement and success. Sometimes, I didn't even have any shoes to wear. But God had a plan for me, and He paved the way for His purposes in my life through the generosity and determination of my father, who saved up enough money to allow me to attend college in the United States. While I was at college in Miami, a fellow student told me about Jesus, and I became a Christian.

Since then, nothing has been able to hinder my progress spiritually, mentally, emotionally, and physically. God found me faithful, removed the curse and shame from me, and blessed me! For example, I became the first person in my family to graduate from college. Then God opened other doors for me, and I was able to attend Bible school. When I went on to serve in ministry, the same process of blessing occurred. At the beginning, our ministry had no finances or other resources. But we always had the Word of God and faith, and that has made all the difference. In terms of numerical growth, our ministry started with twelve people, and now it is a mega-church with a network of more than two hundred associated churches around the world, totaling more than half a million people. Financially, we went from having no property to purchasing land and constructing a large facility—and we have always operated debt-free. Today, we continue to be blessed by the power and grace of our heavenly Father; we are a prosperous ministry with a global impact that transforms lives by the thousands.

Overtaken by Blessings

When we have hearts that are humble and obedient toward God, we can activate His blessings in our lives, and nothing can stop us. God declared to the Israelites, *"And all these blessings shall come upon you and overtake you, because you obey the voice of the LORD your God"* (Deuteronomy 28:2). I can say that I am who I am today because God has blessed me. His blessings have stayed with me and have "overtaken" me. The blessings of God will rise above and beyond anything that seems to stand in our way, including personal crises, adverse government policies, or an unstable global economy. People will know that God is with you when they see that nothing stops you—when you prosper wherever you go and no matter what opposition you face.

The blessing of God
rises above and
beyond all impossibilities.

Concepts and Characteristics Related to Blessings

Let's explore some concepts and characteristics related to blessings so that we can better understand them and how they operate in our lives.

1. Every Blessing Originates from God

Like all other good things in heaven and on earth, blessings come from the Creator God, our Lord and Father. (See James 1:17.) As I mentioned previously, God spoke His first blessing over human beings immediately after creating them. In Genesis 1:28, note that before commissioning human beings to be fruitful and multiply, God first blessed them, because He knew that without His blessing, they could not prosper. Unfortunately, many Christians aren't prospering and bearing fruit today; or, they are prospering in only one area of their lives. If that is your situation, consider your present endeavors and plans, and then ask yourself, "Did God tell me to do this?" Before we start anything, we must be sure we are in the will of God; if we are, then His blessing is assured.

2. God's Blessing Is Supernatural

Since the blessing comes from God, and since He is a supernatural Being who exists above and beyond the laws of nature, we can know that His blessing is a supernatural gift and that its reach is eternal. His blessing possesses and conveys supernatural power to fulfill the destiny of an individual, a family, a nation, and even an entire generation. God's blessing has not only changed my own life but also the lives of hundreds of thousands of people across the world today, and He desires to bless you, as well.

3. God's Blessing Is Transferred Generationally

As we have seen, just as curses can be transferred to subsequent generations, blessings can be passed along to one's children, grandchildren, and later generations. For example, in the Scriptures, God continually emphasizes that He is the God of Abraham (father), of Isaac (son), and of Jacob (grandson). (See, for example, Exodus 3:6.) Thus, the blessings of Abraham's family—of which we are spiritual heirs—were established and strengthened in a tri-generational way. In those three generations, God built and set in motion the promise that He had made to Abraham. He lifted up a great and blessed nation of people that has lasted to this day—the people of Israel. In Abraham's case, in order to initially receive God's blessing and then begin a multigenerational legacy related to that blessing, he had to be separated from the country of his birth and from that of his ancestors. (See Genesis 12:1–3.) Sometimes, we need to start a brand-new heritage in the Lord in our own generation in order to establish God's blessings for the future.

When parents are functioning in the way God intended, their children won't have to begin in the same place they had to; as a result of generational blessings, the children will be able to build on the legacy of their parents. For example, in contrast to my childhood, my natural children grew up lacking no material advantages; they have had proper food, clothing, shelter, and education. They have had no problem getting a good education, and they attend great schools today. The blessing of God has made me successful, and my children will go even farther than I have because they are able to stand upon my shoulders as they move into the future. Likewise, my spiritual children are able to start at the point to which I have progressed and to benefit from what I have learned, received, and overcome. And it is less costly for them. What cost me ten years to attain, costs them only half of that or less. For example, one of my spiritual sons is a pastor in Mexico who began with only forty people three years ago. Now, he has a congregation of about three thousand because of the impartation he receives from the spiritual mantle of our ministry.

Both fathers and mothers are vital to a child's life, and many single mothers are raising children who love God and are being used by Him in remarkable ways—especially as they look to their heavenly Father and to mentors in the church who can help fill the void in their lives where there is no natural father. But God has placed a special responsibility on husbands and fathers as the head of the family, and there are blessings from God that are designed to be conveyed from fathers to their children. This is one of the reasons why the devil aggressively attacks fatherhood and tries to destroy marriages. God wants to lift up the fathers in each generation to transmit His blessings to the generation that follows. Where there is no impartation of fatherhood to nurture succeeding generations—whether for natural or spiritual children—each generation must forge its own path, paying a heavy price in the process. While the children may be very successful, they might not be able to reach the goals they would have achieved if they had started from the accomplishments of the previous generation. Every man carries in his loins several generations, because he has the God-given power to start an inheritance for generations to come. There are times when the blessing jumps a generation, because we must have revelation about God's blessing in order to active it. Therefore, let us be sure to receive the blessings God intends for us, following His plan to use us and our families to bless the world in a multitude of ways.

Faith, the anointing, and the blessing are transferable from parents to their children, from one generation to another.

4. God's Blessing Operates According to Our Choice as We Obey His Principles

As we noted, God asks us to choose between being blessed and being cursed. The Lord desires to bless us, but He cannot make that choice for us. Every time one of His children chooses blessing, that person's life will change for the better; he will prosper and grow, not only spiritually but also in his family life, his profession, his finances, his ministry, and so forth. He will have enough not only for his own needs but also to lift up others in need; and he will leave an inheritance for future generations.

However, let me warn you that to continue in the blessing, you must maintain the principles that activate it. When many Christians start growing and prospering, they cease practicing the principles that led them to prosperity. The principles of the kingdom raised them up from nothing, but once they were blessed, they essentially tossed those principles aside, thinking they did not need them anymore. Their success made them feel important, powerful, and capable in their own strength. As a result, they discarded the foundation that had brought them the blessing. We must take care not to fall into pride or into a sense of self-sufficiency; instead, we must remember that all good gifts come from God.

Even though God has blessed me abundantly, I still need to keep *choosing* the blessing by practicing the principles that activate His blessings. Some of these principles include giving and receiving; sowing and reaping; honoring my heavenly Father; honoring my spiritual parents and other men and women of God; seeking first God's kingdom and His righteousness; defending the helpless; blessing others with whatever God has given me; and serving other people with pure motives of love and compassion.

Accordingly, I choose humility. I choose to show compassion to the sick and afflicted. I choose to work, to show love, and to bear fruit with the gifts God has given me. I choose to stand for justice and truth, never lowering God's standards of holiness, righteousness, and integrity. I choose to seek God's presence and His passion for extending the kingdom. I could never give up doing these things. In pursuing them wholeheartedly, the Lord has blessed me; and I will maintain His blessing by continuing to pursue them. This is what it means to choose the blessing and not the curse. Choose the blessing now!

5. The Blessing Comes upon the Head and Flows Down the Body

"Behold, how good and how pleasant it is for brethren to dwell together in unity! It is like the precious oil upon the head, running down on the beard, the beard of Aaron, running down on the edge of his garments" (Psalm 133:1–2). I believe that Psalm 133 indicates the condition for receiving the blessing, as well as the order in which the blessing comes. The condition is unity, and the divine order, as illustrated in the above passage, is that the blessing first comes upon the "head," or the main authority, and then flows down to all who are subject to that authority. If the proper order is followed, the blessing will flow. If it isn't, there will be a disruption or a stoppage of the flow of blessing. God is looking for people who are in authority in the home, in the church, in the workplace, or in any other area of life who are aligned with His purposes and are living in obedience to Him; He wants to release a blessing over them that will extend to their children, to the members of their congregation, to their employees, and so forth, as well as to subsequent generations.

Accordingly, our own alignment with proper authority is central. If you are in authority in a particular realm of life, and you are not taking responsibility in that area, you will affect not only your own blessing but also the blessing of those who are under your influence. Or, if you have connected yourself to the wrong "head," or if you are not aligned with your proper authority, the blessing will not come to you. However, when the head is in right relationship with God and is fulfilling his responsibilities, then those under him can be blessed. For example, when God supernaturally paid off the mortgage on my house, many of the families and other members of the church had the same thing happen to them. When I started ministering in creative miracles, such as the growth of hair and organs, all my spiritual sons and daughters started operating in same way when they ministered. God wants to bless all of us, but we must first follow the right order.

Consequently, if you are connected with a godly authority, you will prosper as the head prospers. Sometimes, the blessing will reach even to people who are not directly under the covering of that authority but are otherwise associated with it in some way. Such is the power of the divine blessing, as the following testimony illustrates. Pastor Marcelo Salas went from orphanhood and a life of aimlessness and drug abuse to taking hold of the full inheritance that only a genuine son could receive.

"When I was twelve, my father died, resulting in the disintegration of my family. My mother had to work hard to support six children. There was no father figure in our family; thus, we children received little authority or direction, so we all went our own way. I started taking drugs and drinking alcohol at the age of thirteen; by the time I was seventeen, I had dropped out of school. My closest companions were drug dealers and other dangerous people.

"Then I met my future wife, Carmen. We dated for only one month before getting married, and we soon had a child. However, our immaturity, along with my vices, made coexistence impossible. We separated two years later and spent the next seven years apart.

"After this separation, I wanted to change, I needed to change, and knew that if I didn't change, I would die. But I didn't know *how* to change. Desperate, I asked my mother for help, and she took me to a Christian rehabilitation center, where I met God. He forgave my sins, delivered me from my vices, and transformed my life forever. Later, I sought out my wife for reconciliation, and the Lord restored our marriage and family. We both went back to school and graduated as lawyers. Being passionate for evangelism, we visited jails, parks, and anywhere else the Lord sent us to minister to people. We served at our church for a time, but then the apostle of that ministry died, and we were left without a spiritual covering. Our church had few resources. The building had deteriorated, its floor was damaged, and it was full of rats. It was shameful!

"While I was evangelizing and trying to fix up the church building, I would watch Apostle Guillermo Maldonado on TV, and I began to take up his mantle for ministry. I felt that something activated within me when I listened to him. Even without being under his spiritual covering, I took hold of his anointing and put it into practice. One day, a woman came to us whose baby boy had died in her womb; the doctor had told her that the baby would have to be removed, or she would die, too. After we prayed for the woman, the baby's heart resumed beating, and he started to move! It was our first resurrection!

"Two of Apostle Maldonado's books have impacted me greatly—*The Glory of God* and *Jesus Heals Your Sickness Today!* God started performing miracles in our services, and people began to be healed and delivered as soon as they entered the church. Out of gratitude to God, the people of the congregation started tithing and giving offerings. We went from having nothing to having a million and a half dollars, and we were able to buy a new building. We have grown and expanded in a very short time. Additionally, we now have three drug rehabilitation centers—one for men, one for women, and one for children. It has been incredible to see how our small numbers have grown to thousands. It is all due to God and to the vision of King Jesus Ministry, through which our growth has accelerated. Now, people who formerly rejected us and criticized us come to us to find out how we are able to do what we are doing.

"Through his books and messages on TV, Apostle Maldonado challenged me to be coherent and consistent with what I preach. I also learned that receiving fatherhood and covering from a ministry does not mean merely having the use of a ministry logo or being given a VIP seat, but rather using the tools I am being given in order to succeed. Before, I had been a loser, but when I received the benefits of spiritual fatherhood, it brought immense blessing to my life. Today, I am a son, in complete exercise of my inheritance as such, and I am blessed so that I can bless others."

The blessing of God can come through the law of association.

6. God's Special Blessing Comes upon the Firstborn

Under Jewish law, the firstborn son received a double portion of his father's blessing. (See, for example, Deuteronomy 21:17.) We must understand that God has enabled all believers to receive the blessing of the firstborn through Jesus Christ. He is *"the firstborn among many brethren"* (Romans 8:29), and He willingly shares all of the Father's inheritance with us. (See Romans 8:32.)

I believe the principle of the firstborn was in effect even prior to the giving of the law. Esau and Jacob, the children of Abraham's son Isaac, were twins. Yet Esau was the firstborn because he came out of the womb first. By the principle of the firstborn, the fullness of the blessing in double portion belonged to Esau. However, Jacob desired the blessing so much that he decided to fight for it, so he bargained to obtain his brother's birthright and then used deceit to obtain the blessing. (See Genesis 25:24–26, 29–34; 27:1–40.) Although God intended for Jacob to receive the blessing (see Genesis 25:22–23), Jacob took matters into his own hands and suffered various consequences for his actions; for instance, he had to leave his home, and he never saw his mother alive again. If things don't appear to be going according to God's plan for you, you must rely on Him to work things out rather than trying to move things along yourself. You should always earnestly pursue God and His blessing with a pure heart.

7. God's Blessing Depends upon Our Obedience to Him

God blesses us when we obey Him. When we rebel against Him, the fullness of His blessing cannot be manifested. A hindered blessing does not change God's unconditional love for us, but obedience is the foundational kingdom principle for receiving His blessing. If you are rebellious and disobedient, you are acting according to the sin nature, which is cursed; consequently, God's blessing cannot flow in your life.

Ultimately, the blessing of God is based on the fact that He created human beings in His own image and likeness, and everything that God blessed them with enabled them to reflect His glory as they fulfilled their destiny. Then, with Adam and Eve's disobedience and fall, God's image and likeness in humanity became distorted; thus, we lost the blessing and were placed under the curse. But the blessing has been reinstated! Christ redeemed us from the curse and restored God's image and likeness in us, so that we can again reflect His nature and activate His blessings.

Many people today are asking themselves, "Why am I not being blessed in this area of my life?" If you are among them, could it be that, in some way, you are disobeying God in that area? The divine blessing was designed to be eternal, not temporary; therefore, it applies only to that which is within God's eternal will. It is not subject to our whims or temporary desires. Previously, we noted that we are not meant to jump into an endeavor and *then* seek God's approval for it. It is presumptuous to assume that we should be involved in something without first knowing if it is His will. The correct order is to understand the will of God and then to act upon that will in faith, knowing that, from beginning to end, our blessing rests on our obedience. Frequently, if there is no indication of God's blessing (even in the midst of opposition), we can know that whatever we are trying to do is not His will. Let us always start with knowing and obeying the will of God.

From the beginning of our ministry, God made it clear that the ministry was His will for us and that He would be with us. His blessings have come to us in the form of financial provision and other resources, miracles, deliverances, salvations, and special favor. God has been faithful to His Word, and we have never lacked anything. For over twenty-five years, His blessings have been consistent and continuous for me, for my family, and for our ministry. I give all the glory to God for this. And again, the blessing of God does not apply only to me; if it was possible for me, then it is possible for you!

8. God's Blessing Is Transmitted or Imparted by Words, but It Is Often Sealed with Hands

Spoken words of blessing hold supernatural power. God told Abraham, *"And I will make My covenant between Me and you, and will multiply you exceedingly"* (Genesis 17:2). Moreover, the priest Melchizedek, whom the Bible describes as a type of Jesus (see, for example, Hebrews 6:20), spoke words of blessing to Abraham, saying, *"Blessed be Abram [Abraham] of God Most High, possessor of heaven and earth; and blessed be God Most High, who has delivered your enemies into your hand"* (Genesis 14:19–20). The Lord's promises to bless Abraham, and through him to bless all the nations of the earth, were promises that would benefit all of humanity through Christ. (See Genesis 18:18; 26:4.) And all those words of blessing have been fulfilled—and are still being fulfilled today.

Although words hold power, there is also something supernatural about the spiritual laying on of hands or the raising of the hands toward someone; I believe that through these practices, we are able to both impart and seal blessings. For example, in the Old Testament, Jacob placed his hands on the heads of Joseph's two sons as he blessed them. (See Genesis 28:13–20.) In another illustration, after Aaron the high priest, on behalf of the Lord, ministered atonement for the Israelites through various animal sacrifices, he lifted his hand toward the people and conveyed on them a spiritual blessing. (See Leviticus 9:22.) In the New Testament, before Jesus multiplied the loaves and the fish to feed five thousand people, He first took the food in His hands and blessed it. (See, for example, Matthew 14:18–20.) When Jesus healed people, He would sometimes make a declaration of healing, but other times He would place His hands on them for healing, such as when He healed the leper. (See Matthew 8:3.) In a further example, Paul wrote to his spiritual son, Timothy, *"Therefore I remind you to stir up the gift of God which is in you through the laying on of my hands"* (2 Timothy 1:6). The blessing of a spiritual gift was bestowed on Timothy when Paul laid hands on him. Similarly, today, parents can bless their children, pastors can bless the members of their congregation, and other delegated authorities can bless those who are under them through words of blessing—and often through the laying on of hands or the raising of the hands toward them.

For the fullness of the blessing to manifest, it must be spoken and then sealed with the laying on of hands.

9. God's Blessing Is Activated When We 'Have God's Faith'

When you know there is a blessing upon your life that has yet to manifest, you must activate it with words spoken out loud and in faith. Faith is the "currency" of heaven, giving us access to the promises of God. (See, for example, Hebrews 6:12.) Jesus indicated how we can address the challenges and obstacles of life when He said,

> *Have faith in God. For assuredly, I say to you, whoever **says** to this mountain, "Be removed and be cast into the sea," and does not doubt in his heart, but believes that those things he **says** will be done, he will have whatever he **says**.* (Mark 11:22–23)

A more literal translation of the statement *"Have faith in God"* is "Have God's faith." Again, everything begins with God and His eternal will. Only if we start there can we exercise genuine faith to fulfill His will and to see His blessings activated in our lives.

10. God's Blessing Always Comes with Instructions

When God blesses someone, He immediately indicates how that person is to use the blessing; He reveals the purpose of His supernatural favor and how to implement it. Again, God's blessing is intimately tied to our purpose and destiny. For example, even though Saul was a persecutor of the church, the Lord extended to him the blessing of mercy and forgiveness. This blessing was manifested when Jesus appeared to Saul on the road to Damascus and commissioned him as an apostle of the church. (See Acts 26:15–18.)

11. God's Blessing Is a Sign That He Is with Us

When a God-fearing person is blessed, we can be sure that the Lord is working in his life, providing favor and all the resources he needs to carry out his calling. It is true that people who disregard the Lord and engage in evil pursuits sometimes accumulate great wealth and other material advantages. However, the Scriptures tell us that their prosperity is temporary and earthly; in the end, they will lose everything. (See, for example, Psalm 73.) We must choose blessing, so that God's presence will remain with us always.

Supernatural Effects of God's Blessing

In the previous chapter, we learned that curses supernaturally empower people to fail, even if all the conditions for success are present. Conversely, blessings have a supernatural power to lead us to success, despite all odds. Let us take a closer look at the effects of God's blessing.

1. God's Blessing Preserves, Protects, and Provides

If human beings were meant to exist without the blessing of God, why would God's first act after creating Adam and Eve be to bless them? Again, God's blessing includes His continuing presence in our lives. He preserves us from evil, protects us during crises, and enables us to fulfill our purpose in this world and for eternity. For example, one time, after I had ministered at a conference in Honduras, I was followed by seven men with guns and rifles who robbed me and held me and the others who were with me at gunpoint for forty-five minutes. I prayed nonstop for supernatural protection, and the men finally left. God had preserved our lives. Additionally, over the years, God has preserved our ministry spiritually, so that we have continued to preach the pure gospel with pure doctrine. Furthermore, He has provided for all of our material needs; again, we have never lacked anything we needed, and as I wrote earlier, our ministry has always been debt-free.

2. God's Favor Is the Evidence of His Blessing

Favor is the first stage of God's blessing, and we have to keep our discernment exercised so that His favor does not pass by us unnoticed. When you overlook the favor of God, you also overlook His blessing. Likewise, when you reject the favor of God, you reject His blessing.

What forms does favor take? God will place people in your life who are willing to help you and to serve you as you seek to fulfill His purposes. He will open new doors and opportunities for you. The demonstration of His favor is a sign that His blessing is upon you, and your role is to take the opportunities He gives you and develop them for His glory.

God can use someone whom others would least expect—in fact, He often does. Perhaps, in your eyes, that person is "nobody," but to God, he is the right person because God's eyes see what man's eyes do not. (See, for example, 1 Samuel 16:1–13.) Furthermore, God is sovereign, and He does whatever He wants to through whomever He chooses. His favor positioned Joseph in the court of Pharaoh in order to bless His people during a time of famine. (See Genesis 50:20.) And He desires to give us favor, too, enabling us to be a blessing to others. He has given us things that He wants us to share with others—gifts, ideas, resources, visions, callings, ministries, and more—but without the divine favor that accompanies God's blessing, we won't be able to do much, if anything, with what He has given us.

No human being can decide whom God chooses to bless.

3. God's Blessing Is the Line That Divides His Children from Others

That which is blessed never diminishes but rather increases, multiplies, and extends higher and higher, because the blessing of God does not know decline. It enables us to live according to the properties of the kingdom of God, which include stability and expansion. The blessing is recession-proof and hunger-proof; it does not conform to the circumstances or problems of the world but proceeds according to the economy of God's kingdom. That is why, even in the midst of global economic recessions and shortages, the children of God are "the head and not the tail, above and not beneath." (See Deuteronomy 28:13.) Thus, the blessing of God will mark the line between your family and others' families, between your ministry and others' ministries, between your business and others' businesses, and so forth, as you live in obedience to Him.

4. God's Blessing Prospers All Areas of Life

"The blessing of the Lord makes one rich, and He adds no sorrow with it" (Proverbs 10:22). When the blessing of God is upon you, you will prosper in whatever you do. Moreover, it will be impossible for you to fail, because your ability to prosper comes from your very essence as a child of God who walks in his purpose. Again, the principle is similar to the nature of the curse, in which a person is supernaturally empowered to fail. But the power of supernatural blessing is infinitely stronger. The blessing comes from a state of being—from being a child of God who does not try to use worldly methods of success but rather remains obedient to Him and to the principles of His kingdom.

However, keep in mind that when you prosper materially or otherwise, you may be persecuted at the hands of "religious" people who believe that poverty comes from God. Their doctrine teaches that the poorer you are, the holier you are, but this idea is a lie from the devil. Other people believe that prosperity is a sign of vanity or of a lack of humility. But God desires to prosper His people so that they can extend

His kingdom and bring more souls to salvation in Christ. That is the reason He blesses us!

We have seen that the condition for our being fruitful and multiplying, for our having productive lives, is to first be blessed by God. As we noted, He first blessed Adam before authorizing him to be fruitful and multiply, and the same principle is true for us. God has to pronounce the blessing first; this is the key to our productiveness. Jesus chooses us and appoints us to be fruitful for the kingdom, bearing lasting fruit. (See John 15:16.) Thus, when God blesses you, He places you in locations and circumstances where you will be fruitful. If God has told you to do something—He may even give you a direct prophetic word about your assignment—He will bless you in it as you remain obedient and submitted to Him. The moment God speaks to you, blessing you to fulfill a purpose, you are guaranteed to be successful in it as you look to Him for your provision. What "place" are you in right now? Is your life fruitful or barren? Prosperous or stagnant? As I emphasized earlier, before you undertake to do something, you must make sure that God has blessed you in it and directed you to do it.

5. The Supernatural Blessing of God Is Given According to Our Purpose

Understanding your God-given purpose expands your mind, your dreams, and your expectations. Accordingly, prosperity will begin the moment you know your purpose on earth and begin to act on it. Your purpose brings the blessing of the One who called you—your Father and Creator. Essentially, when you find your purpose, you will find your prosperity. And as you enter into God's favor and move further into fulfilling that purpose, you will receive even more blessings and resources—everything will accelerate. Generally, if you live outside your God-given purpose on earth, you might have just enough provision to meet your needs, but you will not have enough to be a blessing to others in the ways God wants you to be.

The blessing of God has the power
to accelerate us in every area of life
and to enable us to bless others.

God told Abraham, "*I will make you a great nation; I will bless you and make your name great; and you shall be a blessing*" (Genesis 12:2). Again, if you have only enough to get by, you cannot be a blessing to others. You will feel a need to keep what you have for yourself. There are people who are content at this level; they represent the servant in the parable of the talents who received one talent and promptly went and buried it for "safekeeping." (See Matthew 25:14–30.) They have a mentality that says, "I want enough for me and my family, and that's it. I do not ask for more." They don't realize that this is a mentality of deficiency and selfishness that does not see past itself or its present circumstances. That is not a kingdom mentality! You must change your mind-set of deficiency to a mind-set of abundance, overabundance…and even more! We develop this mind-set when we step out with faith into our purpose.

When you operate from need instead
of from purpose, you might have enough,
but you will never have abundance.

The Impact of Blessing

When someone is blessed by God, it is as evident as it is impacting. The following is a wonderful testimony from Darvin of Guatemala that clearly demonstrates the blessing of God operating in the life of an individual. "Ever since the Lord allowed us to be under the covering of our spiritual parents, Apostle Guillermo Maldonado and Prophet Ana Maldonado, the blessing has been overflowing. The year 2014 has marked our life forever. Daniel, my fifteen-year-old son, was playing soccer in school when he hit his ahead against the bleachers and died instantly. When the emergency medical technicians arrived and declared him dead, a friend of my daughter Rebeca called her to tell her what had happened. But instead of falling apart, Rebeca went running to her brother and placed her hands on his body. She did not ask God why this had happened but instead thanked Him for His infinite love and mercy, declaring that He would fulfill His purpose in Daniel. At that moment, my son began to breathe again! As a precaution, he was taken to the hospital, but he was soon released. The medical bill for his hospital stay and other medical services was very high, but the hospital informed me that the bill had been taken care of—someone had already paid it electronically!

"Also, in June of 2014, an earthquake struck our city of San Marcos in Guatemala, and there was great destruction. My own house sank half a foot on one side, and the authorities told us we had to evacuate the area, saying it was very dangerous to stay in our home. We decided to go to church to pray, to worship, to praise, and, most important, to thank God, knowing that everything would work out in our favor. We returned to the house, where we anointed the walls, believing for a miracle. A few minutes later, the builders called us, saying that something strange was happening. The house was straightening itself out! Only a short time later, the house had returned to its original position. God had literally straightened my house, and many people were there to witness it!

"In addition, we received a supernatural provision of finances. We had originally taken out a loan of about $270,000 dollars when we built our house. But we received a call from the bank manager who told us, 'I don't know what you have with God, or what God has with you, but I can't go to sleep without first asking you to stop by on Monday to sign the settlement for the house. You owe the bank nothing.' God completely paid off the mortgage for our house. This is why I cannot keep my testimony quiet. God has been good, and His blessing has been poured out over us as His children. I thank Him eternally, and I declare that my family and I will serve Him forever. Let all honor and glory be to God!"

How to Possess the Blessing of God

We need God's wisdom for everything we desire to attain in Him. Our natural mind cannot grasp or decipher the mysteries that belong to the supernatural world. Thus, we need to know and follow the principles of His supernatural wisdom for obtaining the blessings that He has prepared for His children. The following steps will enable you to live in the blessings of God.

1. *Understand and accept that Jesus carried our curses on the cross so that we could receive His blessings.*

> *Christ has redeemed us from the curse of the law, having become a curse for us (for it is written, "Cursed is everyone who hangs on a tree"), that the blessing of Abraham might come upon the Gentiles in Christ Jesus, that we might receive the promise of the Spirit through faith.* (Galatians 3:13–14)

If you believe that you "deserve" God's blessings, you are wrong—and you won't receive them. Every material, emotional, mental, physical, and spiritual blessing has been provided by Christ and has been given to us by grace for the purposes of furthering God's kingdom. We do not deserve these blessings; we could never earn them on our own merits. But, because of His love, God has blessed us, and He enables us to use His blessings on behalf of others. As we have seen, a divine blessing is not given to be selfishly enjoyed, and it is never bestowed without the resources necessary for its operation and usefulness. Therefore, if God has healed you, He wants you to minister healing to others. If God has prospered you, He wants you to sow into His kingdom and be a blessing to other people spiritually, intellectually, financially, and so forth. Remember also that God's purposes are never about only a single individual or even that person's generation; the Father sees multiple generations into the future.

2. Place your faith in the finished work of the cross. Jesus completed the work of the cross in order to reconcile us with the Father; His sacrifice removed the curse from our lives and opened the door for us to receive God's blessing. He redeemed us, He gave us health, and He prospered us. He restored to us everything that had been retained in eternity since the fall of mankind, when sin separated human beings from their Creator. Paul wrote, *"Blessed be the God and Father of our Lord Jesus Christ, who has blessed us with every spiritual blessing in the heavenly places in Christ"* (Ephesians 1:3). Our blessings are in *"heavenly places."* I believe that this expression refers to heavenly areas, domains, territories, nations, and worlds that have counterparts on earth. In other words, the kingdom is manifested in many different realms on earth that mirror those in heaven, such as the realms of business, economics, the arts, education, science, and sports.

The blessing of God will manifest in the primary realm to which we are assigned, according to His purpose. Many believers are not receiving God's blessings because they are functioning outside the realm He intended for them. Others don't receive His blessings because they are not living by faith. They are living by "hope," or wishful thinking; or they living in the past. But faith lives in the now, and only in the now. This means that we can bring God's blessings into our lives today—here and now. If you live according to earthly parameters, you will often find yourself in a continuous state of waiting, when you could be bringing heaven to earth by faith and possessing God's blessings right now.

Faith is the future that
God calls "now."

3. Fight for your blessings. We frequently need to engage in spiritual warfare in order to receive the blessings that have been promised to us. Thus, before God's blessings are manifested in our lives, we have to do battle. Some of our battles will involve our struggle to die to our sinful nature and our self-centeredness so that we can move into God's presence and receive His revelation and supernatural power. Other battles will involve fighting against the attacks of the enemy, who seeks to rob us God's blessings. No matter what battles we face, we cannot give up; we must contend for our blessings!

Although Jesus has completed the work of salvation, He wants us to appropriate that work, a theme we will discuss more in the next chapter. The enemy attacks us by trying to get us to disobey God and thereby to introduce curses into our bloodline. His plan is not to tempt us with a "small" sin today and another "small" sin tomorrow. Rather, his sights are set on our spiritual inheritance; he not only goes after us, but he also goes after subsequent generations. He tries to blind us so that we cannot see the blessings that God wants to give us, because he knows it is impossible for us to enter into God's abundance and to fulfill our purpose without them.

From Genesis to Revelation, we see evidence that the enemy has always fought for territory—especially the territory of human souls— and that, in one sense, human beings have always needed to fight to receive the blessings of God. For example, Jacob wrestled with a powerful *"Man"* the night before he had to face his volatile twin brother Esau for the first time in twenty years. *"Then Jacob was left alone; and a Man wrestled with him until the breaking of day.…And He said, 'Let Me go, for the day breaks.' But [Jacob] said, 'I will not let You go unless You bless me!'"* (Genesis 32:24, 26).

Christ did His part by paying the price for our sin and by defeating the enemy on the cross. He did what we never could have done; He delivered us from the curse, and He opened the door to allow the Father's blessing to flow into our lives. Now, we must do our part, which consists of fighting for that blessing and possessing it, just as Joshua and the

Israelites had to fight for possession of the Promised Land, the land that God had given to them as an inheritance.

Sometimes, we think that our current position or situation is our place of blessing, until we realize that we have outgrown it. We are ready to progress to a new place when the place we are currently in has begun to seem very small to us. We might begin to sense the prompting of God moving us on to the next level; or we might feel the pressure of demonic opposition against the plans that God is unfolding in our lives. But to enter our next territory, we must wage war.

4. *Obey the priorities of God.* Jesus said, *"But seek first the kingdom of God and His righteousness, and all these things shall be added to you"* (Matthew 6:33). God's blessing is activated when we are aligned with His priorities. If we put Him first in our lives, He releases His blessing. Whatever you place first in your life is your "god." What is number one for you? Is it your business, your family, your education, your personal goals, or something else? When you give God the supreme place in your heart, He will never be your second thought or a lesser option. When His priorities become your priorities, you will be a clear vessel in which His blessings can flow, with no obstacles blocking their path.

Prayer and Declaration of Blessing

As an apostle, a pastor, and a spiritual father in the church of Jesus Christ, I want to bless you. Receive this prayer and declaration:

Heavenly Father, I come before Your presence according to the merits of Your Son Jesus Christ. Thank You for the many blessings You have given me so that I can be a blessing to others. What You have freely given me, I freely give to others. Therefore, to this reader, whom You love, I say, "I bless you, and I remove every curse and every negative word that anyone has been spoken against your life. And now, as an authority in the church of Christ, I release God's blessing into your life, and I empower you to prosper. I declare that everything you touch will be successful, and that the favor and grace of God will accompany you. I declare that you will succeed despite any negative or challenging circumstances. May the Lord release over you all the blessings that Jesus won on the cross. I declare that you are blessed with health in your body, health in your mind, and health in your soul. You will be fruitful, and you will multiply wherever you go. Against all odds, I declare that you are blessed and prosperous." In Jesus' name, amen!

10

HOW TO APPROPRIATE THE
BENEFITS OF THE CROSS

There is eternal, supernatural power in the finished work of the cross of Jesus Christ. The cross provides us with numerous benefits in both the spiritual and physical realms, but many believers fail to take ownership of them because they lack revelation knowledge of what actually took place when Christ sacrificed His life on our behalf. If we were to ask Christians what benefits Jesus won on the cross, most would not know how to answer. They might understand that Jesus died for their sins, but that's about as far as their revelation goes. There is so much more for us to understand and receive. God wants us to appropriate *all* the benefits of the cross in our lives and to minister them to others, as well.

The Effects of Jesus' Finished Work on the Cross

Why don't believers know more about the powerful benefits of the cross? The main reason is that the enemy has launched a severe attack against our knowledge of the cross. Satan wants to eclipse the gospel of the kingdom that Jesus preached—a message of power centered on His death and resurrection—with doctrines of men that do not produce power. These doctrines are based on natural thinking rather than on the supernatural; they are focused on trying to change people by human strength or intellectual reasoning rather than by the wisdom of God. Consequently, any changes that occur in people's lives in relation to them are incomplete or temporary. They can never provide the lasting, *supernatural* transformation that the cross makes available to us.

Second, to a great extent, our lack of deeper knowledge about the cross is the result of a serious problem in the church. Although most preachers and other Christian leaders, including those in educational institutions, teach about many godly matters, they rarely talk about the *effects* of Jesus' finished work besides that of salvation from hell. While salvation is vital, being forgiven for our sins so that we can go to heaven one day is really just the starting place in God's plan of redemption for His people.

Essentially, in a number of Christian churches, a *"different gospel"* (see 2 Corinthians 11:4) is being presented. The dynamic message of the cross is being replaced with what is basically a self-help message that is more popular with people, thus winning their favor. Inspirational or motivational messages may be good for the emotions, but they won't change people's hearts or release the inheritance that belongs to the children of God. That happens only when the cross is preached!

Even many leaders in the charismatic church have moved away from the message of the cross. They present a "gospel" of faith for the acquisition of material goods and for achieving other temporary goals rather than a gospel of faith for manifesting the eternal power of Jesus' death and resurrection. Consequently, many of the truths about the finished work of the cross are being excluded from the teaching in our churches and Bible institutes, leaving believers with an incomplete understanding of Jesus' sacrifice. And society as a whole knows even less about the real meaning of the cross.

The gospel of "self-help" has replaced the message of the cross.

The apostle Paul wrote, *"For the message of the cross is foolishness to those who are perishing, but to us who are being saved it is the power of God"* (1 Corinthians 1:18). On the whole, the church of this century seems to consider the message of the cross as *"foolishness."* It has adopted an intellectual mentality based on Greek philosophy in which reality is defined by human reason rather than by God's truth. If we are not careful, our own beliefs and teaching will shift from the power of God's truth to powerless theory. Man-made philosophies sometimes include stirring ideas and fascinating information, but they are ultimately lifeless because, again, they are unable to produce lasting change. The message of the cross may not the most popular message at present, but it is eternal truth; it was given for all people of all times, *"yesterday, today, and forever"* (Hebrews 13:8), and it produces enduring results.

No person can be aligned with the life of heaven outside of the cross.

The Christ Who Died on the Cross

Most people acknowledge the historical fact that a Man named Jesus lived in Palestine in the first century and died on a cross. But many of them dispute Jesus' identity as the divine Son of God, and that standpoint exposes the error of their core beliefs. In many religions, Jesus is considered to be a "great teacher," a "good man," or a "prophet of God." He is certainly all of those things—but much more!

Jesus is the second Person of the Trinity, which consists of God the Father, God the Son, and God the Holy Spirit. Jesus is God in the flesh—the God who is also 100 percent Man, and the Man who is also 100 hundred percent God. God came to earth in the form of a Man to be our Substitute and Savior, because it was impossible for us to atone for our own sins. Jesus' mission was to restore human beings to their original condition before the fall of humanity. If He had not come, we would be eternally lost.

Jesus' death paid the price for the sins of humanity, terminating the consequences of the fall and changing the destiny of all who believe in Him. No other belief system or religion has been founded on a leader, a prophet, or an enlightened individual who has given His life to atone for the sins of the whole world—even the sins of those who hated Him and killed Him. No other belief system or religion in the world can compare with the message of the gospel, which proclaims the benefits of the cross and the power of the resurrection. The philosophies that are the foundation of other groups and religions are based on abstract speculation, but the cross—the foundation of faith for Jesus' followers—is a historical fact grounded in reality. Not only that, but the event of the cross was established in eternity before the world was even created. The Scriptures say that Jesus is *the Lamb slain from the foundation of the world*" (Revelation 13:8). The cross is therefore both an indisputable historical event and an eternal reality.

*The work of Jesus Christ on the cross is an
undeniable, unarguable, unchangeable, irrevocable,
total, permanent, finished, and eternal reality.*

What Is "the Cross"?

When I speak of "the cross," I am referring to much more than two planks of wood nailed together to form a means of execution. The cross is Jesus' sacrifice of Himself, in which He died for the sins of humanity. Jesus Christ humbly surrendered His body to be crucified for our sake. But even before Jesus was nailed to the cross, He was cruelly tortured by Roman soldiers. He was beaten (see, for example, Mark 14:65), His beard was plucked out, He was spit upon (see, for example, Isaiah 50:6), and He was whipped (see, for example, Mark 15:15). The whips used for such purposes were made out of woven belts with small pieces of lead and sharp pieces of bone or sheep's teeth. These fragments pierced the body, ripped out pieces of flesh, and drew blood with each strike. Jesus' tormentors also placed a crown of thorns on His head, causing acute pain. (See, for example, John 19:2.) Enduring all this, Jesus' body was disfigured, and it bled from every wound.

Then, the soldiers placed a heavy wooden plank on His shoulders and upper back—already horribly raw from the whipping—and forced Him to carry it toward the site of His crucifixion, a place called Golgotha. When He finally arrived at the mount of crucifixion, enormous nails were hammered into His wrists and feet, and He was lifted up on that cross to suffer a slow death by asphyxiation.

The cross is Jesus' sacrifice of Himself,

in which He died for the sins of humanity.

Has there been any other suffering and death as torturous and disfiguring as that of Jesus? It would be hard to imagine. But even if there has been, no other human being has ever had to suffer in the way I just described while, at the same time, carrying on himself the crushing weight of all the sins, rebellions, and transgressions of the entire human race. In this way, the "weight" that was nailed to that wooden plank was infinitely heavier than the weight of one human man.

The Son of God's death on the cross was a terrible spectacle, one of such great humiliation and rejection that Satan thought he had won the ultimate victory over God. However, I'm sure that Good Friday is a day the enemy will never forget, because from the moment he made the mistake of inciting the crucifixion of Christ, his reign on earth ended. When Jesus died for our sins, His spirit descended into hell, where He conquered Satan in the spiritual realm. (See, for example, Ephesians 4:8–10.) Moreover, supernatural power was released that enabled us to be free from Satan's grasp, so that we could be saved, healed, delivered, and transformed. I can therefore understand why the apostle Paul declared, in effect, "I do not want to know or preach about anything except the cross; I do not want to hear another perspective or another new doctrine, but only Christ crucified." (See 1 Corinthians 2:2.)

Every deliverance must be

ministered from the cross.

No other death has had the effect on the world that Christ's has, because, as we have seen, His death was an unprecedented event that occurred both in this world *and* in eternity. For this reason, the cross is effective to deal with the sins of our past, our present, and our future; it is able to cleanse the iniquity that travels in our bloodline—the sins of our ancestors and of our parents, as well as our own sins. It has made provision for the mistakes we will make tomorrow, if we believe today in its power of redemption.

The results of the cross are still in effect today, just as they were in the past.

Essential Aspects of the Cross

If we want to receive full deliverance from sin and its consequences, we must have a clear understanding of what Jesus accomplished on the cross, and why. Let's explore some primary truths about Jesus' sacrifice on our behalf.

1. On the Cross, Christ Supplied Total Provision for Humanity

Again, everything we need for the past, for the present, for the future, and even for eternity has been provided by Christ on the cross. He released supernatural power to meet every spiritual, mental, emotional, financial, and material need. What do you require today? What do you lack spiritually, mentally, emotionally, financially, or materially? Jesus provided the solution thousands of years ago—you simply need to *receive* it now.

> When the church is ignorant about
> the finished work of the cross,
> it cannot receive its total provision.

Until we look to the cross, we will always be looking for some other way to solve our individual problems and the problems of the world. There is no other way, there is no other source, that will lead us to full and lasting deliverance than the cross; otherwise, Jesus' sacrifice would not have been required. Nothing but the finished work of Jesus can save, heal, and deliver. I could provide testimony after testimony of those who came to Jesus Christ in order to receive the help they needed when they could not find it anywhere else. In the following account, Alejandro, a thirty-year-old from a Cuban-Colombian background, shares one of these testimonies.

"I had worshipped the devil for sixteen years before I came to know the Truth. I had upside-down crosses implanted into my body, scarification marks of upside-down crosses put on my back, and diabolical images tattooed on me. I also practiced Santeria and witchcraft. I started all of that because, as a teenager, I had a lot of anger. I was always depressed and getting into fights; I would even punch holes into walls. In addition, I went through two failed marriages. I never wanted to go out, and I was usually alone; I just wanted to stay home in the dark. Then I got fascinated with the devil. I would feel his presence and have dreams about him. I split my tongue to be like a serpent's and made other modifications to my body in order to look more like him. I also influenced other people to change their appearance to look like him; I made them color their eyes with injections, implant horns into their heads, and get tattoos. I made them worship the devil; I was making disciples for Satan. Furthermore, I looked for satanic movies to watch, downloaded diabolical music, read the satanic bible, and became a member of the satanic church. I drew pentagrams on the ground with candles and went to graveyards to call Satan to come to me. I wanted to see him. Everything associated with death fascinated me.

"Meanwhile, my family believed in God and wanted me to believe in Him, too; they wanted me to go to church, but I would only laugh at them. I didn't believe in Jesus, and I made fun of Him. But my family prayed for me. The truth was that although I did lots of things associated with the devil, I still was not satisfied. Something was missing. A part of me was empty; I wasn't happy with myself. I had thought the devil was the answer, but he wasn't. It didn't matter what I did, I wasn't able to fill that emptiness.

"One day, I went to the gym and met a guy who talked to me about the gospel. I started going to a House of Peace [home fellowship ministry], then to church and to a discipleship program. Eventually, I went to a CAP [Apostolic and Prophetic Conference], where I experienced God's presence. I felt a burning sensation from my head to my feet. Jesus filled me; His presence was what I had been missing all my life, and was all I needed to fill the void. From that moment, everything started to change. I went to a retreat and received the revelation of the finished work of the cross, learning about what Jesus did there, and was set free from all of Satan's influences.

"Christ defeated the god I had been serving, and He delivered me from his shackles. Thanks to Jesus' work on the cross, I am not angry anymore; I am not down or depressed. I am actually really happy now. I have changed so much that people don't recognize me. Jesus set my life free, and now I evangelize to everyone I knew before, telling them about Jesus. They can see the change in me because they know how I used to be. Before I accepted Jesus, my parents were always there for me, but I didn't care about them, and we did not have the close relationship we enjoy now. My first marriage had lasted two months, and my second marriage three months; now, after having accepted God, my third marriage has lasted for a year, and everything is going well. I love my family. I am now able to show them all my love, and I can receive their love, as well. Thanks be to Jesus and His completed work on the cross!"

2. The Cross Is the Highest Expression of the Love of God

God's sacrifice of His own Son was the highest demonstration of His love for humanity. *"But God demonstrates His own love toward us, in that while we were still sinners, Christ died for us"* (Romans 5:8). While we were still sinners—prideful, selfish, bitter, revengeful, backbiting, gossiping, disdainful, hateful, greedy, envious, arrogant, unjust, pursuers of recognition and fame, sexually immoral, liars, cheats, extortionists, abusers, murderers, and so on—Christ died for us!

Even in our fallen state as sinners, with hearts in rebellion against Him, God chose to love us with His unconditional love. His first and highest expression of that love was a sacrifice, because, again, it took place in eternity—before the foundation of the world—where Jesus, the Lamb of God, was slain for us. Even before creating us, God deeply loved us—loved you and me—and made provision for our salvation and deliverance.

> *God's sacrifice of His own Son was the highest demonstration of His love for humanity.*

To the earthly mind-set, it will always be a mystery why an innocent man should have to die for the guilty. In fact, no death is surrounded with as much controversy as Jesus' death. Perhaps that is because His death changed history, and our acceptance or rejection of His sacrifice determines our eternal future. Similarly, God's love for human beings will always be a mystery to Satan. The Father's plan for humanity was manifested through the death of His own Son. The devil never imagined that Jesus would save the world by dying on that cross; instead, he thought that Christ's death would seal God's utter defeat! In some ways,

God's love is incomprehensible to us, as well. Even in our worst condition, God loved us with the greatest love possible; His love goes beyond
our reason and understanding. But if we can accept God's love for us,
even though we can't fully comprehend it, and if we can understand the
principles of the cross through revelation, then we can receive all the
benefits of Christ's finished work.

> *The cross is a constant reminder that*
> *God deeply loves us and is always*
> *thinking about us.*

3. Jesus Released His Supernatural Grace Through the Cross

The cross satisfied the justice of God, which demands a reckon-
ing or punishment for sin. His righteous nature does not allow for the
restoration of anyone who has offended Him and His Word unless a
sacrifice of blood has been made. This is because, as the Scriptures tell
us, *"the life of the flesh is in the blood"* (Leviticus 17:11). As we have seen,
Jesus' provision on the cross is not something we can earn or deserve;
it is received only by grace. And at the cross, supernatural grace was
released that empowers us to be and do what we can't be and do in our
own strength. Now we can live above sin and above our circumstances.

> *Supernatural grace begins*
> *where human strength ends.*

4. The Cross Releases God's Supernatural Confirmation of His Word

The gospel message carries the delivering power that Jesus released when He paid for the sin—as well as all subsequent sins—that expelled humanity from Eden and from the presence of God. When the message of the cross is preached, God confirms it with miracles, signs, and wonders. Mark 16:20 says, *"And [the disciples] went out and preached everywhere, the Lord working with them and confirming the word through the accompanying signs."*

At a recent Supernatural Fivefold Ministry School conference, Pastors Pablo and Olga Segovia traveled from Granada, Spain, to testify of a creative miracle that occurred in their church. The couple shared that two years previously, a leader from King Jesus Ministry in Miami had brought them some books and other material by Apostle Maldonado that introduced them to the supernatural power of God. They read all the material and also started watching his preaching via the Internet, through which they received God's revelation that they, too, could be used to manifest miracles. They made a commitment to God to bring His supernatural power to their city.

Pastor Pablo and Pastor Olga obeyed, and miracles began to happen in their church. Shortly after this, in one of their services, a twenty-three-year-old woman went to the altar to receive prayer. She was seven months pregnant, and her doctor wanted her to abort the baby because the ultrasound showed that the fetus had spina bifida and that his legs had not developed. Pastor Pablo immediately took spiritual authority over the situation and manifested the supernatural, declaring and decreeing life, health, and a creative miracle for the baby. At that moment, the woman felt a very strong sense of God's presence over her and decided to trust Him and not abort the baby, knowing that she had received her miracle.

The following week, she went to the doctor to let him know of her decision not to abort her baby. The doctor was not happy with that decision and prescribed another ultrasound to convince her that the abortion was needed. To the doctor's surprise, the results of the ultrasound showed that the baby was completely healthy; his spine was normal and his legs were developing just as they should at that stage of the pregnancy. There was no sign of spina bifida or any indication of a medical problem! The doctor consulted with other doctors at the hospital, and they all came to the same conclusion: The baby was healthy, and his development was completely normal. Given the results of the ultrasound, the doctors could only agree that the baby had received a miracle from God. They all began to say, "This is supernatural; this is supernatural…this is supernatural!" Two months later, the young woman gave birth to a healthy baby boy!

> The cross is a constant reminder that,
> in God's mind and in the heavenly realm,
> we are complete in Christ.

5. Through the Cross, the Will of God for Our Spiritual Inheritance Was Activated

Through the cross, our spiritual inheritance—based on our new covenant with God in Christ—was released. To better understand how this transpired, we must know the following truths, or principles:

+ *Only a person's death can activate his will.* As it says in the book of Hebrews, *"For a testament is in force after men are dead, since it has no power at all while the testator lives"* (Hebrews 9:17).

+ *When Jesus Christ died, God's "will" was activated.* What spiritual inheritance do we receive through God's will in Christ? Salvation, healing, deliverance, and prosperity were all activated through Jesus' death. Our debt of sin was fully paid, so that we were transferred from the hands of the enemy, our torturer, back home to the arms of God, our heavenly Father, where we find provision for all things. As we will discuss in more detail shortly, an exchange occurred on the cross—the exchange of our complete poverty for Jesus' eternal riches, which are manifested spiritually, physically, emotionally, mentally, financially, and in all other ways.

+ *We must meet the conditions of God's will.* The matter of our inheritance is not pending on God's part; His will was already decreed on the cross through Christ. Now it is up to us to appropriate Christ's completed work in our lives. But there is a requirement that we must meet or put into practice here on earth in order to receive that work. That requirement is to obey God's commandments. Yes, it is the will of God for you to be saved, healed, delivered, transformed, and prosperous. However, if you need, for example, a financial breakthrough but are not being obedient to God by tithing, the will of God cannot be fulfilled because you are not meeting the conditions of that will.

Jesus initiated His new covenant on the cross,
but we need to carry it out in the now.
We must know, do, and "be" the will of God.

+ *When we accept our inheritance in Christ, God's will is activated in our lives now.* We must believe in and accept everything that Jesus paid for and activated on the cross. We can have confidence that God will do for us what He has promised according to the new covenant. *"God is not a man, that He should lie, nor a son of man, that He should repent. Has He said, and will He not do? Or has He spoken, and will He not make it good?"* (Numbers 23:19).

If God were to fail to fulfill His promises under the new covenant, He would be dishonoring His Word, His eternal purposes, and the death of His own Son. Therefore, let us draw increasingly closer to the Father through the sacrifice of Jesus, with full assurance that we can receive the benefits of the cross. Remember that it was according to Jesus' merits—not our own—that grace was released on the cross, giving us access to the Father. It is no longer necessary for us to wonder if it is God's will to save, heal, deliver, transform, or prosper us, because His covenant with us through Jesus includes all these things (see, for example, Luke 4:17–21), and His will has already been activated.

> *If God were not to fulfill His will,*
> *He would be in violation of His own Word.*

6. The Holy Spirit Is the Revealer of the Cross and of the Will of God

Christ has made full provision for all our needs through His death and resurrection; therefore, if believers lack something, it is because they lack knowledge of the finished work of the cross. Earlier, we talked about some of the reasons why many Christians have this deficiency. One of those reasons is a reliance on natural thinking and intellectual reasoning rather than on God's supernatural power. Consequently, many believers have failed to cooperate with the only Person who witnessed the work of Jesus on the cross from beginning to end, from the inside and the outside, and was later sent by the Father and the Son to the church to be our Helper. I am referring to the third Person of the Trinity, the Holy Spirit. (See John 14:26.)

Jesus told us that when He returned to the Father in heaven, He would send us the Spirit, who would guide us into all truth (see John 16:13)—including the truth of the cross. Without the Holy Spirit, we cannot fully understand the will of the Father, live according to that will, or ensure its fulfillment in our lives. Paul wrote, *"The Spirit Himself bears witness with our spirit that we are children of God"* (Romans 8:16). In keeping with the new covenant, the Spirit makes known the Father's will to His children, those who are *"heirs of God and joint heirs with Christ"* (Romans 8:17). He reveals to us the entire finished work of Jesus. If you don't have an understanding of the completed work of Jesus Christ on the cross, then begin to work with the Holy Spirit, and He will show it to you!

> **The Holy Spirit reveals**
> **what Jesus won on the cross.**

7. The Work of the Cross Is Finished and Complete

"So when Jesus had received the sour wine, He said, 'It is finished!' And... He gave up His spirit" (John 19:30). I believe that the three most powerful words Jesus ever spoke were *"It is finished."* The moment He made this declaration, every curse on humanity was broken. Depression, poverty, sickness—all the powers of sin and death—were nullified. I believe that when the devil heard those words, he suddenly began to understand the ramifications of what Jesus had done. Before that moment, he had not seen it; in fact, he had made the maximum effort to make sure that Jesus was crucified, because again, he believed he could defeat God if Jesus were killed. Then, once the Son of God had been nailed to the cross and had surrendered His spirit to God, Satan could no longer do anything about it. The work was finished, complete, consummated, and irreversible. There was no room for debate or argument about that fact.

Furthermore, Christ was subsequently raised from the dead and seated at the right hand of God the Father (see, for example, Hebrews 10:12) to rule and reign on earth through the church (see, for example,

Ephesians 1:22–23). Satan can never reverse what Christ accomplished for us on the cross—not only to redeem us but also to make us God's *"kings and priests"* (Revelation 1:5–6) who can destroy the powers of darkness.

8. Ever Since the Cross, Everything Is in the Now

Why wait until tomorrow to receive something that is completed and paid for? Faith is *now*. If you think you need to wait for your inheritance in Christ, it is because, in your mind, the work is not finished. Faith does not wait for what is in the "now"; it believes in what has already been *accomplished* in eternity. If you know that the work of Jesus is already complete, you will not sit and wait—you will act *today*. Receive your salvation, your healing, your deliverance, your transformation, your prosperity, or your miracle now!

The members of the heavenly court continuously worship Jesus because they know that His completed work on the cross is an eternal reality. (See, for example, Revelation 5:8–12.) All heavenly beings live in the midst of a perfect, complete, and finished work; they worship a King who was crowned because He overcame sin, sickness, death, and Satan. If the work had not been completed, then Jesus would not have been raised from the dead; He would had not have ascended to heaven; He would not have been seated at the right hand of the Father; and He would not have sent the Holy Spirit to us. Today, Jesus sits on His heavenly throne because His task is complete. When God finished creating the world, He *"rested."* (See Genesis 2:2–3; Hebrews 4:4.) Likewise, when Jesus completed the work of the cross, He "rested" by sitting down in authority at the Father's right hand.

The greatest compliment that faith can give God is to rest in Him.

What Jesus Conquered Through the Cross

Let us now summarize what Jesus conquered through His death on the cross.

1. Jesus Overcame Death and Hell

Following Jesus' resurrection and ascension to heaven, He declared, *"I am He who lives, and was dead, and behold, I am alive forevermore. Amen. And I have the keys of Hades and of Death"* (Revelation 1:18). Jesus' sacrifice has released us from both the fear of physical death and the reality of spiritual death. *"That through death He might destroy him who had the power of death, that is, the devil, and release those who through fear of death were all their lifetime subject to bondage"* (Hebrews 2:14–15).

2. Jesus Overcame Satan and All His Works

On the cross, Jesus dealt Satan a total, irrevocable, permanent, and eternal defeat. (See, for example, Colossians 2:15.) Again, there is nothing the devil can do to change this fact. The only thing he can do is to try to take more souls to hell with him. That is why he works so hard to steal the revelation of the cross from us. If we try to fight Satan outside of the foundation of the cross, we will be defeated. But if we fight him standing on the work of the cross, we will be victorious.

> *Satan is a disarmed, dethroned, defeated, and destroyed enemy.*

Satan is a limited created being. He is not God; therefore, he is not omnipotent, omnipresent, or omniscient. Neither does he have any creative power. In their ignorance, many believers often overestimate

Satan's power while underestimating his ability to deceive them. The devil does not want us to know that he is a defeated enemy who has been stripped of all legal authority on earth.

It is due to the work of the cross that the devil now functions in the world under an illegal status. As we have discussed in previous chapters, the enemy no longer has any authority on earth, although he does retain much of his power. The only authority he can use here is what people give him by their disobedience to God. Since he can't change what Jesus did on the cross, the enemy tries to hide from God's people the truth of what actually took place there in order to prevent us from stopping his evil works. But Jesus gave us *"authority…over all the power of the enemy"* (Luke 10:19). If we remain ignorant of the revelation of the cross, we will not be able to appropriate the victory that Jesus has already won over Satan.

> *The cross constantly reminds Satan of his defeat. Every believer has power and authority over Satan and his works.*

3. Jesus Overcame the World

Jesus encouraged us, *"In the world you will have tribulation; but be of good cheer, I have overcome the world"* (John 16:33). The word *"world"* here refers to the social order, the way in which the world system operates, which is controlled by the *"prince of this world"* (John 16:11 NIV, TLB) in complete rebellion against the kingdom of God. The world is under the influence of Satan. *"We know that we are of God, and the whole world lies under the sway of the wicked one"* (1 John 5:19). On the cross, Jesus conquered this anti-God world system. We Christians necessarily live in the world; accordingly, we live in the midst of that social order, or system, but we should not *conform* to it. (See Romans 12:2.) We are in the world, but we are not of it. (See, for example, John 15:19; 17:14–16.)

In this context, the Scriptures teach that we are not to love the world. Here are some key points in relation to this.

+ To love the world system is incompatible with the love of the Father. *"If anyone loves the world, the love of the Father is not in him"* (1 John 2:15).

+ To love the world is to commit spiritual adultery against God. *"Adulterers and adulteresses!...Whoever therefore wants to be a friend of the world makes himself an enemy of God"* (James 4:4). The world's plans, strategies, values, opinions, standards, priorities, judgments, and attitudes, including its patterns of thinking, speaking, and acting—all these go against God and His kingdom. To love the world is to pursue power, success, fame, position, prestige, influence, wealth, and outer beauty; these pursuits contrast with the priority that marks the citizens of God's kingdom. Jesus declared, *"But seek **first** the kingdom of God and His righteousness, and all these things shall be added to you"* (Matthew 6:33).

The cross of Christ traces a line between the church and the world.

4. Jesus Overcame Sin and Its Spiritual Consequences

Christ made provision for us to receive complete forgiveness for sin and its spiritual consequences through His death on the cross, *"having wiped out the handwriting of requirements that was against us, which was contrary to us. And He has taken it out of the way, having nailed it to the cross"* (Colossians 2:14). Jesus was punished so that we could be forgiven. Every record or evidence of guilt that was against us has been erased. Because Jesus overcame sin, *"sin shall not have dominion over* [us], *for* [we] *are not under law but under grace"* (Romans 6:14). Therefore, the moment we believed in Him, Jesus delivered us from the disobedience that had ruled our lives in the past. Now we have to make the victory of Christ effective in us, and live above sin.

> *On the cross, a remission of sin took place,*
> *which means it is just as if it never existed.*

The Cross Gives Us Victory over all Evil

Every work of Satan has been nullified by the cross. Because of Jesus' sacrifice, we can have victory today against all the evil that previously enslaved us. This is possible for anyone who believes, wherever they are, as the following testimony illustrates.

"My name is Fabiola. I am fifty-two years old, and I am from Italy. I come from a world of witchcraft and occultism in which I was involved for thirty years. One day, Pastor Elena, a spiritual daughter of Apostle Maldonado, invited me to a deliverance retreat at her church in Rome. I knew God existed, but I didn't think He could help me, so I went there a bit skeptically. For six and a half years, I had suffered from depression and severe panic attacks. The doctors had told me that I would have to take pills for the rest of my life. Due to my fear, I had gotten to the point of not driving my car or going to the grocery store anymore. I had to endure horrible thoughts that came to my mind. The only thing that kept me going was my son.

"During the retreat, I learned about the cross and the finished work of Jesus. When they prayed for me, I began to feel a fire inside me.

I didn't understand what was happening, but that fire made me feel great. Then a battle started in my mind. I began thinking about the pills, feeling that I needed them, that it would be very hard for me to go through the day without them. A voice told me, *You don't need the pills anymore; you're healed.* Yet I decided to take them anyway. After I took them, instead of feeling better, I felt really sick, and that is when I realized it was true—God had healed me!

"Since that day, I have not taken those pills. It has now been a year and a half, and I can certainly say that I don't need them anymore. I went to the doctor and told him so, but he insisted that I needed them in order to survive. I felt the boldness of the Holy Spirit inside me, and I told my doctors that I refused to listen to them because I knew I was healed. My psychologist also said it was impossible for me to be healed, but I told him that I had been healed by the power that Jesus released on the cross.

"Today, I thank Him because I found a job; previously, I couldn't find or keep a job because I was sick all the time, but everything has changed. I have also stopped practicing witchcraft, because I don't want to displease my God. He is alive, not dead, as other religions claim. Now I wake up happy. I want to go out and spend time with people. I enjoy the communion and fellowship at my church. I have found a joy in living because the finished work of the cross has been manifested in my life."

The Law of Exchange Was Activated on the Cross

The law of exchange, which was effected on the cross, is one of the most powerful laws of the kingdom found in the Bible. After human beings rebelled against God, evil ruled over us, and we all committed evil acts. There was nothing we could do about our condition because, as Jesus said, *"what will a man give in exchange for his soul?"* (Mark 8:37). Only Jesus Christ could pay the price for the redemption of our souls;

thus, all of our evil and all of its consequences were placed upon Jesus on the cross. Now, according to the law of exchange, all of the good things associated with Jesus' perfect obedience, which He released through the cross, have been placed on us!

The following are some of the benefits we receive from Jesus through the law of exchange:

+ Jesus was punished for our sins so that we could be forgiven. (See, for example, Isaiah 53:5–6.)

+ Jesus became sin for us so that we could become *the righteousness of God in Him.*" (See 2 Corinthians 5:21.)

+ Jesus carried our sicknesses so that we could receive His healing. (See, for example, Isaiah 53:4–5.)

+ Jesus died so that we could receive His life. (See, for example, Hebrews 2:9; Romans 6:22–23.)

+ Jesus became a curse so that we could receive His blessing. (See Galatians 3:13–14.)

+ Jesus endured our poverty so that we could enjoy His prosperity. (See 2 Corinthians 8:9.)

+ Jesus took our iniquities so that we could receive His spiritual DNA. (See, for example, Romans 6:7–8.)

+ Jesus suffered our rejection so that we could receive His acceptance. (See, for example, Ephesians 1:6.)

+ Jesus endured our guilt and shame so that we could be carriers of His glory. (See, for example, Colossians 1:27.)

+ Jesus conformed to our human nature so that we could be transformed into His image. (See Philippians 2:7; Romans 8:29.)

+ Jesus bore our bondage, our captivity, and our oppression so that we could receive His freedom. (See, for example, Galatians 5:1.)

Take Ownership of the Benefits of the Cross

The biggest obstacle in many believers' lives is not the actual problem or challenge they are dealing with but the fact that they don't know how to take ownership of the finished work of the cross to overcome that problem or challenge. To appropriate the benefits of Jesus' finished work, we must do the following:

1. Get to Know the Contents of God's Will, or Testament

"But now [Jesus] *has obtained a more excellent ministry, inasmuch as He is also Mediator of a better covenant, which was established on better promises"* (Hebrews 8:6). If you were to inherit a large fortune, but you did not know what was written in the will of the person who bequeathed it to you—and nobody ever informed you of it—you would not be able to claim your rightful inheritance. I encourage you to take ownership of the finished work of Jesus, not only by learning what is in this chapter but also by searching the Scriptures to find out more about what Jesus won when He died on the cross, as well as about the promises that are written in God's will. Right now, ask the Holy Spirit to reveal the finished work of the cross to you as you read God's Word.

2. Use Faith as the "Master Key"

Faith is the "master key" that allows us access to the inheritance we have in Christ Jesus. Let us review several aspects of faith that will help us to understand how this key works in relation to the benefits of the cross.

- ✦ *Faith serves as our entrance to the spiritual realm.* It enables us to bring things from the eternal realm into the present day, and it carries things out in the now that we would have to wait for according to the natural realm.

+ *There is no true faith outside of the Person of Jesus Christ.* Before our faith can exercise supernatural results in any situation or matter, we must always first place our faith in the Person of Jesus Christ. If we were to remove Jesus from our faith, we would be left with just empty illusion. Jesus is *"the author and finisher of our faith, who for the joy that was set before Him endured the cross"* (Hebrews 12:2). The word *"author"* signifies that He is the Originator of our faith. The word *"finisher"* indicates that He is the One who also completes our faith. Therefore, we can say that faith begins with the revelation of who Jesus truly is; and everything that God has promised and that you believe in, Jesus is able to carry out and complete.

+ *Faith proceeds from the finished work of the cross, on which Jesus shed His blood.* Jesus' atoning blood is the basis of our faith in His finished work. If His blood had not been spilled on the cross, our faith would have no substance (see, for example, Hebrews 9:22); thus, the devil could legally ignore our faith. But because of the blood, we have access right now to the supernatural faith that was released the moment Jesus said, *"It is finished!"* (John 19:30). His work being complete, all our sins are forgiven; all our bondages are broken; all our generational curses—whether of alcoholism, disease, poverty, or anything else—are nullified. We receive all these benefits by faith in the blood of Jesus, according to His finished work on the cross.

Without a revelation of Jesus' finished work on the cross, our faith has no real basis, and Satan can still legally keep us in bondage.

+ *Faith is established upon the finished work of the cross.* We have seen that faith begins with the Person of Jesus and proceeds from trusting in His shed blood. But faith is also *established* upon the reality of Jesus' finished work by manifesting the supernatural. It is impossible to say that you believe in the finished work of Jesus, in all its power, and not do supernatural works. Paul wrote, *"And my speech and my preaching were not with persuasive words of human wisdom, but in demonstration of the Spirit and of power, that your faith should not be in the wisdom of men but in the power of God"* (1 Corinthians 2:4–5).

What did Paul mean by *"the wisdom of men"*? He was referring to human doctrines, philosophies, and intellectual knowledge. These are the means by which people who operate according to the world system determine their destiny. Fields such as science help us to function in the natural world, but they cannot activate us in the supernatural or provide miraculous healing; likewise, getting an education can prepare us to work a job, but it cannot reveal our calling and purpose in God. Sometimes, the answer to your problem will not be found in intellectual knowledge or even in common sense but in the supernatural. I believe that you will do more with God's revelation than with any other type of knowledge, because the supernatural is above and beyond anything offered by the natural world. The question is, on what is your faith founded? Is it established on human wisdom or on the power of God, which is accessed only through the finished work of Christ?

When your faith is not firmly established on the victory of the cross, you can easily be shaken, because you are open to opinions and viewpoints that divert you from the truth. But when you rest on Jesus' completed work, you can say, "My healing, my deliverance, my protection, my prosperity, and my freedom are complete. I do not have to wait until later to receive them. I take my authority in Christ to receive all the benefits of the cross now." That is when your faith will have substance to produce miracles. If you proclaim the finished work of the cross with that kind of faith, you will manifest supernatural power!

3. Confess and Continuously Testify About the Finished Work of the Cross

"And they overcame [Satan] by the blood of the Lamb and by the word of their testimony" (Revelation 12:11). We overcome the devil when we confess and continually declare what God's Word says and what the power of Jesus' blood has accomplished both in us and for us. A wonderful way to do this is to share your personal testimony about what Jesus has made possible in your life by His sacrifice on the cross. I urge you to tell people how you were saved and delivered, how your family was restored, how you became financially prosperous, and so forth. The enemy cannot argue against your testimony, because it is evidence of the finished work of Christ on the cross, by which he has been thoroughly conquered. Every testimony related to Jesus' completed work is a spiritual wound to the devil; it reminds him that he has been defeated and that the power activated through the cross of Jesus continues even today, overtaking territory that formerly belonged to his dark dominion.

Our testimony about the power of the completed work of the cross in our lives is what makes us credible.

4. Make the Decision to Obey; Then Act On and Fulfill the Work of the Cross, Here and Now

"Thus also faith by itself, if it does not have works, is dead" (James 2:17). You are a believer in Christ, appointed by God to this earth to do His will—to enforce the finished work of the cross here and now. Thus, starting now, activate salvation, healing, deliverance, transformation, and prosperity in your life and in the lives of those around you. Everything that Jesus won on the cross is available to you, but

you must manifest it now. Take ownership of it! Make the decision to obey God by manifesting the power of the cross through faith; then act upon Jesus' finished work, bringing God's will on earth as it is in heaven.

The following testimony of one woman's blessing through the finished work of the cross might surpass anything you could have imagined. Maria attended the Apostolic and Prophetic Conference (CAP) sponsored by our ministry. There she received a prophetic word that radically changed the state of her finances.

"I came from Brazil to CAP, where Apostle Maldonado prophesied that God had anointed me for riches and would give me creative ideas in dreams for a new business. That night, I dreamed of a series of formulas. Since I didn't understand them, I wrote them down and then woke up my son to help me search the Internet to find out what I could about them. I needed to know what those formulas meant and how to develop them. As I searched, I realized they were cosmetic formulas. My son and I jumped for joy because we knew that God was fulfilling what He had just prophesied though the apostle. As soon as we returned home, we started developing these formulas, and they resulted in a keratin product for the treatment of hair. This product has revolutionized the hair and beauty industry around the world!

"I had immediately thought about renting a place to develop the business, but I lacked the money to do so and couldn't get a loan because I had bad credit. However, we declared the work of the cross in this project, where everything had already been provided for, and we kept working to complete it. God opened all the doors and gave us the needed contacts. By His grace, we established our own factory, and my dream came true. The formulas were so excellent that, within one year, we were in thirty-two countries with sales of $2.3 million—and that was only the first year! It was then that I remembered the words of Apostle Maldonado, who had taught us that when God gives riches, they are not only for us but for the kingdom and for the purpose of serving others. Every day, people would affirm to me that I would own a beautiful house and a luxury car, but I said to God, 'Not yet, Lord. First I want the church I attend to have its own land and a building in which to worship You.' And so it happened. We donated money to the church, and God has kept blessing us financially. Today, we have everything we need in abundance because we believed and loosened the power that Jesus Christ released on the cross."

Appropriating Your Deliverance

We have seen that on the cross, according to the law of exchange, Jesus already took on Himself all our sin and all our curses; at the same time, He released all the good things that are associated with His perfect obedience, so that they could be applied to us. Therefore, if you need any type of deliverance, don't wait to receive it; appropriate the power of the cross right now. Do you need forgiveness from sin and a brand-new life in Christ? Do you require physical healing from a sickness or disease, like asthma, chronic fatigue syndrome, heart disease, cancer, diabetes, the restoration of an organ, or anything else? Do you suffer from a generational curse, such as poverty, addiction, barrenness, or abuse? Are you oppressed by a spirit of fear, anger, lies, or compulsive behavior? Has an emotional or mental trauma derailed your life? Do you feel controlled by a destructive power, such as a lust of the flesh or a desire for revenge? Do you have ties to witchcraft or the occult? Is your life full of stagnation and frustration, so that you always seem to be pushing and struggling but never seem to make any progress? Are your thoughts entrenched in a pattern of worldly reasoning and arguments, unbelief, or stubbornness that blocks your spiritual growth?

Whatever you need, receive your deliverance now! Repent of all your sins, including rebellion, iniquity, sexual immorality, witchcraft, soul ties, jealousy, unforgiveness, fear, self-pity, or anything else. Then activate the power released by the finished work of the cross as you repeat the following prayer.

Prayer of Activation

Heavenly Father, I draw close to You on the merits of Christ's sacrifice on the cross. By faith, I take ownership of His finished work. I believe that Jesus carried my sin so that I could be forgiven, and I receive that forgiveness today. I believe that Jesus became a curse so that I could receive His blessings, and I receive those blessings today. I believe that Jesus become poor so that I could be enriched, and I receive His abundance today. I declare the work of Christ in my physical, mental, and emotional health; I establish it in my finances, my work, my company, and my projects. I confess it in all of my family and ministry relationships. I declare prosperity in every area, because Christ took the curse so that I could be blessed in all things. I believe I will receive this prosperity by faith in the finished work of the cross. In the name of Jesus, amen!

If you do not yet have a personal relationship with the living Christ, who gave Himself on the cross for you, accept Him into your heart and receive His life as you repeat this prayer:

Heavenly Father, I recognize that I am a sinner and that my sin separates me from You. Today, I believe that Jesus died on the cross for me and that You raised Him from the dead. I repent of all my sins, and I willingly confess Jesus as my Lord and Savior. I break every pact I have made with the world, with my flesh, and with the devil, and I now enter into the new covenant with You that Christ has made possible. Jesus, I ask You to come into my heart and change my life. I know that if I were to die today, I would be in Your arms. Amen!

Praise God for your salvation and deliverance! When Jesus healed the ten lepers, only one came back to worship Him and to express his gratitude. (See Luke 17:11–19.) Whenever we receive deliverance or healing, we need to give God the glory and thank Him for His super-natural grace in our lives.

Now That You're Delivered

As we conclude this book, let me encourage you in three specific ways in regard to your deliverance, because this is only the first step in God's plan to save you and release you from the powers of darkness.

1. Sustain Your Deliverance

I want you to retain all the benefits of your deliverance and heal-ing. I see so many people who are set free, only to lose what they have received because they didn't understand how to maintain their deliver-ance, or because they believed they could go back to their old ways of living without experiencing any consequences. To maintain your deliv-erance and healing, you must keep spiritually alert. Stay in constant communication with God through prayer, and make a commitment to fully obey Him. Study the Word and be intentional about renewing your mind according to it. Continually deny your flesh, resist the enemy, walk in forgiveness, and be filled with the Holy Spirit.

Do not allow the "old man" to control your life any longer. Be watch-ful so that you do not open an entry point for demons to oppress you. As you repeatedly submit your flesh to the finished work of Jesus on the cross, you will receive God's grace to live in His righteousness. In this way, the kingdom of God will be fully established in your life. This is my prayer for you: *"May the God of peace Himself sanctify you completely; and may your whole spirit, soul, and body be preserved blameless at the coming of our Lord Jesus Christ"* (1 Thessalonians 5:23).

2. Be Empowered to Deliver Others

From the beginning of creation, God blessed people so that they could be a blessing. He blessed Adam and Eve so that they could be fruitful and multiply and fill the earth with His glory. God blessed

Abraham so that through him and his descendants, the whole world could be blessed through Jesus Christ, our Savior and Deliverer. And God has blessed us so that now we can be carriers of the authority and power of Christ to bless this world.

You have been delivered to be a deliverer. You have been healed to be a healer. You have been set free to free others. You have prospered in order to sow into the kingdom of God. Jesus said, *"Freely you have received, freely give"* (Matthew 10:8). Whatever you have received, you are to give to others. That means that whenever we are blessed, we are to be a blessing. This is the purpose to which God calls us.

Be the blessing you were meant to be. Recognize that you have been empowered to be a blessing to the world. You have this authority because of what Christ accomplished through His cross and His resurrection. This is my declaration for you: "Receive all the blessings that Jesus won on the cross for you. Be blessed with health in your spirit, your mind, your soul, your emotions, your body, your finances, and all other areas of your life, so that you can bless and deliver others."

3. Go Forth!

Now that you understand that you have been blessed in order to be a blessing, you need to do something about it! You have been empowered, but now you must use that power; otherwise, it will remain only potential. I want you to put all that potential into action. Don't just receive God's blessing and then "bury it" until Jesus returns. (See Matthew 25:14–30.) Instead, give it away; invest it in the lives of others. Take the authority and power that the Lord has given you, and destroy the works of the devil wherever you see them. Bring deliverance and healing to your family members, your friends, your neighbors, your co-workers, your community, and your nation. This is my declaration for you: "Go forth with all the blessings of God. Be fruitful and multiply, filling the earth with His glory!"

ABOUT THE AUTHOR

Apostle Guillermo Maldonado is a man called to bring God's supernatural power to this generation at the local and international levels. Active in ministry for over twenty years, he is the founder of Ministerio Internacional El Rey Jesús (King Jesus International Ministry)—one of the fastest-growing multicultural churches in the United States—which has been recognized for its development of kingdom leaders and for visible manifestations of God's supernatural power.

Having earned a master's degree in practical theology from Oral Roberts University and a doctorate in divinity from Vision International University, Apostle Maldonado stands firm and focused on the vision

God has given him to evangelize, affirm, disciple, and send. His mission is to teach, train, equip, and send leaders and believers to bring the supernatural power of God to their communities, in order to leave a legacy of blessings for future generations. This mission is worldwide. Apostle Maldonado is a spiritual father to a growing network of over 200 churches, the New Wine Apostolic Network, which he founded.

Apostle Maldonado has authored many books and manuals, a number of which have been translated into several languages. His previous books with Whitaker House are *How to Walk in the Supernatural Power of God*, *The Glory of God*, *The Kingdom of Power*, and *Supernatural Transformation*, all of which are available in Spanish. In addition, he preaches the message of Jesus Christ and His redemptive power on his international television program, *The Supernatural Now* (*Lo Sobrenatural Ahora*), which airs on several networks, thus reaching millions worldwide.

Apostle Maldonado resides in Miami, Florida, with his wife and partner in ministry, Ana, and their two sons, Bryan and Ronald.